FACE TO FACE WITH
SERIAL
KILLERS

FACE TO FACE WITH
SERIAL
KILLERS

My Conversations With the
World's Most Evil Men

CHRISTOPHER BERRY-DEE

JOHN BLAKE

Published by John Blake Publishing Ltd,
3 Bramber Court, 2 Bramber Road,
London W14 9PB, England

www.blake.co.uk

First published in paperback in 2007

ISBN: 978 1 84454 367 0

British Library Cataloguing-in-Publication Data:

A catalogue record for this book is available from the British Library.

Design by www.envydesign.co.uk

Printed in the UK by CPI Bookmarque, Croydon, CR0 4TD

3 5 7 9 10 8 6 4

Papers used by John Blake Publishing are natural, recyclable products made
from wood grown in sustainable forests. The manufacturing processes
conform to the environmental regulations of the country of origin.

Every attempt has been made to contact the relevant copyright-holders,
but some were unobtainable. We would be grateful if the appropriate
people could contact us.

Some names have been changed in the text.

Face to Face with Serial Killers
is dedicated to my lovely wife Tatiana

Acknowledgements

Special thanks to my colleagues and friends: Steve Morris (co-editor and publisher with me of *The New Criminologist*), Phillip Simpson, Kirstie McCallum, Sarah Brown, Ruth Sands, Simon Beal (webmaster of *TNC*), my parents, Patrick and May, and Martin Balaam.

Much gratitude is also extended to all of the professionals who have assisted me in the writing of this book.

For John Wayne Gacy: Joseph R Kozenczak, former Chief of Police, Des Plaines PD, Judge Louis B Garippo and attorney William Kunkle.

For Kenneth Bianchi: Frances Piccione (Bianchi's adoptive mother). Kenneth Bianchi, Veronica 'VerLyn' Compton, Professor Donald T Lunde, MA, MD, Professor David Canter, Professor Elliot Leyton, Judge Roger Boren, Bellingham PD, LAPD Homicide, Captain Lynde Johnston, Rochester PD Homicide, Det Richard Crotsley LAPD Homicide, Agent Robert Beams FBI,

Katherine Yronwode, Whatcom Security Agency, former SOCO Bellingham PD Robert Knudsen, the staff at Western Washington Correctional Centre for Women (WWCCW) and the Washington State Penitentiary (WSP) Walla Walla.

William Heirens: The Vienna Correctional Centre, Ill, William Heirens, Dolores Kennedy, attorney Thomas Epach and Betty Finn (sister of Suzanne Degnan).

John Cannan: the Avon and Somerset Police, DCI Bryan Saunders, Dorset Police, SO II Metropolitan Police – DCI Jim Dickie and DI Stuart Ault, John Cannan, Professor David Canter, Mrs Cannan, Robin Odell and Sharon Major.

Patricia Wright: Arletta Wright and Patricia Wright.

Finally, to all of my staff at www.newcriminologist.co.uk, my publisher John Blake and Lucian Randall.

Christopher Berry-Dee,
2007

Contents

Introduction

With 5 per cent of the world's population, the United States produces more serial killers than the rest of the world, accounting for 76 per cent of the total. Europe produces the second-highest number of serial killers at 17 per cent. England leads with 28 per cent of the European total, followed by Germany with 27 per cent.

California has the highest serial homicide rate in the USA, followed by New York, Texas and Illinois, while Maine has the lowest.

Over 90 per cent of serial killers are white males, usually from low- to middle-class backgrounds; these men are usually intelligent but, as students, have generally had difficulty in focusing. Most have experienced a traumatic childhood, often having been abused psychologically, physically or sexually. Typically, they may have been raised in unstable families, often with criminal, psychiatric and alcoholic histories. As a result, children raised in such families often spend a great deal of time on their own with many of them indulging in animal cruelty at a very young age.

Most people who suffer as children grow out of it and become upstanding, decent human beings. But serial killers such as John Cannan, Kenneth Bianchi and John Gacy, who all suffered as children, repeat the same mistakes over the course of their lives. They cannot make their transition into adulthood; they have trouble making the transition in middle age and, at the very time they feel they should be reaching the pinnacle of success, they find they are sliding downhill fast. They want to feel important, they want to feel special; they crave the sense of power, dominance and control. But they simply cannot achieve it in any respectable way, so they kill, torture, sodomise and dismember, and this makes them feel good about themselves.

The typical sado-serial killer appears extraordinarily ordinary. He's a white, middle-aged man who has an insatiable appetite for power, control and dominance, and he kills not for money, nor for revenge, but because it makes him feel good. He does it because he enjoys trawling for prey, entrapping them, restraining and torturing them; he has fun killing, because he likes the thrill, the excitement and the exhilaration that he gets from squeezing the last gasp of breath from his dying victim's body.

Killers such as John Wayne Gacy and Kenneth Bianchi enjoy the suffering on the part of the victim, and they try to make it slow and painful. It makes them feel superior to the extent that it makes their victims feel inferior.

Sixty-five per cent of serial homicide victims are women. In the USA, there are, at most, 200 victims of sexual serial killers a year. That number, although very large, pales into insignificance compared with almost 18,000 single-victim murders in the USA on a yearly basis. The problem is not serial murder, it is domestic violence, or workplace homicide, or two guys going into a bar, where one takes out a gun and shoots the other.

The problem, on the other hand, is that serial murderers amass a large body count – a small number of men who do a lot of damage. They may kill five, ten or even twenty or more. Some of them have killed hundreds, and that is enough to terrify anyone.

Randy Kraft drugged many of his victims and then inserted cocktail sticks into their penises, or car door handles into their bodies, and flayed them alive. And, as we will soon learn, John Wayne Gacy, Kenneth Bianchi and Angelo Buono also inflicted terrible, extended suffering upon their hapless prey.

It is this sadistic impulse that feeds the real and fragile ego of the sado-sexual serial murderer who desires so much, so desperately, to achieve a sense of power over other human beings – sexual sadism is the means by which that happens.

JOHN WAYNE MICHAEL GACY

17 March 1942–10 May 1994

Smaller than I imagined, he bustles into the interview room, shackled and scrubbed as clean as a new pin. He smells of cheap disinfectant; a prison odour not unlike that exuded by a mortuary attendant. He has a slight, almost effeminate lisp. Potato-faced, round-shouldered, porcine blue eyes, he is two inverted cones joined together, bulging at his gut, a repugnant sight indeed.

I have some patience for killers like Kenneth Bianchi because they are least able to communicate at length. However, for this doughy monster, a creature that tortured and slaughtered at least 33 young boys, I have little time at all.

Gacy, among all other serial killers I have met, repulses me the most with his presence; his self-important attitude, declaring, 'I grant you an audience at my behest,' was all too apparent.

His handshake was like touching a damp cloth, his fingers feminine, the nails oh so carefully manicured like the words in his day-to-day diary, so well clipped and cleaned for the observer's consumption.

It was not so much his catalogue of mind-sickening crimes that troubled me, it was more this gutless bisexual who degraded the word 'humanity' that turned my stomach; how weak and pathetic can a 'real' man be?

Christopher, I wish you much success in your current project. *Former Chief of Detectives, later Chief of Police, Des Plaines PD, Joseph R Kozenczak (the officer who captured John Wayne Gacy), to the author, June 1995*

In his book *A Passing Acquaintance*, former Chief of Detectives and, later, Chief of Police of the Des Plaines PD Joe Kozenczak chillingly writes, 'Gacy, to the casual observer, was a pillar of the community. He was active in the Jaycees (the Junior Chamber of Commerce) for whom he dressed as a clown and entertained children. He was a precinct captain for the Democratic Party, and a member of the local lighting commission. But Gacy had an odious hobby: he forced boys to perform deviant acts and then murdered them, sometimes sleeping with the dead body for a day or two. Gacy was convicted of killing 33 young men, 27 of whom he buried in his basement.'

Opened in March 1878, Menard is second-oldest prison in Illinois. Up until Saturday, 11 January 2003, it boasted the 'Green Mile', the Death Row for the State, upon which date the then soon-to-depart Republican governor had a sudden change of heart. With his conscience getting the better of years of witnessing men going to their executions, George Ryan told the 156 condemned inmates that they no longer faced the death penalty.

'I can't live with executed men on my conscience,' said Ryan. If John Wayne Gacy had been more fortunate, he would have been a beneficiary of the governor's farewell gift, too!

JOHN WAYNE MICHAEL GACY

Most of the things all of us value, John had no value for at all.
John didn't value other life. John didn't value other emotions.
John didn't value any institutions. John didn't value the feelings
of other people.

Greg Adamski, John Gacy's attorney 1990–94

ONE

Living up to Expectations

BORN on a Tuesday, and executed on Tuesday, blue-eyed John Wayne Michael Gacy came into this world at Edgewater Hospital on St Patrick's Day, 17 March 1942. He was to be the second of Marion and John Stanley Gacy's three children and their only son. Joanne was born two years earlier and, two years later, along came Karen.

Marion Elaine Gacy, *née* Robinson, was an outspoken and gregarious woman from Racine, Wisconsin. A vivacious lass, she loved to dance, sing and enjoyed a few drinks with her friends. She was also hard working, having supported herself as a pharmacist prior to her marriage at the age of 30. Her upbringing had been solid to the core, so here we find no abusive, hard-drinking butterfly; indeed, our focus is on a thoroughly decent woman.

The family patriarch, John Stanley Gacy Sr, was born in Chicago, the son of Polish immigrants. Quite the opposite of his wife, he was serious, known to be self-contained, sombre and largely incapable of displaying the gentler emotions such as happiness or sorrow.

Nevertheless, he was applauded by colleagues as an industrious machinist, a perfectionist in a perfectionist's trade, and he earned a good living.

At home, John Sr could do anything with his hands – carrying out household repairs, decorating, even creating his own tools and beating his wife, which he did frequently. Quick-tempered, he could explode without any warning. At dinner, he would lash out at anyone who said so much as a word that displeased him. He also drank heavily and believed that to spare the rod was to spoil the child.

> I've always looked after my children – even now. A lot of things my dad did, I refuse to do 'cos… I… I… don't believe in hitting children… I always felt that service to the community… and community service to others, you know, in my religious background. If you serve other people, it will come back to serve you.
>
> *John Wayne Gacy, Death Row, 1993*

It would be fair to say that John Jr had had the shakiest of starts, as he barely lived through a difficult breech birth. The Gacys' home on Opal Street, Norridge, Chicago, a location that gave a nod to suburbia, was one of six houses on the street but retained its rural charm. Visitors noticed that prairie grass grew like electric hair in every direction.

Norridge was a small community of proud, like-minded people who cared for their homes and their children. They kept livestock, including chickens and goats, and carefully tended their vegetable gardens. Doors were never locked, curtains never twitched with gossip, for they attended to their own business and expected their neighbours to attend to theirs.

With a near-death birth, John Jr's start in life was not without further problems. One day, as John Stanley worked on his car, his four-year-old son wanted to help. However, he messed up a pile of parts that his father had neatly laid out in a specific order. Mr Gacy liked things orderly. He was expected to deal with tolerances of a thousandth-of-an-inch at work, and that, in his view, was the way things should be done at home. His detail for tolerances, however, didn't extend to the treatment he meted out to his family, and little John was no exception. For this slight infraction, Gacy yelled at his son and gave him a whipping with a belt. It was a thrashing John Wayne would remember for the rest of his life.

Around the same time as the thrashing, a neighbour's 15-year-old daughter, who had minor learning difficulties, took John out into the long prairie grass and pulled his pants down. The lad ran off home, shrieking at the top of his little voice to blurt out an account of what had happened to his mother. Much acrimony existed between both sets of parents for years afterwards.

John Jr loved animals and, aged six, he was given a mongrel named Pal. In a drunken rage one day, John Stanley Gacy shot and killed the dog to punish his son, leaving the dead animal on a riverbank, where young John found it. The boy stole some flowers from a funeral parlour and gave Pal a proper burial.

The Gacy children enjoyed a Catholic education in the north of the city. Regarded by his teachers as a good student, John wasn't much liked by his schoolmates. He was overweight, clumsy and inclined to be dreamy and unimaginative. He was useless at sports and he wasn't good with his hands, either. Added to this was the fact that he was a sickly child. His mother had told him that he had a heart problem from birth, an 'enlarged bottleneck heart', which kept him away from the rough-and-tumble play of childhood. The doctors could find nothing of this bad heart, but they were soon to have cause to wonder.

John was subjected to a pitiless campaign of mental and physical abuse from his bullying father in the years to come. It seemed that never a day passed without the boy getting into trouble. The elder Gacy never missed an opportunity to let his son know he was a disappointment, and was always berating the lad for the slightest mistake, calling him 'dumb' and 'stupid'. This label must have fixed itself in Johnny's psyche like an unwelcome mantra.

Aged around five, Johnny started to have seizures, causing him to pass out for no apparent reason at all. The doctors who examined him did not immediately settle on a precise diagnosis; nevertheless, advising caution, they prescribed large quantities of strong barbiturates along with anticonvulsant drugs such as Phenytoin (Dilantin) and Phenobarbital, which are used to treat seizure disorders and status epileptics.

Taken in small doses, these drugs have few harmful side-effects. However, John Jr was packed full of these pills and, if he wasn't well before he started taking them, he was most certainly a lot worse off under their influence, because Dilantin produces a veritable harvest of side-effects.

First was gingival hyperplasia of the gums; apart from being uncomfortable and socially embarrassing, he noticed an uncontrollable growth of rapidly reddening gums which spread throughout his mouth, and this was followed by ataxia, nystagmus (involuntary movement of the eyeballs), slurred speech, decreased co-ordination with an inability to execute fine motor skills or manipulate objects, and unpredictable muscle movements. Not surprisingly, John suffered insomnia, dizziness, transient nervousness and was plagued with headaches, nausea, vomiting, constipation and, quite understandably, chronic depression. To cap it all, he also ran a very high risk of suffering toxic hepatitis and liver damage.

John's father had his own ideas about what was causing the seizures, putting it down to malingering, in an effort to miss out on school and gain attention. Marion Gacy thought differently. She knew her boy was ill and she did the best she could to protect him. As an experienced pharmacist, she should have known that her pre-adolescent son was growing steadily more dependent on the painless highs of these mood-altering drugs, and she would have noted the

7

adverse side-effects. However, her main concern was directed at the ceaseless friction between the boy and his father. She acted as a buffer to such an extent that John Stanley taunted the lad about being a 'mamma's boy' and told him he was going to be a 'queer'. Calling the child a 'he-she' was another of his favourite labels of derision.

It was not until John was ten that the doctors eventually diagnosed his malady as a form of motor epilepsy. By then, the damage had been done, for he had been taking the powerful anti-seizure drugs for five years.

When he was nine, John Wayne claims he fell prey to sexual molestation from a friend of the family, a contractor who began giving the lad rides in his truck. These trips always included episodes of tickling and wrestling. Invariably, these sessions would end up with the boy's face caught between the man's legs, John claimed while on Death Row. He knew in some way that he was being victimised, but he felt powerless to do anything about it. Telling his father was out of the question.

Although the precise date is unavailable to us, circa 1952 the family moved to a more spacious house at 4505 Mamora Street, in the north-west region of Chicago. John later recalled that his father had a 'secret place' – the large basement. Here, the man would soak up music by Richard Wagner and a lot of drink. The basement was off-limits to the rest of the family, however, when drunk, Gacy Sr would talk to himself in two different voices.

Before long, young John had found a secret place of his own underneath the front porch where he could see others but not be seen himself. Like his father who enjoyed his own private den, the lad now had his own lair and what he did there was his secret, too. That was until he took an item of his mother's underwear to his playhouse and hid it in a paper bag. In later years, Gacy would explain to interviewers that he had not used the underwear for sexual purposes; as he had previously told his parents, he just liked the feel and smell of it.

When discovered for this infraction, John was subjected to yet another beating. He was to get yet another hiding when his younger sister, Karen, found her panties in his bed. After being thrashed by his father, his mother compounded the punishment and, in an effort to end this troubling habit, she forced him to wear women's panties to school under his clothes.

So, without doubt, John Wayne Michael Gacy staggered with faltering steps into his teens, only managing to get by with the support and the partial protection from even more fatherly abuse that his mother offered him. Nevertheless, even with the storm fence in the form of the matriarch around him, the psychological battering from John's father continued relentlessly. There would be no let up until Gacy Sr died.

Aged 11, young John Gacy was doing quite well at school. He had few friends among his peers, although, again, his teachers considered him a good pupil. With that being said, he was a withdrawn lad who kept himself to himself. He wanted, indeed desperately needed, to meet his dad's high expectations, paralleling Mr Gacy's desire that he wanted a son who shared his own interests and did things the way he did. To some extent, John met some of the criteria – he was always neat and well turned out, he kept his room orderly and clean, but his father demanded so much more.

John Stanley Gacy took his 11-year-old son on a week's fishing trip to Wisconsin. This was the boy's first real chance to prove himself. Unfortunately, it rained the entire time. The fishing was ruined with the result that Gacy Sr retired to the tent and drank to excess, all the while brooding and blaming his son for the failed adventure. He never took his son fishing again.

In the same year, John was playing by a swing when he was hit in the head by one of the seats. The accident caused a blood clot in the brain; the trauma wasn't discovered until he was 16 when the blackouts ceased after he was prescribed medication to dissolve the blockage.

The tough, brutal, hard-working, hard-drinking perfectionist and disciplinarian that was Mr Gacy admired his own attributes in others, so young John set out to prove he could work hard. And it would be fair to say that, throughout his life, the 'good' John Wayne Gacy was a slogger who never let up.

At school, he ran errands for the teachers; he helped the school truant officer by telephoning parents to check up on absentees; aged 14 he took on odd jobs after school; he had a paper round; and he worked as a stock clerk and delivered groceries for a local store, and this work gave him his first salary.

John was a diligent lad, anxious to please. He helped his mother paint the house and do chores, and he made sure his school homework was still excellent. But this was still not enough in his father's eyes. Nothing the lad did was right.

This is Christ as I see him in myself. And it is monolithic because Christ to me is monolithic; he's all things to all people.
John Wayne Gacy, Death Row 1992, describing one of his paintings of Christ

Although not commonly known, least of all agreed upon, it seems probable that Gacy started killing in his fourteenth or fifteenth year, for years later he admitted stabbing a young lad to death when he was about 15. This startling claim made by Gacy can also be supported by an unimpeachable source – none other than the former Des Plaines Chief of Police, Joe Kozenczak, who was the prime investigator in the 33 murders.

In the summer of 1989, Joe Kozenczak says he was sitting at his desk when Sergeant John Sarnowski of the Chicago PD called on him. The officer had read Russ Ewing's book on Gacy called *Buried Dreams*.

In 1955, Sarnowski had been a detective with the CPD. Furthermore, in the October of that year, John and Anton Schuessler and their friend Robert Peterson were found brutally murdered.

In his book *A Passing Acquaintance*, Joe records that 'the boys' battered bodies were found in a forest preserve area on the north-west side of Cook County. About a year after the murders, Sarnowski was assigned to the case, and now thirty years later, he was still haunted with it.'

While the CPD sergeant had been reading about the young John Gacy in Ewing's book he suddenly realised that Gacy, Peterson, the Schuessler lads, aged 11 and 14, had lived within close proximity of each other on the north-west side of Chicago.

Gacy lived at 4505 North Mamora. The Schuesslers at 6711 North Mango Avenue; Robert Peterson at 5519 Farragut Street. Therefore, Gacy lived about a mile from the Peterson household, and a very short distance from the Schuesslers. Of some added significance, the school John Gacy attended at the time was at Prussing, which was close to the Farnsworth School attended by Peterson.

What had also piqued Det Sergeant Sarnowski's interest was that, as a youth, Gacy had frequently visited the Monte Cristo Bowling Alley. Coincidentally, this was the same bowling alley attended by the three other lads.

John Sarnowski had seen a photo of Gacy taken shortly after his arrest for serial murder, and he couldn't help but notice the strong resemblance between it and an artist's conception of a boy who used to meet with Robert Peterson when he took his sister to an eye doctor's surgery. According to the sergeant, the drawing was developed with the help from the eye doctor who described the boy [Gacy] as looking like Mr Potato Head and having a limp.

At first, Joe Kozenczak couldn't believe his ears. The very notion that Gacy might have become a serial killer at the age of 14 was completely alien to him. It would have probably been alien to the entire US law enforcement system as it is extremely rare to find a person committing serial murder at such a young age.

Sergeant Sarnowski persisted, continuing to add weight to his theory by suggesting that the *modus operandi* used to murder the three boys seemed to reflect a young serial murderer who had not yet perfected his method.

But that was not the end of it. Sarnowski added that Peterson had been strangled; that there was an indentation on the front of the throat from a sailor's knot, or from something else. (Gacy would often kill his victims with a ligature twisted tight with a length of dowel rod, which would have caused similar trauma to the throat area.)

The evidence found on the boys' bodies in 1955 indicated that they might have been killed in a machine-shop type of environment. Sarnowski reminded Kozenczak that the Gacys had had a machine shop in the basement of their house on Mamora Street.

There were a few other correlations, some which interested Kozenczak and others that didn't. The idea that one boy could overpower three boys at the same time seemed most unlikely, yet it was not impossible.

Sarnowski had brought this matter to his superiors, who found no reason to pursue the theory.

Shortly after their meeting, Kozenczak and Sarnowski visited the crime archives at Maybrook. The officer in the records section pulled down a box – a cardboard box that should have contained the complete files on the three murders. When they blew the dust off, they found to their utter dismay that the container was empty. The vitally important files were lost for ever.

At the age of 17, Gacy was diagnosed with a non-specific heart ailment. He was hospitalised on several occasions for this problem throughout his life, but the doctors were not able to find an exact cause for the pain he was suffering. Although John complained frequently about his heart, even more so after his arrest for serial murder, he never suffered any serious heart-attack, and many thought it was an attempt to gain sympathy votes, of which he received none.

The year 1960 started on a sound note for 18-year-old John Wayne Gacy, for by now he had learned that people admire volunteer workers. He knew that trusted and respected public servants such as law officers and firemen were at the top of the list. Deprived of respect by his father at home, he had gained respect at school from his volunteer work. The grocery-store boss admired him for being a hard-working and industrious young lad, and this was sufficient reward for the moment.

John formed a civil defence squad at his high school. As the organiser, he awarded himself the rank of captain. He even attached a flashing blue light to the dashboard of his car and, wearing his cop-type uniform, he delighted in racing off to a fire or traffic incident. It made him feel important, needed, respected. It gave him a sense of belonging, a kind of acceptance that came with his new responsibilities, something he'd sought so frequently from his father at home, to no avail.

In his late teens, it would seem that, at last, the friendly and earnest John Wayne Gacy was starting to succeed and move up the social ladder. However, in one area, he considered himself an abject failure – he was useless and pathetic with the opposite sex.

John was an unappealing sight; his doughy shape and potato head simply didn't appeal to the girls. On the rare occasions when he did find himself starting a sexual encounter, his nerves got the better of him and he failed. On one occasion in his car he passed out, just as he had done so many times before when under stress. The girl had partially stripped and they were groping each other when he fainted. The girl was shocked, Gacy was mortified, and, when he told his father, Gacy Sr was furious with his weak son. Mr Gacy hated homosexuals, and told young John he was becoming a queer. He was a sissy and a weakling. But 18-year-old John refused to give up trying to please, so he threw himself into politics.

John ventured into political life by placing one toe in the water, starting volunteer work for an alderman candidate in the 45th Ward. For such a young man, he had taken on a great responsibility, yet, despite his success, his father ridiculed him. 'Politics is all bullshit,' his father ranted, 'politicians are phonies; you are a patsy for working for free.'

Nevertheless, John loved the work and long hours. He had found new friends who trusted and admired him. He had found another home in politics, a place where he was wanted and respected. Here, he could succeed and make his mark, so he dropped out of high school in 1961. Now, aged 19, the rift between himself and his father widened more than ever before.

Anyone that I've had sex with, so far as I know, is still alive.

John Gacy to the Des Plaines PD

We could never accuse John Wayne Gacy of being workshy. Despite all of his faults, here we find a young man who was driven to hard toil by his brutal and domineering father – not so much because Mr Gacy demanded it of his son, but because John wanted to please in any way he could.

Not merely content with his political work, John laboured away on behalf of the Catholic Church, turning his hand to anything asked of him with zeal. Carrying out repairs, picking up the elderly and dropping them home after services, collecting and delivering their groceries – nothing was too much trouble. In fact, he spent so much time at church, he considered the priesthood. He even became a member of the St John Berchmann's parish bowling team and showed some promise.

John recognised that the church was not meeting the needs of some parishioners, particularly the young ones. And, while it is easy for us to denigrate John's well-intentioned ambitions, knowing as we do now that he was to become one of the most heinous serial murderers of all time, it's true that he formed a young adults group called the Chi Ro Club. Ever the organiser and eager to please, he put together social events, ran yard sales to raise cash and scheduled a formal winter dance.

> I really wanted to become a priest. Even went to confession and hinted this. But all they wanted was someone to do plumbing and carpentry. Stuff like that. One time, during confession, all the priest wanted to discuss was a building quote from my father.
>
> *John Gacy to Lt Joe Kozenczak*

Then Gacy's world fell apart. During one of his more generous days, it is claimed that Mr Gacy Sr purchased a new 1960 Chevrolet Impala for his son. It was to become John's pride and joy and he kept it spotless. However, there was a catch. The truth was that Mr Gacy loaned John the money for the car and John suddenly found himself in debt to his dad. Now John's father had more control over him than ever before.

After one argument, Gacy Sr removed the distributor cap, saying he would replace it when the arrears were up to date. John was not only humiliated but also inwardly fuming. Unable to get to and from work to carry out his tasks for the church or fulfil his other social obligations, he brooded. After three days, he paid his father back and the distributor part was replaced. This time, though, John had had enough. Telling his mother that he was off out to put air in the tyres, he vanished for three months.

Having by now dropped out of no less than four high schools and with no diploma, John Jr drove to Las Vegas where he found work as an ambulance driver for the Palm Mortuary and Memorial Park. This employment was soon terminated when the staff discovered that John was too young to drive ambulances; John was 20 and the minimum legal age was 21. However, rather than lose the enterprising young man, his boss assigned him to the mortuary; work that necessitated contact with dead bodies.

Not knowing where her son was, Mrs Gacy was beside herself with worry and couldn't sleep. Knowing that John was physically and emotionally sick, she fretted for his wellbeing. For his part, John Gacy Sr could not have cared less, that is until a letter about medical bills from his insurance company dropped through the letterbox.

Mr Gacy flipped.

Marion called the hospital where her son had been receiving treatment and was informed that young John was paying off the bill, and that he was working at the Palm Mortuary in Las Vegas.

There was something about the detached, professional way the morticians went about their work that appealed to John Gacy. He found himself fascinated with cadavers and death. The stillness of the corpses, white, bereft of life, skin batlike tight over fragile bone, touched something primitive in him. He learned how the bodies were cleaned, treated and embalmed. And, because he had no proper lodgings, he slept on the premises, which gave him access to the deceased at night.

Alone in a strange city, without friends and no social life, John Gacy became a ghoul. When all was secured in the funeral home and the staff had left, he would shuffle over to the cabinets and pull out a drawer. In the weak, yellowy light, he would converse in hushed tones with the corpses, explain his troubles and touch the bodies ever so gently, curiously examining them. Sometimes he would undress them, neatly fold the clothes and leave them next to the caskets. He did this night after night until the director became suspicious and telephoned the Las Vegas Police to get some advice on what to do, but nothing was ever proven, and Gacy soon moved on to another job.

The Des Plaines Police eventually learned that the John Gacy was a necrophiliac. He enjoyed having sexual relations with his victims both before and after he killed them, sometimes keeping their bodies around and sleeping with them for a day or so after their deaths.

Tiring of Las Vegas, John phoned his mother and asked if he could come home. It would take him three months to save enough money for the trip back to Chicago.

In 1963, with the newfound confidence he had found by living and working in Las Vegas, John Wayne Gacy enrolled in a year-long course at a local business college, and moved in with a maternal uncle and aunt. When he completed his studies, he found a position as a management trainee for Nunn Bush, a large shoe company based in Illinois. Here he proved to be a born salesman, a hit with the staff and customers alike. Easy-going and hard-working, he soon was promoted to departmental manager for the company at the Robinson department store, 821 E Cook Street near Springfield.

Then John discovered the Junior Chamber of Commerce – the Jaycees. Established in 1920 to provide opportunities for young men to develop personal and leadership skills through services to others, the Jaycees helped establish Air Mail services in the USA with Jaycee Charles Lindberg, and have raised millions of dollars for causes such as the Muscular Dystrophy Association and the March of Dimes, a charitable organisation which fights the growing crisis of premature childbirth in America.

Jaycees can be found in all walks of life, ranging from past presidents Bill Clinton and Gerald Ford, business tycoons such as Domino Pizza mogul Tom Monaghan, registered nurse and former Miss America, Kay Lani Rafko-Wilson, to sports heroes like basketball player, the great Larry Bird.

In 1963, the Jaycees enrolled 21-year-old John Wayne Gacy. John took to the Jaycees like a duck to water and was in his element. Out of the reach of his domineering father, he blossomed, for he was now in the company of like-minded young people whose watchwords were 'honour' and 'achievement'. And, as he had done previously while working as a volunteer for the Catholic Church, he threw himself into the organisation with such determination that he won the 'Key Man' award for April 1964; no small achievement for he had only been in Springfield for three months.

Indeed, John was now on a roll. He met a young woman, Marlynn Myers, who worked at the Robinson store and they dated. 'It was kinda like love at first sight,' Gacy later claimed.

But he then discovered other highly charged feelings. John had been out drinking with a male colleague – a young man several years older than himself – and, at the end of the evening, they returned to the man's house for coffee. A homosexual encounter soon followed with the two men ending up naked and Gacy receiving oral sex.

After his arrest for murder, Gacy said somewhat hypocritically to the author, 'Although I enjoyed it at first, I felt ashamed and violated. He outsmarted me and I felt used.'

In September 1964, Gacy, now 22, married Marlynn, whose father, Fred Myers, was a successful franchiser of Kentucky Fried Chicken with outlets in Waterloo, Iowa.

The year 1966 found Gacy being named as the first Vice-President of the Jaycees, the outstanding first-year Jaycee in his area, and the organisation's third outstanding member state-wide. His wife became pregnant with their first child, Christie, although his father remained tight-lipped – perhaps secretly he was somewhat impressed by his son's exceptional achievements.

Gacy's new father-in-law was not overly impressed with his daughter's choice of husband. He didn't regard Gacy as good breeding stock; nevertheless, he was crazy about his daughter, so he offered the couple a house and his son-in-law a job managing three chicken franchises in Waterloo.

The position paid $15,000 a year, plus a percentage of the profits. John went on to take a course at the Kentucky Fried Chicken University, joined the Waterloo Jaycees and revelled in the best years of his life.

1966 brought even more success for John Gacy. His son, Michael, was born. He worked 10–14 hours a day, and maintained his tireless devotion to the Jaycees, organising events, recruiting new members, co-ordinating fundraising efforts, and devoting his skills to community projects. At meetings and events, he always arrived with buckets of chicken to hand out in a well-meant public-relations exercise. John also joined the Waterloo Merchant Patrol, a kind of auxiliary made up of citizens who helped augment the police protection of businesses. He carried a sidearm and even had a red flashing light put on the dashboard of his car. And John also liked being around young boys. If they had blond hair, all the better.

John Gacy was voted the Jaycees' outstanding member for 1967, and he was chaplain of the local organisation. In line for presidency of the Waterloo club in 1968, Gacy was almost there. He had political connections, boasting friends in just about every type of business, and many of his pals were in the police and fire department. Married with two adorable children, a nice house and a secure income, what could possibly go wrong now?

Everything seemed to be looking good for John Wayne Gacy Jr. Yet his lucky streak would not last too much longer. Rumours were spreading around town, more importantly among Jaycee members, regarding Gacy's sexual preferences. It seemed that young lads were always in Gacy's presence. Everyone in town had heard the stories that Gacy was a homosexual – or, more correctly, bisexual – and that he made passes at the young boys who worked for him at the fast-food franchises. However, people close to him refused to believe in the gossip.

That was until May 1968 when rumours became truths and the world of John Wayne Gacy imploded.

TWO

Hunting... and Hunted

It was all their [his victims'] fault. They stalked and came on to me.

John Wayne Gacy, Death Row

20 MAY 1968 – WATERLOO, IOWA – SODOMY – 10 YEARS
09 SEPTEMBER 1968 – CONSPIRACY – ASSAULT WITH ATTEMPT TO
COMMIT FELONY DD 3036939
12 SEPTEMBER 1968 – BURGLARY AND ENTRY
11 DECEMBER 1968 – (REF # 26526 BLACK HAWK COUNTY)
Extract from Gacy's FBI rap sheet # 585181 G

IN the spring of 1968, Gacy was indicted by a Grand Jury in Black Hawk County for allegedly committing the act of sodomy with a teenage boy named Donald Voorhees.

The story which developed was that Gacy was driving along when he heard a young lad call out, 'Hey, Mr Gacy...' He pulled his

JOHN WAYNE MICHAEL GACY

car over and, when he realised that the boy was the son of another Jaycee, he offered him a ride. Donald had been at his girlfriend's home and was walking home. Gacy seized the moment to bring up the subject of sex. He mentioned some stag films which several of the Jaycees had allegedly been watching. Donald said that he had never seen such a film, and by now Gacy's heart was racing. With Marlynn out of town, he had his house to himself so he invited Donald to join him at home.

They had a few drinks, and Gacy manipulated the lad into exchanging acts of oral sex. Indeed, after that night they met several times for sex. Gacy claimed that these liaisons were at Donald's request and he paid him some money in return.

But Gacy had crossed the line. In March 1968, Donald learned that Gacy was planning to run for Jaycee president and that his own father had been approached by Gacy to act as his campaign manager. Ron spilled the beans about his relationship with Gacy, and soon police were hammering on Gacy's front door.

While executing their search warrant, officers found pornographic videos portraying oral sex, so they charged Gacy with sodomy. Donald told the court that Gacy had tricked him into being tied up while visiting Gacy's home a year earlier, and had violently raped him. Gacy denied all the charges, claiming that Donald had willingly had sexual relations with him in order to earn extra money. Gacy further insisted that Jaycee members opposed to him becoming president of the local chapter organisation were setting him up.

Rapidly, the case moved on to a Grand Jury, where, for the first time, Gacy learned that he was in even more trouble. In late August 1967, another boy, Edward Lynch, a 16-year-old employee of one of the chicken franchises, had been invited to his boss's home while Marlynn was away.

First, they went to the basement, had a few drinks and played pool, the lecherous Gacy watching Edward's every move. The winner would give oral sex, and Gacy lost each frame. Gacy would

21

argue that the suggestion of the prize was the lad's idea, however, after the game, the boy baulked, so they repaired to the front room where Gacy played a few videos. Now extremely sexually aroused, Gacy suggested that they go to the master bedroom and he pulled out a kitchen knife with which to force the lad into submission. The boy was terrified and tried to run. A short scuffle ensued, during which Gacy lost possession of the knife, and Edward suffered a few cuts. Then the steam went out of the older man and Gacy apologised.

Having calmed the lad and himself down, Gacy insisted on showing another film. Edward reluctantly agreed. After all, he wanted to keep his job, and Gacy had apologised. The next thing he knew, the boy's boss had produced a padlock and length of chain; Gacy also wanted to bind the boy's hands.

Reluctantly, the lad agreed and was lucky to escape with his life.

Once again, Gacy would later argue that the idea of the chain and padlock came from Edward; however, Edward claimed that, when Gacy tried to sit on his lap, face-to-face, he head-butted Gacy, who tried to force the boy's face down on to a cot and began to choke him. He released his grip only when the boy fell unconscious for a few seconds. Then Gacy reverted back to normal – Dr Jekyll and Mr Hyde had arrived. He apologised again, then drove Edward home. Despite Gacy's promises that there were no hard feelings, Edward was fired from his job a few days later. Gacy was now facing charges relating to Edward as well as those arising from the case brought by Donald.

Despite it all, Gacy persisted in his bid to become president of the Jaycees. He even volunteered to take a lie-detector test to prove his innocence to his friends. He undertook two polygraph examinations and failed both.

Notwithstanding this, many of his fellow Jaycees rallied around Gacy, refusing to believe that such a 'fine, upstanding brother' could be a sexual deviant. He stayed in the running for president until he was nominated and then, quite suddenly, he did the decent thing – he fell on his sword, emotionally announcing his withdrawal 'in the interests of the organisation and my family'.

Moral support for John Gacy had all but evaporated by now. His wife could hardly hold her head up in her beloved community. John's father was incandescent with rage and Fred Myers was on the verge of sacking his son-in-law. For his part, Gacy thought he could wheedle his way out of his problems by the simple expedient of threatening Donald with his life if he testified against him.

In September, with the court case looming, Gacy hired an 18-year-old thug called Russell Schroeder to persuade Donald not to testify. Without this witness, Gacy reasoned that he could beat the rap against him for assaulting Edward. The police had the chain and padlock as evidence, and they had also recovered the stag movies, but John Gacy maintained that there had been no sex, only a fight, which had merely been a high-spirited tiff between young men after a drink.

Gacy, with his high social standing in the community and supported by his powerful friends, thought he could win the case hands down. He convinced himself that he would resume his social and business life as if nothing had ever happened.

For his part, Schroeder jumped at the chance to earn the $300 offered by Gacy for his services. It was money he could use to pay off the loan on his car. He approached Donald, who dismissed the threat out of hand, so Schroeder fired a Mace spray at the lad, burning his face. In agony, the lad rushed home sobbing. His parents took him to the hospital and reported the incident to the police.

Under questioning, Schroeder soon cracked and implicated Gacy, who was manifestly now in more trouble than before.

As the investigation into the sodomy allegation was being prepared, other witnesses lost their fear of Gacy and came forward. At the front of the queue was 17-year-old Richard Westphal. He had worked for Gacy, and he told investigators that Gacy often played pool with him, the prize being oral sex, which the lad declined. Gacy had also coerced his wife, Marlynn, into sleeping with Richard, who was a virgin. After they had finished in bed, Gacy ambled into the room saying the boy 'owed him one'.

Another 18-year-old who worked at the same restaurant as Richard reported that Gacy had threatened him with a pistol. Gacy played a bluff game of Russian roulette with him because the boy had talked to Richard and knew too much about Gacy's perverted sex life.

A 15-year-old lad came forward claiming that Gacy paid him and other boys $5 each for helping out in 'sex experiments' which he claimed he was conducting for the Governor of Iowa.

John Wayne Michael Gacy, aged 26, was ruined.

As with the majority of sex offenders, the courts may order that a person attend a psychiatric hospital for evaluation prior to a court case. Gacy could not make the $10,000 bail bond so he was packed off to the Psychopathic Hospital at the State University of Iowa to await his trial. There, he was examined over a period of 17 days. Apart from being overweight, the doctors could not find anything physically wrong with him.

Dr LD Amick was one of the psychiatrists assigned to Gacy at that time. He found that Gacy had an IQ of 118, which was 'bright and normal'. But the shrink also concluded that Gacy enjoyed a total denial of responsibility for anything that went wrong in his life. He had an excuse for every accusation; he would twist the truth about every wayward move to deflect blame from himself, and make himself look good, however damning the circumstances.

As to molesting boys? Gacy had 'no remorse over his admitted deeds', Dr Amick penned in his trial report. 'We regard Mr Gacy as an antisocial personality – a diagnostic term for individuals who are basically unsocialised and whose behaviour pattern brings them repeatedly into conflict with society.' Dr Amick concluded, 'No known medical treatment can help such people because they do not learn from experience.'

So, it could be argued that John Stanley Gacy Sr had much to answer for. He had created a sexual psychopath, a young man who would later turn into a creature of monstrous proportions.

Days before his trial, Gacy changed his mind and decided to throw himself at the mercy of the court by pleading guilty to the sodomy charge. This was a calculated move by Gacy to wheedle his way out of a prison sentence, and he almost succeeded.

Investigating probation officer Jack Harker had been so impressed by Gacy's convincing manner that he supported John, arguing that a period of supervised probation would serve just as well as any prison term. Also in Gacy's favour was the fact this was his first offence and he had agreed to move back to Illinois, well away from Iowa.

Judge Peter Van Merte had been a sitting judge for years. Here was a hardliner who had heard this type of claptrap before. Sitting patiently while the defence made its argument in favour of a lighter sentence, the judge thought long and hard about John's abuse of his position at work, and how the respected Jaycees had been brought into disrepute in his own city. The judge took a very dim view of the accused, more so because there seemed to be a pattern of molestation, which, if not stopped now, would only escalate.

To exacerbate the issue, Gacy was not an Iowa homeboy. Facing the judge was a city slicker from out of town, a man who had abused his position in the judge's own community to abuse young boys.

The judge sentenced Gacy to ten years in the grimly ornate Iowa State Reformatory for Men at Anamosa – 25 miles east of Cedar Rapids, in the heart of 'Nowhere Land'.

That very same day, Marlynn Gacy filed for divorce. She later remarried and John Wayne Gacy would never see his wife and children again. Somewhat shamefully, however, this pervert was released back into the community after serving just 18 months of his sentence, being paroled back to Chicago on Thursday, 18 June 1970. His rap sheet informs us that his parole was discharged on Tuesday, 19 October 1971.

Prisoner #26526 John Wayne Gacy threw himself into prison life with the same degree of enthusiasm as he had done when at liberty. In fact, not a day passed when Gacy was not organising or doing something. He passed the examinations for a high-school equivalency, something he had failed to achieve before, and took college credits in psychology.

Setting out to impress inmates and staff alike, John toiled in the prison kitchen and was thrilled to find that the facility had a Jaycee chapter. Working all the hours allocated to him, he spearheaded the design and building of a miniature golf course for the inmates' use, and prepared Jaycee banquets. He won a number of Jaycee honours, including the club's 'Sound Citizens Award', and the roles of chaplain and legal counsel became his.

In a controlled environment, John was as good as gold.

However, prison life had not all been a complete bed of roses. Of course, on 'the outside' he had lost everything he had worked for, and then he lost something else. On Christmas Day 1969, John Stanley Gacy died of cirrhosis of the liver. The man had been completely broken by his son's crimes and the disgrace John had heaped on his family. Several times, John Sr had been reduced to tears – the only times he had cried in his life.

Upon his release from Anamosa, the prison warden shook Gacy's hand, explaining that, while he had been a model prisoner, he was sad to see him walk out of the gates.

Gacy travelled to Chicago, moving back with his mother who now lived in a new condominium. Finding work as a cook at a popular restaurant called Bruno's, his employment brought him into contact with members of the Chicago Black Hawks hockey team and a number of Cook County Police officers, many of whom he befriended.

In February 1971, having only been out of prison for eight months, 29-year-old Gacy was in trouble once again. He picked up a teenager near the Greyhound bus station and tried to force him to have sex. Gacy would later claim, once again, that it was the lad's fault. The boy, he alleged, had offered sex. Despite this, Gacy was arrested and charged with assault but, for reasons unknown, the complainant didn't show up at court so the case was dismissed. Gacy had escaped returning to prison by the skin of his teeth. Had he been found guilty, perhaps 33 young men would not have lost their lives.

By the time his period of parole expired, Gacy was found hanging around with a young man named Mickel Reid. They had met on a street corner as early as November 1970 while Gacy was trawling for sex. The two men had talked about setting up a home-maintenance business and they chose to name it 'PDM Contractors' (Property Development Maintenance Contractors), a name that John's mother had suggested.

Trade boomed and the backyard at the condo soon became too small for all of the building materials, so mother and son bought a three-bedroom, ranch-style place at 8231 West Summerdale Avenue, Des Plaines. The financial arrangement meant that John owned half of the property, while his mother and two sisters owned the other half. Two lads then moved into the spacious house – they were Mickel Reid and one of John's co-workers at Bruno's called Roger.

Like most of Gacy's homosexual relationships, the one between Reid and John was destined to fail. For some bizarre reason, one evening when the two were working in the garage that adjoined the property, Gacy struck Reid over the head with a hammer. This assault, as we may imagine, drew some blood and, when the older man raised the weapon a second time, Reid fought him off. Gacy stopped and apologised, but the incident terrified Reid and he left immediately. Roger followed.

If we are to believe Gacy, his first murder – other than any killings committed when he was in his middle teens – took place on New Year's Day in 1972.

John, now 30, had joined his mother at a family party and he got drunk on Scotch. That night, Marion Gacy stayed with friends, while her inebriated son sat around brooding. Then he suddenly got into his car and disappeared into the night. 'I just went looking around,' Gacy later told police.

By Gacy's own admission, he drove to the Greyhound bus station in Chicago where he spotted a light-haired youth whom he remembered as 'the Greyhound Bus Boy'. Tim McCoy was from Omaha, Nebraska, and had just arrived in Illinois. Gacy invited him back to his house where they had drinks and sandwiches, followed by sex. According to Gacy's later statement – which can be safely taken with a pinch of salt – he retired to his own room while Tim slept in the guest room.

Gacy said that he awoke to find the youth walking towards him brandishing a butcher's knife in his hand. He claimed that, in the ensuing struggle, the boy fell on the knife and stabbed himself to death.

In a second version of the story, Gacy claimed that the boy didn't fight back; rather, Tim seemed surprised and frightened. As Gacy grappled for the knife, he was accidentally cut on the left forearm and felt 'a surge of power from my toes to my brain'. Then he said he plunged the knife into Tim's chest. 'When it was all over,' Gacy claimed, 'I looked down at the pants he'd worn to bed. They were covered with blood – but with something else, too. During the struggle, I had experienced a powerful sexual release.'

After the stabbing, Gacy had a problem, and that was how to dispose of the body. No one would believe it was self-defence, so he cleaned up the blood, dragged the corpse to the foyer closet, opened the crawlspace trapdoor and pushed it through. He would bury it later. However, the truth of why the lad was walking towards Gacy with a knife soon became patently clear. When Gacy went into the kitchen, on the worktop were a carton of eggs and a joint of unsliced bacon. The young guest had not been planning murder, but was preparing breakfast for his host.

On Thursday, 22 June 1972, the Northbrook Police booked Gacy on charges of aggravated battery and reckless conduct SOL (Stricken on Leave to Reinstate). This incident stemmed from an accusation that Gacy had fought with one of his sex partners, and then attempted to run the boy down with his car.

It transpired that, posing as a police officer, Gacy had lured the young man into his car and handcuffed him. After a short conversation, Gacy said, 'What's it worth to you to get out of this?' When the lad explained that he didn't have much money, Gacy asked, 'Would you suck my dick?'

Fearing for his life, the passenger consented. Gacy drove to the restaurant where he worked and forced the boy into the toilet. It was between 3.30 and 4.30am. Once inside the building, the lad resisted Gacy's attempts to make him perform oral sex and he was hit on the head several times and kicked. Somehow, handcuffed though he was, the lad managed to open the door to the toilet and ran off down the road. Gacy followed in his car and knocked him down. The victim survived to testify, but the overworked court system got into plea-bargaining and finally granted Gacy the disposition 'Stricken on Leave to Reinstate'. This meant that Gacy had been issued with a warning that if he were brought in front of the courts again the charge would be reinstated. Once again, the criminal-justice system had failed the community, for, if the case had gone ahead, a number of young boys would not have been slaughtered and ended up, their remains rotting, in the crawlspace beneath Gacy's home.

There are many who claim that John Wayne Gacy was a homosexual. To be accurate, he was bisexual and, to prove this point, he married a woman named Carole (Huff) Lofgren on Saturday, 1 July 1972 – just nine days after the Northbrook Police had arrested and bailed him.

Gacy and Carole had known each other from their school days. Carole, herself recently divorced, found John 'a very warm, understanding person, easy to talk to'. She claimed that he was comforting to her and her two daughters, four-year-old Tammy and

April, aged two, from her first marriage, and she accepted the fact, when he told her, that he was bisexual.

What we do know is that Gacy was a Dr Jekyll and Mr Hyde. His mind had split in two. On the one hand, there was Gacy the successful contractor, community builder, event organiser and friendly neighbour, while, on the other hand, he was a sexual pervert, a sexual sadist, whose murderous compulsions were growing out of control. The stronger personality, the killer, would soon dominate, to turn John Wayne Gacy into one of the most heinous serial murderers of all time.

Carole, her two daughters and her mother, Jean Cienciwa, moved into Gacy's home on West Summerdale. Carole would later tell police that she was aware that he had been married previously with two children, and had been in trouble in Iowa. She had believed John when he had told her that the charges were primarily concerned with pornography. She knew nothing of the sodomy charges. Had she known the truth, she would have never married him.

Initially, the two little girls were pleased to be around John Gacy. They tried hard to please him and readily climbed on to his lap to share what they had done with him during the day or just in an effort to communicate with their new father. However, Carole recalled that her daughters quickly discovered that the man they called their 'Daddy' had no time for their affection and they, in turn, eventually stopped trying.

John was mirroring the lack of affection and the rejection his own father had meted out to him. Carole and her mother now sensed something was very wrong.

After John Gacy's arrest for murder, Detective Lt Joseph Kozenczak and Detective Greg Bedoe spoke to Carole at length. She recalled that her husband's unusual behaviour didn't stop with his rejection of Carole's daughters, and that it was not uncommon for John to lounge around the bedroom, naked, and to masturbate while flicking through homosexual magazines. When she taunted him, he would push her across the room. There were stag magazines everywhere, even under the sink in the kitchen. She found semen-stained silk bikini underwear behind the bedroom dresser and under their bed. Initially, she thought that he was trying to arouse her, however, around the same time, she began to notice some other unusual activities involving her husband. He was staying out late and, occasionally, he would pull his car into the driveway up to the garage with its lights out, park the vehicle and go into the garage. Often, he had a young, blond-haired boy with him.

Carole was scared; although she loved John, her suspicions were now truly aroused. She told the detectives that on one occasion she took the key to the garage and had a look inside. What she found shocked her. The interior had been decorated. There were mattresses over the floor, red lights plugged into the walls and mirrors on the ceiling.

And there was something else. The new bride started to smell a strange, sickly sweet odour emanating from the crawlspace under the house. Carole called upon neighbourly Mrs Grexas, who thought that a rat had died under the floor. John blamed the stench on the damp crawlspace.

On one occasion, Carole claimed she awoke at around 4.00am when she heard his car entering the driveway. When John turned on the light, Carole's presence startled him. He became angry and ordered her back to bed. She asked him what he was doing, but he became madder, so she retired without another word being said. Sometimes, he would arrive home during the early hours and sleep on the couch in the recreation room, which he had fitted out with a bar and a pool table.

Later, she learned that John was having sex with young men who worked at PDM. Not all were compliant, however, and one strong lad beat up Gacy in the driveway. Gacy told Carole it was merely a dispute over money. Years later, she would learn the truth. Gacy had tried to rape the lad and had come off much the worse for wear.

Despite his bizarre and depraved domestic behaviour, by 1974 the Mr Hyde in Gacy had well and truly ingratiated himself into the community. While some considered that he was a loud-mouthed braggart, he was generally popular, and always willing to help his neighbours out, even if this meant shovelling snow from their driveways when he had more pressing matters at hand. To the locals, he was a great guy, even more so when he started to host theme parties.

One event had a Hawaiian *luau* theme, another had a cowboy Western flavour; with around 300 guests attending each one, they were usually held on Independence Day – 4 July – and his barbecues became the talk of the town.

By now, John's reputation had outgrown Des Plaines. At one function – the groundbreaking of a new retirement centre for the elderly he had helped raise money for – Gacy had his photograph taken with the then mayor, Michael Bilandic. As he had a criminal record, Gacy could never aspire to such high office, but he was able to nourish his longstanding taste for politics in less influential ways.

It was not long before Gacy caught the attention of Robert F Matwick, the Democratic township committee member for Norwood Park. As a free service to the community, Gacy and his employees volunteered to clean up the Democratic Party headquarters.

In 1975, Gacy achieved an appointed post, his first political position: Secretary-Treasurer of the Norwood Park Township Street Lighting District. He headed up Chicago's Polish Constitution Day Parade, and it went like clockwork. He ran the River Grove Moose Lodge – aged 33, he was now too old to be a Jaycee – and, as part of the organisation's 'Jolly Jokers Club', Gacy further impressed Matwick when the contractor dressed up as Pogo the Clown to entertain children at parties and hospitals.

Indeed, Gacy invented two clown characters. One was the tattered Patches and the other was Pogo. 'Pogo was the happy clown,' he said, 'while Patches was more serious.' Gacy's interest in clowns remained with him right up to his execution.

But Dr Jekyll was never very far away.

Trouble started to brew again when gossip began to circulate about Gacy having a homosexual interest in teenage boys. One of the rumours stemmed from an incident that took place during the time Gacy was involved with cleaning the Democratic Party headquarters. A teenager who worked with Gacy on that particular project was 16 years old and, according to the boy, Gacy made sexual advances towards him, yet backed off when the youngster threatened to hit him with a chair. Gacy joked about the situation and left him alone for a while.

The following month, while the boy was visiting Gacy's home, Gacy again approached him. Gacy tried to trick the young man into handcuffs and, believing he was securely cuffed, he began to undress the boy. However, the boy made sure that one of his hands was loosely cuffed and he was able to free himself and wrestle Gacy to the ground. Once he had Gacy on the floor, he handcuffed him, but eventually let him go after Gacy promised he would never try touching him again. Gacy honoured his promise, and the boy remained working for Gacy for another year following the incident.

At his office in Chicago, Joe Kozenczak recalled that one of the most significant things Carole had told him related to an event that took place on Mother's Day 1975. John had risen early and told her that he was going to give her a Mother's Day gift, and that, when he had done so, he would tell her something interesting. He started to have intercourse with her and, when they had finished, he announced that she should never expect sex again. 'I am through with women,' he said. Carole thought that this was a morbid joke but, as time marched on, it turned out to be the truth.

After this Mother's Day incident – her gift being intercourse – John had no qualms about commenting on young men and their bodies. He'd sit at a bar and lewdly comment on a 'guy's tight ass' or describe the hair and build of the type of young man who turned him on. Of course, at this stage, no one knew just how far John's obsession had actually taken him… or would take him.

THREE

Bodies of Evidence

That Butkovich kid owed me money for the damn apartment carpeting... carpeting... oh, the bloodstains... that happened when I stored one of the guys upside down... it usually ran out of his nose or mouth or something... but Butkovich, usually takes three knots and the stick to kill these guys with the rope... it only took two with him. I covered his body with tarp before the concrete.

John Gacy to Detective Larry Finder

Seventeen-year-old John Butkovich was like most young men who enjoy cars and he took great pride in his 1968 Dodge upon which he was continually working. He particularly loved to race his car. It was an expensive hobby and, in order to pay for new parts, he knew he had to get a job.

Butkovich, who had lived at 4835 North Kenmore, Chicago, began doing remodelling work for Gacy at PDM Contractors. It was a position that he enjoyed and one that paid well. He and Gacy had a good working relationship, which made the long hours pass by more quickly. However, their working relationship ended abruptly when Gacy refused to pay Butkovich for two weeks' work. Gacy often refused to pay his employees in order to save money for his own purposes.

On Tuesday, 29 July 1975, angered that Gacy had withheld his pay, Butkovich went over to his boss's house with two friends to collect what he believed was rightfully his. When Butkovich confronted him about his paycheque, Gacy refused to pay him and a heated argument erupted. Butkovich threatened that he was going to tell the authorities that he was not deducting taxes from earnings. Gacy was enraged and screamed at him. Finally, John and his friends realised that there was little they could do, so they eventually left Gacy's house. John dropped off his friends at their home and drove away, never to be seen alive again.

Gacy later told police that he had called Butkovich back to his house on the promise of payment. He apologised about the disagreement and they had a drink. Then the argument started again, and Gacy, now alone with the lad, handcuffed him and said nothing more.

When Gacy awoke in the morning, he said the boy's body was just where he had left him, alive, but now he was dead. There was a rope around the lad's neck. Gacy rolled the body up in a tarpaulin and dragged it into the garage. He planned to dump it later. When his wife returned home, he told her Butkovich had left his employment and that was the end of the matter.

However, disposing of the body was not as easy as John would have liked it to be. With his wife now on the premises, there was no way he could get it down into the crawlspace unseen, and the corpse was beginning to stink. So Gacy dug a hole in the only part of the garage that was not concreted, a section three feet by one- and-a-half feet, where he had planned to install a drain.

The corpse was stiff and, as much as John jumped up and down on it, it would not bend in half and compress enough to get it into the small grave. Eventually, after an hour of strenuous exertion, Gacy managed the task and covered the grave with concrete.

Butkovich's car was later located by police approximately one block from his home. Inside was his wallet, the cash intact, his jacket and many other personal items.

The marriage between Gacy and Carole had now completely broken down so Carole asked for a divorce. Gacy was thrilled and even sent her to his own lawyer and helped her move out. After their divorce in 1976, Carole occasionally met John for dinner. The divorce was finalised on Tuesday, 2 March 1976, and she finally stopped seeing him after she remarried.

The 17-year-old Michael Bonnin was not too different from John Butkovich in that he enjoyed working with his hands. He especially liked doing woodwork and carpentry and he was often busy with several projects at a time. On Thursday, 3 June 1976, he had almost completed work on restoring an old jukebox, yet he never had a chance to finish the job he'd started. While on route to catch a train to meet his stepfather's brother, he disappeared.

Ever since his parents could remember, Billy Carroll Jr was the kind of boy who seemed to be always getting into trouble. At the age of nine he was in a juvenile home for stealing a purse and, aged 11, he was caught with a gun. Billy was mischievous and spent most of his time on the streets in uptown Chicago. At the age of 16, he was making money by arranging meetings between teenage homosexual boys and adult clientele for a commission.

Although Billy came from a very different background to that of Michael Bonnin and Johnny Butkovich, they all had one thing in common – John Wayne Gacy Jr. Just like Johnny and Michael, Billy also disappeared suddenly.

On Sunday, 13 June 1976, he left his home saying that he was going out to paint a friend's garage. He was never seen alive again.

When talking later about another of his victims, Gacy recalled that 17-year-old Gregory Godzik loved his job with PDM Contractors and, although he had been working at PDM for two weeks, he didn't mind doing the extra odd jobs that his boss required of him. His wages allowed for him to buy parts for his 1966 Pontiac car, a time-consuming hobby. He was proud of his car and, although it was a bit of an eyesore, it served its purpose.

On Sunday, 12 December 1976, Gregory dropped his date, a girl he had had a crush on for some time, off at her house, then drove back towards his own home. In fact, he intended to visit Gacy and take him some marijuana, but he hadn't been able to buy any, and needed to apologise.

Gacy stated that he retired to bed and, in the morning, he had found the lad dead, sitting in a chair wearing only his underwear. There was a rope around his neck.

The body of Gregory Godzik ended up in the crawlspace with the others. The following day, police found the boy's Pontiac. The windows were open and the doors unlocked, but Gregory was missing. John Gacy later remarked to Detective Larry Finder, 'One guy, Godzik, dug his own grave.' Godzik's parents had last seen their son on 12 December 1976, and had reported him missing the following day.

Towards the end of December 1977, 19-year-old department-store employee Robert Donnelly was walking along a north-west Chicago sidewalk on his way to a bus-stop when a black Oldsmobile pulled over to the kerb. It was late at night and the boy suddenly found himself fixed in a spotlight shining from the driver's side of the car. Gacy played a tough cop and asked for identification, then he pointed a gun at the lad and shouted, 'Get in or I'll blow you away.'

Placing handcuffs on the young man, Gacy drove him back to West Summerdale, forced whisky down his throat when he refused a drink, and anally raped him. Gacy then dragged Robert into the bathroom and repeatedly dunked his head into a bath full of water until the boy lost consciousness. After Robert came to, Gacy urinated on him, dragged him back into the recreation room to watch homosexual movies and continued the torture.

Robert would later testify in court that Gacy made him play Russian roulette with a revolver, spinning the cylinder and pulling the trigger 10–15 times until the gun finally went off. It was loaded with a blank round.

Gacy then bound and gagged his terrified victim and raped him again. His rage nearly spent, Gacy ordered the weakened youth to take a shower and get dressed, then he put him in the car for what he promised would be Robert's last ride.

'How's it feel, knowin' you're going to die?' he taunted as he drove Robert back downtown. But then, inexplicably, Gacy released his captive with one last threat – 'If you go to the cops,' he said, 'I'll hunt you down.'

Robert, who was afflicted with a stutter, and had been receiving treatment from a psychiatrist following the death of his father, did report the attack to the police, describing the black car and the distinctive personalised number plate – 'PDM'.

As had happened three times before, the police interviewed Gacy, who corroborated the incident, but claimed that it was a 'slave routine', and the sex was consensual. The prosecutor who reviewed the case dropped it because it was one person's word against that of another. Gacy had slipped through the net again with further terrifying consequences.

On Thursday, 20 January 1977, a 19-year-old street hustler called John Szyc – Gacy called him a 'he/she' – also disappeared, much like the other young men before him. Cruising in his 1971 Plymouth Satellite, he was never seen alive again. Gacy had spotted him while he was driving through North Chicago, and the lad told the contractor that his Plymouth was up for sale. Gacy said that he might be interested so they drove to West Summerdale Avenue, supposedly to settle the deal. Szyc died that night and he, too, was buried in the subsoil of the crawlspace.

Interestingly, a short while after the young man vanished, another teenager, Tom Costa, was picked up by police in a 1971 Plymouth Satellite while trying to leave a gas station, allegedly without paying. A police chase ensued, which started in Cicero and ended in Chicago. He was charged with running a stop sign, eluding the police and reckless driving. The theft charge was dropped through 'lack of evidence'. The charges for running the stop sign had been SOL. He had pleaded guilty to eluding the police and reckless driving and, as a result, had his driving licence suspended for two years and was fined $50.

Tom Costa had originally worked for a plumber called Max Gussis, but found the pay inadequate, so, when Gacy offered him $10 an hour, he jumped at the offer. Prior to his marriage in 1977, he had moved into Gacy's house, with the agreement that he would pay his boss $25 a month rent. He would later describe Gacy as 'a workhorse whose first concern was business'. Tom had apparently slept at Gacy's home on the night of the Szyc murder but says he saw nothing untoward.

Tom and Gacy soon struck a deal of their own – Tom would buy the dead lad's car from Gacy for $300, and pay him back at $50 a week until the bill was settled. After he had paid $200, he could take possession of the vehicle. Costa and Gacy went and picked up Szyc's car near Clark and Ohio Street in Chicago. It had been parked close to a gay movie house, and they took it for a 'test drive'. According to Gacy, Tom forged the title, signing the vehicle over to the two of them. Tom Costa would later deny the forgery and he was never charged with the offence. A television and a clock radio, taken from the trunk of the Plymouth, went home with Gacy, but Szyc's transvestite wardrobe of clothes and wigs was left behind a dumpster.

Jeff Rignall, a 26-year-old homosexual, was walking to a Chicago gay bar when Gacy picked him up in his black Oldsmobile. Though

Rignall climbed into Gacy's car willingly, Gacy chloroformed him for the drive back to West Summerdale Avenue. There he stripped the man and strapped him to what the victim would later describe to the police as a 'pillory device' that held his head and arms immobile. His attacker then forced him to perform oral sex and repeatedly raped him with a number of blunt objects.

Rignall was later dumped in the snow at the base of the Alexander Hamilton statue in a downtown Chicago Park. He was bleeding from the rectum and his face felt as if it was on fire; he had suffered facial burns and liver damage from the chloroform, and spent several days in hospital.

In a later television interview, Rignall changed his story, albeit slightly, saying, 'I got in the car with him [Gacy] and a short way after I got into the car with him he placed a rag over my face which turned out to be chloroform, and proceeded to have a lengthy drive and every time I came to the rag would go back over my face, and I remember him carrying me into his house. And then he put the rag over me and that's the last thing I remember until I found myself at about 5.30am at the steps of Lincoln Park, half-dressed, my face completely burned.'

This attack transformed Jeff Rignall into an avenger bent on tracking down Gacy. However, once the police realised that the complainant was a homosexual, they lost interest in the case. Undeterred, Rignall hired a civil lawyer and sued in civil court. Gacy counter-charged that Rignall had abused him verbally and had pushed him. In September, Gacy settled the suit for $3,000.

In May 1978, Gacy was in charge of the Polish Constitution Day Parade, which was attended by Rosalynn Carter, wife of the then president, Jimmy Carter. Thirty-six-year-old Gacy was in his element. At a reception, he was even photographed shaking hands with the smiling First Lady. This was an extraordinary lapse of security, for the Secret Service had even given him a lapel pin as a sign that he had been cleared as having no criminal record.

Up to this point, an astonishing number of young men had either been listed missing, or had been discovered as murder victims, pending enquiries. The official records from various morgues stated:

CLOTH-LIKE MATERIAL IN THE THROAT. MALE, WHITE, FIVE FOOT THREE, 119 POUNDS. IDENTIFIED 14 NOVEMBER 1978, AS FRANK LANDINGAN, AGE 20.

MALE, WHITE, FIVE FOOT TWO, 140 POUNDS. IDENTIFIED 20 DECEMBER 1978, AS JAMES MAZZARA, AGE 20.

MALE, WHITE, FIVE FOOT SIX, 130 POUNDS. IDENTIFIED 29 DECEMBER 1978, AS RICK JOHNSON, 17, STUDENT.

MALE, WHITE, SIX FEET, 165 POUNDS. IDENTIFIED 6 JANUARY 1979, AS JOHN PRESTIDGE, AGE 20, A STUDENT.

MALE, WHITE, FIVE FOOT TEN, 130 POUNDS. IDENTIFIED 6 JANUARY 1979 AS JOHN SZYC AGED 19.

LIGATURE AROUND THE NECK. MALE, WHITE, FIVE FOOT SEVEN, 150 POUNDS. IDENTIFIED 6 JANUARY 1979 AS MICHAEL BONNIN, AGE 17.

CLOTH-LIKE MATERIAL IN HIS THROAT. MALE, WHITE, SIX FOOT, 175 POUNDS. IDENTIFIED 6 JANUARY 1979, AS ROBERT GILROY, AGE 18, A STUDENT.

MALE, WHITE, FIVE FOOT SEVEN, 135 POUNDS. IDENTIFIED 9 JANUARY 1979, AS TIMOTHY O'ROURKE, AGE 21.

LIGATURE, A ROPE AROUND HIS NECK. MALE, WHITE, FIVE FOOT EIGHT, 145 POUNDS. IDENTIFIED 27 JANUARY 1979, AS JOHN MOWERY.

LIGATURE AROUND NECK. MALE, WHITE, FIVE FOOT EIGHT, 140 POUNDS. IDENTIFIED 29 JANUARY 1979, AS MATTHEW BOWMAN, AGE 19.

CLOTH-LIKE MATERIAL ON THROAT. MALE, WHITE, FIVE FOOT NINE, 145 POUNDS. IDENTIFIED IN THE SPRING OF 1979 AS RANDALL REFFERT, AGE 15, STUDENT.

PAPER-LIKE MATERIAL IN THE THROAT. MALE, WHITE, FIVE FOOT EIGHT, 140 POUNDS. IDENTIFIED 9 APRIL 1979, AS ROBERT PRIEST, AGE 15.

CLOTH-LIKE MATERIAL ON HIS THROAT. MALE, WHITE, FIVE FOOT EIGHT, 155 POUNDS. IDENTIFIED 16 MAY 1979, AS WILLIAM KINDRED.

ROPE AROUND HIS NECK. MALE, WHITE, FIVE FOOT SEVEN, 145 POUNDS. IDENTIFIED 11 SEPTEMBER 1979, AS ROBERT WINCH, AGE 16, A STUDENT.

MALE, WHITE, FIVE FOOT SIX, 145 POUNDS. IDENTIFIED 14 NOVEMBER 1979 AS SAM STAPLETON, AGE 14.

LIGATURE AROUND NECK. MALE, WHITE, SIX FEET. IDENTIFIED 16 NOVEMBER 1979 AS DAVID TALMA.

CLOTH-LIKE MATERIAL ON THROAT. MALE, WHITE, FIVE FOOT FIVE, 140 POUNDS. IDENTIFIED 18 NOVEMBER 1979 AS DARRELL SAMPSON, AGE 18.

CLOTH-LIKE MATERIAL IN HIS THROAT. MALE, WHITE, FIVE FOOT SEVEN. IDENTIFIED AS RUSSELL NELSON, AGE 21, A STUDENT FROM MINNEAPOLIS.

Of Robert Priest, a victim discovered in April 1979, Gacy said later:

> Well, the Priest kid never fit in... he probably would have told someone, though... even if he wanted fast money... that's the truth... the kid was scared I was going to kill him. He couldn't do anything – no erection – sometimes we used Amyl nitrate... Godzik and I would smoke marijuana and then take it... more kicks... no females, no Blacks, no Puerto Ricans.'

> **John Gacy to Detective Larry Finder**

With 16 years on the Force, and promoted to Chief of Detectives on 1 July 1978, Lt Joe Kozenczak had never been a cop to treat a missing-person's report lightly, and there was something that immediately troubled him early on the Tuesday morning of 12 December that year.

Midway through a stack of paperwork, he came across a missing-person's report numbered 78-35203. It concerned a 15-year-old lad named Robert Jerome Priest. The complainant was Elizabeth Priest, the boy's mother, and she had reported him missing at 11.00pm on Monday, 11 December.

Scanning the report, Kozenczak noted that Robert, DOB 16 March 1963, was described as having brown hair, brown eyes, five feet eight inches, 140 pounds, with a 'shag' haircut. Rob, as his friends and relatives called him, was a student at Maine West High School and a stockroom boy at the Nisson Pharmacy in Des Plaines.

On the night he disappeared he was wearing tan pants and a blue down jacket. By a remarkable coincidence, Mrs Priest had taken a photo of her son outside the pharmacy a year earlier. Even more remarkably, the very day that Rob went missing, his father, Harold, had bought him his own camera and, anxious to see what kind of photographs it would produce, he purchased a roll of colour film and took a snap of his son, who was wearing exactly the same clothes as when he disappeared.

It was roll of film that would catch a serial killer.

Lt Kozenczak soon established that Rob worked from 6.00 to 9.00pm, when usually his mother would pick him up. This Monday was special to the family because it was Elizabeth's birthday. Earlier in the day, Harold had bought a birthday cake, and they would cut it when Rob arrived home.

Mrs Priest arrived at the pharmacy dead on 9.00pm. Rob asked her to wait a few minutes while he went outside to talk to a man about a summer construction job. She waited for 20 minutes then went outside to find him gone. After hanging around for a further five minutes, she drove home and started to phone her son's friends as well as the co-owner of the pharmacy, Phil Torf.

Torf seemed to recall that Robert might have been talking to a local building contractor called John Gacy of PDM Construction. He had heard part of a conversation about 'summer employment'. To help Elizabeth, Torf telephoned Gacy, who had been in the store about a refurbishment contract, but he could only leave a message on the answering machine. Tragically, and unknown to Torf, at that precise moment Robert was restrained in handcuffs. At 11.00pm, Elizabeth Priest contacted the Des Plaines PD.

After Lt Kozenczak had tidied up his morning paperwork, he summoned Sergeant Ken Fredericks, the supervisor of the Youth Bureau, to his office. When the sergeant arrived, he told Kozenczak that Mrs Priest and her children – Ken, 21, and Carrie, 22 – were downstairs talking to Detective Ron 'Ronnie' Adams. The time was around 9.10am.

At around 9.30am, Adams phoned Gacy at home, and asked him what he had been doing at the Nisson Pharmacy. Gacy confirmed that he had been there to discuss renovation work, and had enquired if there were any materials left over from previous work he had carried out on the premises. He was adamant that he had not had any personal contact with the missing boy.

On face value, Gacy's account was honest enough. However,

Adams double-checked with Kim Byers, a young girl who worked with Rob at Nisson. She recalled Rob saying when he left the store at 9.00pm that the contractor wanted to speak to him outside. Now Adams knew that Gacy was lying... but why?

At lunchtime, Kozenczak, Fredericks and Adams met up for lunch at The Pot and Pan restaurant, where they discussed the Priest case. Adams hadn't wasted a moment, for he had already phoned the pharmacy and had spoken to the co-owners who were brothers. The Torfs had told the detective that Gacy had been in their store twice on the Monday. Possibly, Rob had overheard a conversation with Gacy regarding hiring high-school students for summer work. But the Torf brothers also revealed something else. They believed that Gacy ran a Christmas tree lot on the north-west side of the city.

When he returned to his office after lunch, Lt Kozenczak assigned Detectives Mike Olsen and Jim Pickell to the case, and by 1.30pm they had traced Gacy's address to 8213 West Summerdale, Norridge, Illinois.

Pickell drove out to a Christmas tree lot and the detective soon learned that the Torfs' information was incorrect, so he went to Gacy's house. Although a black 1978 Oldsmobile, four-door sedan, licence PDM 42, was parked in the driveway, no one appeared to be at home. A neighbour thought that Mr Gacy might be out in one of his two black company vans.

It is possible that after Detective Adams's phone call to Gacy in the morning, the contractor, now forewarned that the police were being proactive, put the corpse into his black van or his car and disposed of the body that day. It later became clear, though, that he actually did the deed at night.

On his return to the police station, the detective checked out Gacy's name and was mortified to learn that he had a significant criminal record, which included a lengthy prison term for committing buggery on a boy.

Throughout the rest of the afternoon, detectives phoned round Rob's school friends. Everyone said that Rob was a stable, intelligent lad who did not appear to be having problems at school or personally. He had, however, recently split up with a girlfriend, but the relationship was coming back on track.

At around 4.30pm, Joe Kozenczak went home for dinner and then, at 5.30pm, he received a call from Ronnie Adams who wanted to know what he should do next. Joe asked him to call back. Joe was sufficiently worried to feel that he needed to interview Gacy as a matter of urgency, so he called the duty state's attorney in downtown Chicago for advice.

Joe explained about the missing boy. He recognised that, for the moment, he had no grounds for arresting the man, but it was important to interview him at home without telling Gacy that anything he said could be used against him without issuing the Miranda warning.

It was a sticky problem.

The advice that came back from the DA was simple. Kozenczak would merely treat Gacy as a witness and he would avoid accusing him of anything. Gacy was not required to say a word and, as the attorney put it, 'If he says go, you go.'

At 9.00pm, Kozenczak met up with Detectives Olsen, Pickell and Dave Sommerschield. They drove to Gacy's residence in two unmarked squad cars, and Olsen and Sommerschield went to the side of the premises where they waited. After knocking several times on the door, Kozenczak and Pickell saw the shape of a head move behind the glass of the front door. It was an eerie sight and sent a chill through them. Then, at that very moment, a black van turned up and out climbed Tom Costa. The officers identified themselves and Costa explained that Gacy never answered the front door, and that they would have to try the side entrance. They did, and saw through a window Gacy reclining in a chair watching television.

Gacy invited the detectives into his home. He confirmed that he had been at the pharmacy the previous day, initially claiming that he had returned home at around 8.45pm, 15 minutes before Rob had vanished.

Upon his arrival home, Gacy said he had listened to his answering machine, upon which was a recorded message from his aunt stating that his uncle was dying at the Northwest Community Hospital in Chicago. Gacy drove to the hospital to meet her but he was informed that his aunt had gone home. He followed her there to discover that she had gone on to a neighbour, a relative, to discuss the funeral arrangements. He had stayed with them for a while, and then drove home, arriving between 12.30 and 1.00am.

What Gacy didn't say was that he had, in fact, left the store at around 7.15pm and returned at 8.00pm to pick up his appointments book, and that he had then left the store at 9.00pm when, outside, he spoke to Priest.

Kozenczak had noticed that Gacy's clothing was 'rather strange'. Over a flannel shirt he wore a thin navy top, similar to those worn by joggers. Nevertheless, Joe was sympathetic and suggested that Gacy might like to accompany him back to the police station where they could take a statement. Gacy refused the offer, saying that he was expecting a call from his mother in Arkansas about his uncle's death. Kozenczak was persistent, though. He explained that Rob's parents were very upset and that anything that John could do to help would be appreciated.

'Why don't you call your mother, rather than wait for her call?' Joe asked.

Gacy looked sullen and was annoyed.

Joe Kozenczak remembers, 'Gacy was forty or fifty pounds overweight, around six foot tall, and every inch of him matched the description of a slob.'

After more persuasion, Gacy agreed to phone his mother and spoke to her for ten minutes. Kozenczak furtively looked around the room, then his eyes settled on a piece of office paper. Moving closer, he made out the words 'Nisson Pharmacy' written on the bottom of it. He slipped it into his jacket pocket.

As Gacy was preparing himself for the drive to the police station, Tom Costa walked into the room. Until then, the other two detectives had been talking to him outside, but the weather was cold, and Costa had had enough. Gacy's confidence was obviously boosted by the arrival of his co-worker and, standing up, he suddenly said, 'I have more important things to do. I am not going with you. Haven't you got any respect for the dead?' The police had to leave.

Rob Priest's body was just yards away and John Wayne Gacy was minutes away from taking the biggest gamble of his life.

There was little point in the four detectives watching the Gacy residence all night, so while Sommerschield and Olsen set up an observation point half a block east on Summerdale, Kozenczak and Pickell made their way back to the police station. They had gone only a few miles when their radio crackled. It was Olsen saying that Gacy was on the move, and in a hurry.

It had been a clever ruse because the killer had rightly assumed that the cops would be watching him. He arranged for the van to pull up to the front of the house so that the contractor could walk along the length of the property without being seen, then he ran to his car and sped off with the van in close pursuit.

Sommerschield and Olsen followed, requesting assistance from their two colleagues. Kozenczak spun his car around and drove back across the Robert Kennedy Expressway to try to intercept Gacy, who was obviously up to no good. Unfortunately, moments later, they heard Sommerschield's garbled words over the radio: 'Bureau 6 to Bureau 1... we lost him!'

At 11.00pm that night, Gacy phoned the Des Plaines Police Station demanding to know if Kozenczak still wanted to see him. The Chief of Detectives said that he did and that he would wait for the contractor to turn up. After two hours, Gacy had still not arrived so the detectives asked the desk officer to inform the man that they would see him the next day.

Gacy eventually turned up at the police station at 3.20am. The contractor looked dishevelled. He had mud on his pants and shoes. His eyes 'were glassy', and the desk officer, Jerry Loconsole, reported that the man had claimed he had been in an auto accident near his house. He had skidded in the snow, and had had problems getting his car moving.

On reading all of the available material on this case, confusion seems to exist as to when Gacy actually killed and disposed of Rob Priest's body. The murder had to have taken place between 9 and 11 December, when Rob was abducted, and before Gacy left his home at about 10.00pm, and drove to the Northwest Community Hospital in Chicago after he was notified that his uncle was dying. Or, if the lad had been restrained and gagged, Gacy might have killed him after he arrived home at around 1.00am the following morning, and most certainly before the police arrived to talk to him at around 9.30pm that night.

When questioned by police after his arrest for murder, Gacy claimed that at around 8.30pm on the evening of 12 December – the day after Rob Priest vanished – he phoned Tom Costa and asked him to come over. They were going to look for a Christmas tree, he told him. This is of some significance because the Torf brothers had told the police that Gacy owned a Christmas tree lot, which he didn't.

While he waited for Costa to arrive in the van, Gacy says that he brought the body down from the attic and laid it in the hallway, an extremely bizarre action knowing that his co-worker would arrive at any moment and see the body. However, when Costa rang the doorbell, Gacy says he told his visitor that he couldn't go and sent Costa away. The killer then claimed that he wrapped the body up in an orange blanket and placed it in the trunk of his car, before driving south to throw the corpse into the Des Plaines River. According to Gacy's later statement, Costa had come and gone, and the body had been disposed of in the Des Plaines River before the police arrived.

Lt Kozenczak recalled that they had been ringing John Gacy's doorbell for some time and received no answer. And, rather chillingly, the two detectives had seen 'the outline of a human head moving on the other side of the door for a fleeting moment'.

Costa then arrived and told the officers that Gacy never opened his front door. Shortly after the police left, two vehicles left the Gacy residence at speed. Gacy drove off into the night and was unable to account for his movements other than turning up at the police station at 3.20am with mud on his clothes, and a yarn that he had been involved in an accident.

Costa has always maintained that he knew nothing of any murders, or the disposal of any bodies. It is generally claimed, and agreed by most observers, including the police, that, at around 8.30pm on the evening of 12 December, Gacy had phoned Costa – whom we already know had purchased murdered John Szyc's car from Gacy – telling him that he wanted to get a Christmas tree and the two men decided that they would drive the black company van to one of the wooded areas off Cumberland Avenue. Gacy said that they might possibly spot a tree and cut it down themselves.

Costa says he turned up at Gacy's place and they drove off in the van. He was at the wheel while Gacy rode as passenger, giving directions. They were driving north on a street east of Cumberland Avenue when they passed a sparsely wooded area used for dumping trash. The area, Costa told police, 'looked something like a prairie, and almost the size of a city block'.

Costa told Joe Kozenczak that Gacy, who had been staring out of the windscreen with intense eyes, told him to drive along the perimeter of this area. As they drove slowly north, Gacy suddenly ordered Costa to stop the vehicle and turn the lights off. Not understanding why, Costa did so and eyed the contractor who sat motionless, gazing into the open prairie. This incident seemed rather peculiar, claimed Costa. They stayed there for a few minutes, and Gacy seemed to be in a trance. Then he came out of this trance and they drove off. The two men did not find a Christmas tree, so Costa drove his boss back home and left.

FOUR

Into the Net

AT 11.00am on the morning of Wednesday, 13 December 1978, sounding businesslike and co-operative, John Gacy telephoned Lt Kozenczak. 'Did you still want to see me?' he asked.

'Yes,' replied the detective.

Forty minutes later, Gacy arrived at the Des Plaines Police Department, while Joe was still making arrangements with District Attorney Terry Sullivan to obtain a search warrant for the suspect's home. Detective Pickell took the man through his movements on the evening Rob Priest had vanished, and Gacy was adamant that he had not spoken to the missing boy.

With the search warrant now in his possession, Kozenczak asked Gacy for his house keys. The man looked shocked and was angry. He refused.

'Either give me the keys, John, or you'll have to buy a new door,' said Kozenczak, and Gacy threw them across to him.

A short while later, seven officers – Lt Kozenczak supervising, along with Detectives Pickell, Adams, Olsen, Kautz, Tovar and Evidence Technician Karl Humbert – assembled at Gacy's red-brick ranch house. The place was in darkness.

Kozenczak remembered that the house 'had an aura of coldness and neglect. It lacked a woman's touch... it felt barren and uncomfortable. The interior decoration, if you could call it that, was unco-ordinated and chaotic.'

As Kozenczak scanned the rooms, he noticed a small grey terrier that moved about apprehensively. 'What seemed really ironic,' says Joe, 'was the dog's physical appearance, particularly its enlarged anus.'

The house had three bedrooms (one of which Gacy used as an office), a very large dining room, a combination family/living room, and a kitchen and bathroom. The seven detectives went everywhere, opening closets, pulling out drawers and photographing everything as they went along. One of the officers also went into the garage while another checked out the attic.

Kozenczak walked into the kitchen. He saw a red photo receipt lying in the bottom of the trash basket. Picking it up, he made out 'No. 36119, Nisson Pharmacy Inc., 1920 Touhy Ave., Des Plaines, Illinois'. This was later to become an invaluable clue in the Priest murder.

Detective Kautz had been checking out the closet in the hallway. As he pulled things in and out, he noticed a crack in the floor running alongside the edge of the closet door. He called Kozenczak over and, after removing a golf bag, they put a screwdriver into the crack and found that they were lifting up the closet floor. Indeed, the entire floor was a trapdoor that led down into the crawlspace under the property.

While Kautz held a flashlight, Kozenczak and Humbert climbed down looking for signs of a freshly dug grave. There was nothing unusual except the smell of damp soil.

John Wayne Gacy was released and placed under surveillance.

The highly trained surveillance team – Delta Unit – was made up of the Force's most experienced drivers. Formed into two teams and supervised by Sergeant Walter Lang, it was mobilised at noon on Thursday, 14 December. Officers Shultz and Robinson were assigned to watch Gacy's house until 1.00am, when they would be replaced by Hachmeister, who would work alone.

Although a specialised squad, it was widely agreed that the equipment they used was not the best. 'The Delta cars,' records Joe Kozenczak, 'were items which we referred to as "Article 36", from the Illinois Revised State Statutes, having belonged to an individual who has been convicted of a serious crime.'

One of the cars, a Plymouth, had been used in the abduction of a girl – so the vehicles were ill-equipped for such work and not suitable for high-speed pursuits.

While every move Gacy made was being watched and recorded, back at the police station, Lt Kozenczak was leaving no stone unturned in his hunt for Rob Priest. He interviewed a number of people, while his colleagues conducted more enquiries into Gacy's shady background. They had heard a rumour that Charles Hattula, a former co-worker of Gacy's, had been found drowned in a river some 60 miles south-west of Chicago. They also discovered that Gregory Godzik was missing – Godzik's car was found in the possession of Tom Costa, and the vehicle identification number (VIN) had been slightly altered.

Another workmate of Gacy's, David Cram, was also brought in for questioning. He explained that his boss had been down in the crawlspace and said that there was a drainage problem. Gacy kept wallets and driver's licences from dead people, he told the investigators. There were also a number of watches that had mysteriously come into the contractor's possession.

On Saturday, 16 December, John Gacy's former wife, Carole, came into the Des Plaines Police Station where she was asked about her life with her former husband. She told officers all about his perverse ways and that he liked to have sex with young men. John Butkovich's name came into the conversation. He had been missing since 21 July

1975. Other young men had worked for Gacy and had vanished – Bruce Dorc, Donny Bingham, Chris Cottles, Don Bacon, Chris LaCore, Jerry Caldwell, as well as Gregory Godzik. The names were piling up thick and fast.

Other officers followed up a lead that their prime suspect had buried bodies at the Maryland Cemetery. Extensive searches found nothing.

Following up the information on Charles Hattula, on Monday, 18 December 1978, Detective Tovar managed to get a lead. Hattula had driven a van with Texas plates, so Tovar contacted the driver's licence division of the Public Safety Department in Texas. Tovar was informed that Charles Antonio Hattula resided at 50567B Val Verde Lane in Houston, Texas. He was described as a white male, blond with blue eyes, six feet tall and 170 pounds. His date of birth was 24 April 1953. After failing to obtain a telephone number, Tovar contacted Sergeant Cooper of the Harris County Sheriff's PD, of which Houston is a part. Cooper sent an officer to the residence. In the meantime, it appeared that there was neither a missing report nor any criminal history on Hattula in Texas.

Having apparently reached a dead end, Tovar tried something else. He conducted a driver's licence check on Hattula in the State of Illinois. Charles Hattula resided at 3120 North Western Avenue, Chicago. He had had a driver's licence but it had been revoked on 14 April 1978. He also had a criminal history.

Hattula had been arrested for possession of a controlled substance and marijuana at his home on 20 April 1976. At the time, he was employed by PDM Contractors as a carpenter. He had also been arrested in Freeport, Illinois, on 12 March 1971 for a curfew violation and possession of marijuana. Charles Hattula's aunt explained that her nephew had drowned in Freeport on Mother's Day 1977. His body was recovered from the Pecatonica River on 13 May 1978. Cause of death was listed as asphyxia by drowning. But had he been a Gacy victim?

Officer Tovar and Detective Ron Adams also interviewed Mrs Szyc. They showed her the Maine West ring found at Gacy's property (Item No. 24). She positively identified it as the property of her missing son; however, she went one step further. Missing from her son's apartment – and later from the trunk of his car – was a 12-inch screen black-and-white Motorola television set. She had found the warranty card and had brought it with her.

A large number of photographs had been taken when the police searched Gacy's home, and among them was a snap of Gacy's bedroom. It clearly showed a light-coloured Motorola TV sitting on an ornate jewellery box between two dressing mirrors.

Not wasting a moment, the officers called at the Motorola corporate headquarters at Schaumburg, not far from Des Plaines. They were told that the television in the photograph was a Model BP-3050KN, which matched the number on the warranty card in Mrs Szyc's possession. There was also an identification number for the actual television set on the card. Would it match the TV in Gacy's bedroom?

Lt Joe Kozenczak recalls, 'On the morning of 19 December 1978, I was confronted, once again, with the hardcore reality and horror of a case which, from all indications, would make history in the world of criminal justice.' The Priests had come to see him.

Ever since their beloved son had gone missing and from right under the nose of his mother on her birthday, the distraught parents had been conducting enquiries of their own. They had staked out Gacy themselves, followed him, watch him, fretted and cursed. Now they were at their wits' end. Their patience had run out and they were at the police station to demand answers, for there was little doubt in their minds that Gacy had killed their Rob.

Over coffee with Kozenczak, Elizabeth Priest mentioned Kim Byers, the girl who had worked with Rob at the pharmacy. It was an off-the-cuff remark, but one which, as is so often the case, oiled the creaky wheels of justice.

'Does she have any new information?' asked Kozenczak.

'No, not really. She was just telling me that Rob had something of hers that day, he…'

'Yes, what was that?'

'Well, it's a little complicated, lieutenant. She says she got cold and so she decided to put on Rob's jacket while she was working. And then she decided to leave some film for developing and, well, she thinks she forgot and put the receipt for it in Rob's jacket pocket, because she's never seen it since. So, I just thought maybe that would help.'

'You mean the jacket he was wearing when he disappeared?'

'Yes, of course. Kim gave him back the jacket later, but she left her film receipt in his pocket.'

Kozenczak says his heart missed several beats. He rushed down to the property room and retrieved, 'like a piece of gold', the bright-red receipt which he had found in Gacy's trash bin. It was possibly the only item of evidence to show that Rob had been in Gacy's home.

Within minutes, Kozenczak summoned a marked patrol car and, with lights flashing, the envelope containing the film receipt was on its way to the Cook County Crime Laboratory in Maybrook. Another officer rushed over to the Nisson Pharmacy. Here he would look for Kim Byers's entry in the log sheets. They were able to match the receipt number to the order number. Meanwhile, lab technicians determined, through analysis of the fibres, that the receipt and the envelope had been joined.

Kozenczak would later say, 'When this was going on, I was giving the Priests hope, but I knew that I was killing all hope. It was a bad time.'

Rob Priest's jacket was later found hidden in a wall when police demolished the house.

While the noose was tightening around Gacy's neck, he was giving the police plenty to think about. At times, he was convivial to the extent that he invited the surveillance team into his home for drinks, while at other times he was obnoxious, full of hollow threats and boastful.

'Fuck you, halfwits. I am gonna sue ya fuckin' ass,' was one of his favourite outbursts. 'Tell that fuckin' shithead Pollack, Kozenczak, that I'm gonna have his shield.'

On one occasion, when he left his home, he shouted, 'What am I doing this afternoon? Oh, I've just got to drop off a few bodies behind the railway bridge in Chicago. Care to lend me a hand?'

With the temperature well below zero, Wednesday, 20 December became a hectic day as all of the threads linking John Wayne Gacy to the murder of Rob Priest were slowly coming together. While Kozenczak interviewed Tom Costa using the polygraph machine – the results were inconclusive – Jim Kautz was developing a complete roster of names, addresses, phone numbers and record checks of young men whom the police knew had been in contact with Gacy. 'It was a massive project,' Kozenczak remembered.

However, the final interview of the day produced an amazing result when they again talked to David Cram, Gacy's workmate, who said that he had dug trenches in the crawlspace under Gacy's house.

'Can you draw a sketch for us?'

'Ya, sure.'

Cram took a pencil and drew a rough plan showing trenches around the perimeter of the foundation on three sides. Looking from the north wall, where there were none, they formed a sort of 'upside-down "U"'.

'You notice anything down there?' asked Greg Bedoe.

'Ya, sure, it stunk.'

'What d'ya mean?'

'It smelled real bad, man, like nobody would want to stay down there long. I came up every chance I could.'

Upon hearing this conversation, Kozenczak recalled a remark made by Sergeant Walter Lang, the Delta boss who had said that, when Bob Shultz had used the bathroom, on the invitation of Gacy, he had noticed a 'peculiar odour that seemed to be coming from the heat vent directly in front of the toilet'. While he was standing there, the furnace kicked on, and the smell came up so rich and strong it almost choked him. It reminded Shultz of some unsavoury odours he had encountered when his duties had sent him over to the Cook County Morgue.

The surveillance quickly took its toll on Gacy. For years, he had been sinking into the habits of a confirmed pill abuser, knocking back handfuls of Valium tablets to calm down, then amphetamines to pep himself up. He swilled beer and whisky. During this last week of freedom, he was on a roller-coaster ride of liquor and drugs. He openly defied traffic laws, smoked a joint in his car and drank heavily as he led officers on a merry chase. He introduced the surveillance team to his pals from the Moose Lodge, calling them his bodyguards. He also delighted in eluding his pursuers and succeeded on a number of occasions. Once, after openly joking with his attorney about taking a long vacation, Gacy vanished and a squad car rushed to O'Hare Airport to block his departure. It was only a trick; Gacy had spent the time driving around, making a brief stop to see a friend who sold Christmas trees.

The Thursday morning started bright and early with Joe Kozenczak and DA Terry Sullivan putting together a fresh application for a second search warrant. Despite all of the evidence, which appeared to implicate Gacy, they still had to convince Judge Marvin Peters, who was soon on their side.

At 10.00am, the surveillance team reported in. Gacy, it appeared, was 'cracking up'. He had spent the night at the office of his attorneys, Stevens & Amirante. Soon after he had arrived, Sam Amirante came out of his office visibly shaken. He walked down the hall to the two surveillance officers, and said, 'Whatever you do, don't let this guy get away.'

The astonished officers then watched while the attorney took out a cigarette and tried to light it, only to discover that he had been trying to ignite the filter end. Then he turned his back, still visibly shaking, walked slowly back to his office and quietly shut the door.

Early that morning, Gacy left the office and, driving like a maniac on the slick icy streets, led the members of the surveillance team to the gas station in Park Ridge. Hachmeister and Albrecht watched him give four marijuana cigarettes – 'Thai sticks' – to the station attendant. As soon as Gacy left, they recovered the cigarettes and reported it to Sergeant Lang.

Things out on the street were happening quickly, too. Gacy, feeling the effects of stress, fatigue and the pills he kept taking, seemed to be making the rounds of his friends' homes, bidding them goodbye.

By 11.30am, Gacy, carrying a rosary, had called on David Cram at his apartment. At 11.45am, the two men drove through the snow to De Leo's Restaurant to meet Attorney Leroy Stevens. While Gacy went inside, Officer Shultz spoke to Cram. The contractor had been popping pills and drinking all morning, Cram said, and was going next to the Maryland Cemetery where his father was buried. The man had a knife with him and was talking about suicide.

'Anything else?' asked Shultz.

'Sure… he says he's killed more than 30 people,' came the blunt reply.

Gacy's confession was quickly transmitted to Sergeant Lang, who, having heard about the drug deal at the gas station, knew he could arrest Gacy at any time. He also knew that his suspect was falling apart at the seams and might kill himself.

'Walter Lang, westbound on Elston Avenue, phoned me,' remembers Joe Kozenczak. 'He called me on the red phone and related all the facts.'

'Do you want him arrested?' asked Lang.

'Yes, pull him… now,' Kozenczak replied.

The actual arrest took place at Oakton Street and Milwaukee Avenue in Niles at 12.15pm. In this highly congested and commercial area, Shultz managed to block Gacy's car with his own and, drawing his revolver, searched Gacy and found a bottle of Valium tablets in his pocket. By 12.45pm, Gacy was in the custody of the Des Plaines Police Department. Aged 36, he would never be a free man again.

Lt Joe Kozenczak obtained a second search warrant and arrived at Gacy's home at 6.30pm. Alone, he went inside.

'When the door opened,' Joe recalls, 'I saw nothing but darkness – total darkness. I felt a chill, the kind that makes your entire body jolt. I quickly walked down the hallway to the front foyer area where the closet was. By now, Lang was in the house. We didn't waste time. I opened the closet door, threw all the contents on the floor outside it and lifted the cover to the crawlspace.'

The search team entered the crawlspace expecting horrors, but the reality, if anything, exceeded their worst forebodings. What they found was a hellish graveyard that assaulted both their noses and their sanity.

After an hour of preparation, during which they had to remove the ground water using submersible pumps, the evidence technicians finally got down to digging. Ice-cold water kept seeping into the crawlspace, turning the search area into a sea of viscous mud. The pumps spluttered and clogged on bits of floating, greasy, soap-like flesh, called 'adipocere'. When the pumps finally stopped, the officers used buckets to bail out the water.

Suddenly there was a muffled yell.

'What in the hell have you found?' shouted Kozenczak.

David Genty answered, 'I've got a body down here.'

Having informed the press that bones that had been found in the house were indeed human, the Cook County Medical Examiner Dr Robert Stein, Chief Investigator Francis J Flanigan and the Cook County Medical Examiner's Photographer, dressed in overalls, set to work on the house. This meant that the property would be carefully processed by Cook County personnel. The evidence technicians were Genty, Humbert, Zakas, Cox and Jones.

Floodlights illuminated the work and made it more ghastly. The men labouring in the lurid glow wore heavy protective clothing, including surgical gloves; contact with the noxious matter that they were unearthing made blood poisoning and gangrene dangerous possibilities. But the flimsy gloves were soon torn by the bones and gravel, exposing the workers' hands to the sting of the many bags of lime that Gacy had poured into the water.

The digging continued. The officers down there spoke of hair protruding from the ground which was still covered with remnants of lime. Small red worms scattered from the shock of the light. There was the unforgettable stench of death and decaying flesh. Genty unearthed three bodies in less than ten minutes.

Right from the outset, the police tried to impose some order on the chaos. They sawed through the floorboards and joists to allow easier access to the burial space. They divided the area into a grid, and, when a bucket was lifted from a particular grid, it was taken behind the house and placed in a corresponding grid to dry. No one imagined that it would freeze instead of drying.

The police soon realised that it was impossible to remove bodies methodically one at a time; in most cases, decay had left little intact. Technicians merely searched through the mush for bones, which were crudely rinsed – using a bucket of water and Gacy's own deep-frying basket – before they were passed along for inspection by Dr Robert Stein. It soon became clear that small bones from wrists, fingers and toes would be lost. Only when shoes or socks survived could evidence technicians recover the tiny remains.

As the law prescribed, Dr Stein wrote a death certificate as each body was exhumed. Then he and his assistants piled the bags near the front door to be picked up for daily delivery to the morgue. Each body was reduced to a number, each number was placed on a wooden stake, and the stake driven into the mud of the crawlspace as near as possible to where the skull had been found. As the graves emptied, the number of stakes increased, the chill ground water seeping relentlessly in, pooling around the posts.

In a bizarre deal, Gacy agreed to help the searchers if the police allowed him to visit his father's grave. This done, the contractor was taken to his house where he railed at the officers for wrecking his property. There was mud on the carpets, the houseplants had been knocked over, and his neatly ordered tools had been messed up. He began cleaning up, petulantly announcing that he would not co-operate with the police any longer if they were going to be so careless.

State's Attorney Terry Sullivan, in charge of building the prosecution's case, screamed, 'Cuff him.' He was furious and ordered Gacy out of his home. 'Drag the bastard out, if you have to,' he shouted.

Police coaxed him to spray-paint an 'X' on the spot in the garage where he'd poured concrete over Butkovich's grave. The body, preceded by a cloud of noxious gas, was chipped out of the floor by members of the North Investigation Unit of Cook County, Lundquist and Swartz.

By Saturday, 23 December, Joe Kozenczak received a 'mittimus', a legal order remanding Gacy to the custody of the Cook County Sheriff, from Judge Marvin Peters, which authorised the Des Plaines PD to take John Gacy to Cook County's Cermak Hospital where he would be segregated from other prisoners and subjected to psychiatric examination.

Identifying the bodies was a nightmare. Only after developing a technique of defining each grave site by depth and length could searchers be reasonably sure they were lifting parts of one corpse and not another as they explored. In some graves, Gacy had buried one body on top of another. In one grave, the skeletons were so jumbled together that the two skulls were almost touching. The problem was resolved by simply placing bags between the corpses, and removing the soil by the handful.

The search team fought the horror of their work with black humour. Officers warned against throwing chicken bones into the pit, saying that Dr Stein might flip out. Then there were the inevitable John Gacy jokes – Gacy wouldn't be going out this New Year's Eve because he couldn't dig up a date. Officers held a 'Ghoul Pool' on the number of bodies. The guesses ranged from 5 to 14 – all too low.

On Sunday, two more bodies were recovered and, keeping with a directive issued by Chief Dobbs of Cook County Police, the next day would be a holiday.

On Tuesday, 26 December, six more bodies were recovered from the crawlspace. One was found under a concrete slab. Several had only socks on their bodies. Ligatures were around the throats of a few, and some had what resembled underwear or cloth in their throats. In many instances, a plastic bag, like those used in dry-cleaning establishments, was wrapped around the victim's upper body and head. Gacy had learned as he went along. Cloth in the throat and plastic bags made things neater for him.

Police were taking souvenirs such as bricks, ballpoint pens with the PDM logo and Gacy's business cards. Photos of the diggers and technicians were taken for posterity. They posed in front of a huge blow-up of Gacy adorned with Polish flags and a collection of dildos. Officers postured before this grotesque background, their riot helmets under their arms, while a colleague displayed the day's body count on a film-style chalk clapper-board.

Scuba divers were brought in to supplement the helicopter search of the Des Plaines River around the bridge in Grundy County where Gacy had said he had disposed of a body. Nothing was found.

Five more graves were added to the police diagram the next day. Officer Ralph Tovar found a blue Parka jacket between the floor joists adjacent to the laundry room. The jacket wasn't the only item hidden by the contractor. Like so many serial killers, Gacy kept and hid souvenirs of his murders. Several pieces of jewellery, various items of clothing, adult books, smoking materials – including pipes and bongs – 25 badges and stars, a folding knife, pieces of rope and items used for torture were collected up.

Heavy snow blanketed the upper Midwest. Later, highway diggers excavated the entire crawlspace down to undisturbed clay. In April 1979, the house now unsafe from all the digging, was razed to the ground. But still the digging continued. The total number of bodies unearthed from the house, the garage and driveway eventually totalled 29. Six of the bodies have never been identified.

James Mazzara's body was recovered from the Des Plaines River on 28 December 1978.

On 9 April 1979, a man strolling along the river's towpath, five-and-a-half miles downstream from the I-55 bridge, found Robert Priest's corpse. Joe Kozenczak remembers the day as if it were yesterday: 'It was late afternoon when Ron Adams and I started the trip down I-129 in back of Bedoe and Sullivan's car. They had detailed directions from the Sheriff's Department as to where we were to meet our escort in Grundy County. Bedoe decided to use his red light and siren, and we zoomed down the interstate like that until we reached the Morris exit and found the Sheriff's police car waiting for us.

'The body was being held in a nearby hospital where a dentist was comparing its teeth with Rob Priest's dental charts. It was a positive match.'

FIVE

Judge and Executioner

When they paint this image that I was this monster that picked up those altar boys on the street and swatted them like flies, this is ludicrous. Whether it's Berkowitz, whether it's Bundy, whether it's Wayne Williams down in Atlanta, or any of the others, or Charlie Manson, I don't comment about any other cases because of the simple fact I wasn't there. I hate it when they [the public] put me in the same club with them.

If the people want to know the truth, or the honesty of it ... that they want to be brainwashed into what they want to believe, then, OK, fine, go ahead and kill me. But 'Vengeance is mine' sayeth the Lord, because you will have executed someone who didn't commit the crime.

John Wayne Gacy, Death Row, Menard CF, 1992

THE trial of John Wayne Gacy started at the Central Criminal Court in Chicago on 6 February 1980, Judge Louis B Garippo presiding.

Terry Sullivan and William Kunkle, Chief Prosecutor for the county, were to face Sam Amirante for the defence.

Judge Garippo has since retired from the bench, but recalled the trial clearly. 'It was a straightforward murder trial,' he said. 'There was, from a judge's point of view, nothing unusual in the proceedings. Jury selection was very fast, only taking four days.'

And what of Gacy's defence? 'Well, there is no doubt that he had suffered a bad childhood. That undoubtedly created some sympathy in my courtroom. But, unfortunately for Mr John Gacy, it no doubt occurred to the jury that millions of people have similar abusive childhoods, and very few of them have some thirty bodies buried on their property.'

As for the death sentence Judge Garippo handed down, he said that he had no qualms, 'none at all. I have my own private thoughts, of course I do. I was merely an instrument of the criminal-justice system. My job was to see that John had a fair trial, which he did. Based on the evidence, it was overwhelming, the jury found him guilty, and I passed the only sentence for his crimes prescribed by the law in Illinois.'

William Kunkle's team brought in one expert witness, in the form of James Cavanaugh, who evaluated Gacy at Cermak Hospital. He recalls, 'My impressions of him during these approximate 18 hours were that he was a well-organised, very intelligent man who was very particular about the way he organised his environment. He made the best possible use of all the space he had in Cermak Hospital. He had decorated it. He had worked out an exercise programme that was quite interesting, showing a great deal of imagination. Walking a number of miles each day, which he kept track of by flipping and checking cards out of a deck and each card represented a certain amount of feet. My impression was that this was a person who was a little compulsive, meaning he had to do things over and over and over again in a ritualised manner.

'Other general observations were that, after we got over the hurdle of the ground rules for us during the examination, meaning that we, in a sense, capitulated to his desires to sign this form that we wouldn't release our work product, he was generally quite co-operative and answered questions quite fully and was able in about 18 hours of interview to retrace many of the pertinent details of his life up to the time when these evaluations began.'

Cavanaugh's general conclusions about Gacy were that he showed a sexual-sadistic behavioural pattern, was narcissistic – meaning he had 'a grandiose sense of self-importance or uniqueness' – and was antisocial. In layman's terms, all of this added up to a mixed personality disorder. But Cavanaugh didn't feel Gacy's mental problems in any sense met the state's legal definition of insanity.

Dr Helen Morrison, forensic psychiatrist for the defence, claimed that Gacy was insane, while other psychiatrists labelled him as 'very dangerous, borderline personality, amnesiac and schizophrenic'. Then the final nail was put in Gacy's coffin when a defence psychiatrist said that, if Gacy was found insane, he would be put back out on the streets because 'he cannot be hospitalised against his will'.

In 1995, William Kunkle offered this insight into the case: 'Basically, the defence claimed that John was a deeply sick individual who was crazy all of the time. That one doesn't wash. He certainly wasn't crazy when he was working at his job and socialising. He wasn't crazy at all … According to Illinois law, John was sane. He was just evil.'

And what of Gacy's claim that someone else had killed and buried the victims without his knowledge? 'Within hours of his arrest, John was confessing to the murders. He drew a very accurate diagram of where the bodies were in his crawlspace before the digging started. It was very accurate. He told police where he had disposed of Mazzara and Rob Priest. This was correct, too. Yes, John Gacy was guilty. I lose no sleep over this.'

Kunkle also had an opinion on Gacy's state of mind. 'A real medical, model psychiatrist who treats patients and understands mental illness will never believe that you can turn this type of serious mental illness off like a faucet. Did he have personality disorders? Absolutely. Was he a sexual deviant? Of course. But psychotic? Not even close.'

And, of course, William Kunkle is correct. If not premeditated, why would Gacy have burial trenches dug in advance? Why did he keep handcuffs and a rope ready? If he didn't understand the criminality of his behaviour, why did he choose victims who might not be missed. If he had amnesia, how did he draw a precise sketch locating each body on his property?

William Kunkle added, 'Clearly, when you have this kind of behaviour, the pre-planning for all those things, the covering up, the post-planning, the post-conduct for all these things, and all this going on against the backdrop on the surface of what appears to be a perfectly normal existence ... just doesn't fit.'

Do you realise that, by 1993, 50 per cent of American families will be single parented? And that shows a breakdown in the Church in not being able to hold families together. And, for this reason, children run away from home and seek love in other places.

John Wayne Gacy, Death Row, 1992

The prosecution had called 79 witnesses, the defence 22. Now, on 12 March 1980, at 4.40pm, the jury presented 35 signed verdicts of murder. They also found Gacy guilty of taking 'indecent liberties with a child upon Robert Priest' and guilty of 'sexual assault upon Robert Priest'.

Because the Illinois death penalty statute became effective on 21 June 1977, it applied to the 12 murders that occurred after this date, and affected the sentencing. In fact, the final verdict stated that Gacy, who had 'attained the age of 18 years at the time', murdered 12 individuals after 21 June 1977 and was sentenced to death.

Judge Garippo, with his black robe and grey hair, sat looking distinguished and stately behind the bench, announcing that the execution date would be 2 June 1980.

On 13 March 1980, Gacy was sent to Menard Correctional Center in Illinois. He would remain there for just over 14 years until he was transported by helicopter to the Stateville Penitentiary near Joliet for execution.

Gacy, ranking among the most notorious killers in American history, would become the hundredth person executed in Illinois since 1928, when the state took control of executions. Before that, county officials executed criminals. Between 1928 and 1962, the state electrocuted 98 people. The executions stopped when the US Supreme Court struck down capital punishment. That decision was reversed in 1976, and Illinois officials reinstated the death penalty the following year.

Thirteen years passed before anyone was executed in Illinois, and that only happened when Charles Walker of Mascoutah dropped his appeals. Walker died by lethal injection on 12 September 1990. Had Walker continued to appeal his case, he probably would be alive among 154 other killers, the latest count from the Illinois Department of Corrections.

Barring any last-minute delay, Gacy was to be the second person to die by injection, and the first killer whose appeals had run out since the reinstatement of the death penalty.

John Szabo was the first person sentenced to death under the state's new death penalty. Szabo, 36, has avoided execution since 1979 through various legal challenges. He was convicted of four murders in Will County. Court challenges have also kept alive George Delvecchio, James P Free Jr, Kenneth Allen and Hernando Williams, the other killers sentenced to death before Gacy.

During the evening of 9 May 1994, Gacy sat down for his last meal – fried chicken, French fries, Coke and strawberry shortcake. Prison officials later described his demeanour as 'chatty... talking up a storm'. In a phone interview shortly before his execution, he told a *Knight-Tribune* reporter, 'There's been 11 hardback books on me, 31 paperbacks, two screenplays, one movie, one off-Broadway play, five songs, and over 5,000 articles. What can I say about it?' But, of course, he quickly protested, 'I have no ego for any of this garbage.'

Hours after having exhausted legal appeals that had filled and perpetuated his life, Gacy, aged 52, was strapped to a gurney in the execution room shortly after midnight. For his last words, Gacy snarled, 'Kiss my ass.' His execution was a minor media sensation, and large crowds of people gathered on the grounds of the penitentiary where it occurred. In a display of what has been called 'shocking bad taste', vendors sold T-shirts and Gacy merchandise, and the people cheered at the moment when Gacy was pronounced dead. But all had not gone as planned. There was a problem with the machine.

Executioners had started the chemicals flowing at 12.40am. The process was scheduled for ten minutes, not eighteen. The first injection causes sleep, the second stops the breathing and the third stops the heart. Gacy was not unconscious when the problem occurred and suffered a great deal of distress when there was a 'blow-back' and his blood and chemicals sprayed around the death chamber.

Howard A Peters III, Head of the Department of Corrections, said that the second of the three chemicals that were to flow into Gacy's arm apparently 'gelled', or were blocked by a clot of Gacy's blood. Officials attached a new tube to the needle and resumed the execution.

At the time of my arrest, there were four other suspects, all employees of PDM contractors, all with keys to the house … if you've lived your life the right way then you have nothing to fear in my case. I am fairly comfortable with Him. I've been at Catholic services for the past ten years. I've had confession. I've had communion. I've no qualms about that. I am at peace with myself.

John Gacy at interview

I do not consider myself unique in that I managed to interview John Wayne Gacy prior to his execution. Many other criminologists, psychiatrists and friends of John managed this, too.

I cannot say that his correspondence with me was of much assistance either. As with everyone who visited this man on 'The Row', most had to complete a two-page questionnaire which was subject to his approval before he would even consider agreeing to the visit. Nevertheless, by taking a lateral approach in examining what we do know about John Gacy, we can learn much about the workings of his mind.

On a number of occasions, individuals who wanted to meet with him – those whom he thought worthy of the effort – would be sent his 'Bio Review'. I was considered important enough to receive one, and it makes for an interesting read. I have included it here verbatim, without his permission, for the obvious reasons.

BIOGRAPHICAL REVIEW

Full name:	John Wayne Michael Gacy
Date of Birth:	17 March 1942
Age, Height, Weight:	50; 5' 9"; 220 pounds
Home:	Menard, Death Row, Chester, Ill.
Marital Status:	Twice divorced
Family:	2 sisters, 5 children
Wheels:	Last car '79 Oldsmobile 4 dr.
Brothers:	None
Sisters:	Two
Most Treasured Honor:	3 times Man of the Year, Jaycees, 3 different cities.

Perfect Woman or Man:	Woman – independent thinker, self-starter, mind of her own. Man: Bright, bold, honest, dependable, says what he is thinking.
Childhood Hero:	JF Kennedy, RW Daley
Current Hero:	M Cuomo, Donald Trump
Favourite TV Shows:	Unsolved Mysteries, National Geographic specials
Favourite Movies:	Once Upon a Time in America, Good Fellas, Ten Commandments
Favourite Song:	'Send in the Clowns', 'Amazing Grace'
Favourite Singers:	Judy Collins, Bob Dylan, Neil Diamond, Roy Orbison, Sha Na Na
Favourite Musicians:	REO Speedwagon, Elton John, Zamfir
Hobbies:	Correspondence, oil painting, study of human interests
Favourite Meals:	Fried chicken, deboned lake perch drawn in butter, salad, tea
Why you wrote JW Gacy:	I don't, I just answer for him. [sic]
Recommended Reading:	Texas Connection, Question of Doubt
Last Book Read:	Naked Lunch and Wild Boys, William S Burroughs
Ideal Evening:	Dinner and concert or live show, drinks and a quiet walk by lake.
Every 1 Jan I Resolve:	Correct things that I let go the year before.
Nobody Knows I'm:	A character who loves to tease and joke around (sic).
My Biggest Regret:	Being so trusting and gullible, taken advantage of.

If I Were President I'd:	Make sure the people of this country had jobs and a place to live before worrying about other countries.
My Advice to Children:	Be yourself, think positive, respect parents.
What I Don't Like about People:	Phonies, people who don't keep their word.
My Biggest Fear:	Dying before I have a chance to clear my name with truth.
Pet Peeves:	People who say things they have no intentions in doing.
Superstitions:	None, it's for negative people.
Friends Like Me Because:	I am outspoken and honest, fun-loving and dependable.

John Gacy married two independent-thinking, self-starting women with minds of their own, and they were clearly not right for him. Where he describes his ideal man, of course, he is suggesting his own self-perceived attributes.

Gacy was a man with political aspirations who considered himself as a hard-working entrepreneur, so his childhood heroes will come as no surprise to us: JF Kennedy had been President of the United States; RW Daley was a well-liked Mayor of Chicago; Mario M Cuomo, a State of New York Governor, was the youngest child of poor and illiterate immigrants whose father worked cleaning sewers until he had enough money to start a small grocery store; and Donald Trump needs no introduction.

With his various preferences, the reader will note that he has conveniently omitted to include the masses of stag magazines, pornographic literature and perverted homosexual videos that must have taken up a great deal of his free time. The real John Gacy is also apparent when he refers to the last books he has read; these publications would not have been supplied to him in prison.

Naked Lunch by William S Burroughs was published in the USA in 1962 and sparked a landmark obscenity trial that served to end literary censorship in America. *Wild Boys*, also written by Burroughs, contains shocking, pornographic imagery of a violent world of renegade homosexual boys; it was a book well thumbed by John Gacy.

John's ideal evening seems somewhat out of sorts with his true self, for it is known that he rarely attended a concert or live show. This preference suggests decent sensibilities with the 'drinks and a quiet walk by a lake'. Nowhere here do we find any reference to swilling back bottles of whisky and six-packs of beer, smoking reefer after reefer of marijuana and constant pill-popping to either knock him out or wake him up.

The reader does not have to be a psychiatrist or psychologist to realise that John's 'Bio Review' has to be taken with a pinch of salt. It is what John *doesn't* say which is of more importance to us when trying to understand him and this can no better be illustrated than in his New Year resolutions – 'Correct things that I let go year before' – a well-intended resolution maybe, yet one which, for some decades, he singularly failed to realise.

Of course, as Pogo the Clown, John loved to tease and joke around, while once again neglecting to mention that he loved to 'tease and joke' around with his many young victims – the ploy in getting them to try on his handcuffs to see if they could escape was one of them. Of course, John, as Dr Jekyll and Mr Hyde, could easily get out of them because he had the key secreted in the palm of his hand. When a victim was cuffed, he was doomed.

Towards the end of John's review, we see a little more of the psychopathic personality coming through. Ever the hypocrite, he claims that his biggest regret was 'being so trusting and gullible, taken advantage of'. We can say without any doubt that his many victims were trusting, gullible and taken advantage of… but John Gacy? He was the ultimate user and abuser. And, of course, he has the gall to suggest that he hated phonies and people who didn't keep their word!

His greatest fear was of dying before he had a chance to clear his name with the truth. But, with his having confessed to all of the murders – and, at one point, John Gacy claimed to have killed up to 50 young men all over the United States – and, having described in great detail the locations of the corpses under his home on Summerdale, which turned out to accurate, going on to say where he had thrown at least five bodies into the Des Plaines River, that, surely, must be where the real truth lies.

One might ask oneself, what more truths had to come out which would 'clear his name'? Indeed, he nails his hypocrisy to the cell door when he says that his pet peeves are 'people who say things they have no intention of doing'. It's clear that Gacy had more than sufficient time to come up with the truth – to be precise, between 12.15pm on Thursday, 21 December 1978, when he was arrested, and 12.40am on Tuesday, 11 May 1994, when he was executed.

It is up to the reader whether Gacy might be deemed 'outspoken and honest, fun-loving and dependable'.

John Wayne Gacy was emotionally stunted as a child and, as he grew older, where there should have been a conscience there developed a void. During this period – his formative years through to his very early teens – I would suggest that John's mind split in two, for as he developed he held two differing sets of thinking processes, values, attitudes, emotions and aspirations. There was the hardworking, honest, upright pillar of the community with his social and political dreams. But, on the other hand, he harboured dark and perverted secrets – the Mr Hyde was always there, vying to overpower Dr Jekyll.

There is little doubt that John Gacy harboured two sets of attitudes and emotions. I think that even he agreed that he was an abject failure with women and he developed homosexual tendencies from an early age.

Of course, John loved his mother. As he grew older, he probably regarded her as a strong, gregarious woman who had turned weak. He had witnessed how his domineering father had heaped verbal and physical abuse upon her. And, with almost overwhelming ambitions to be like his methodical father, to be able to prove himself as a 'real man', he would subsequently have subconsciously had little respect for women in general.

His father was a precise patriarch, whom the impressionable young John secretly looked up to, despite the beatings and abuse meted out to him. He would do anything to please his father, and it is interesting to note that John was devastated when, while in prison, his father passed away and he wasn't allowed to attend the funeral. We will also recall that, on the day he was arrested, John Gacy was on his way to his father's grave where he intended to place a rosary and possibly commit suicide.

Mr Gacy Sr was a control freak and a perfectionist. It is no mere coincidence that John would become a perfectionist in his work and a control freak, too. He aimed for perfection in organising social events, his dedication to fine detail and long hours gained him high recognition with the Jaycees. This was no mean feat and we must give John Gacy credit for that.

This 'perfectionist' spent his ten years at the State Reformatory for Men at Anamosa constructively. He designed and organised the construction of the inmates' mini-golf course; incarceration didn't prevent him from tirelessly bettering his education, nor did it stop him from earning a number of Jaycee awards, including the club's Sound Citizens Awards and the roles of chaplain and legal counsel.

There may be those who smirk at these achievements, but the Jaycees do not give out honours lightly. We may also recall that he organised the Polish Constitution Day Parade in 1978 – one of the few years that this event has gone off without a hitch. And John did not gain the position in 1975 of Secretary-Treasurer of the Norwood Park Township Street Lighting District because he was a fool. It may also be argued, though, that, because he could not succumb to the temptation of young boys while in prison, he was destined to become a model prisoner anyway.

It could be suggested that the torture, sexual abuse and seething anger Gacy directed at his helpless victims was an echo of the way his father treated him as a youth. The victims were John himself. He became his father, heaping ridicule on them and exercising power and control over them, punishing them for his own weaknesses in mind, body and soul.

It is also of some interest to note that John never assaulted a woman, nor did he attack older males – he was too much of a coward to strike out at mature men. His targets were young male prostitutes, runaways, the innocent and often gullible. They were his desired prey.

But why, if John thought so little of women, did he marry? I suggest that he married because this was the socially acceptable thing for him to do. The 'good' Mr Gacy wanted to be a successful businessman, a politician – these were his dreams. To fit in with the social set and political circles in which he needed to mix, a wife was an asset to him, a tool he could use to promote himself as an upstanding member of the community. And it is of interest to note that both of his marriages failed when the 'bad' John Gacy came out of the closet.

His first wife quite rightly left him when he went to prison for sodomising a young lad; his second wife left him when she ran out of patience and refused to condone his homosexual leanings and perversions a day longer. John had no choice when Marion left him because he had effectively dug his own grave and was on his way to prison; things were different, however, when he lost his second wife. Our aspiring politician was now aware that, because of his previous prison sentence, he was barred from high office. PDM Contractors was doing very well; effectively, his second wife, Carole, and her two children were unwanted baggage. He was managing in his social and business circles quite well without her now. In fact, the 'bad' John Gacy would have viewed her as a hindrance, one which prevented him from fully exploiting his carnal desires. Once she had left, the leash was taken from around his neck and the monster inside his head could now run amok – which it did.

John would later claim that his alter ego – 'Mad Jack' – committed the murders and, in a strange way, with the great gift of hindsight, it appears that John Gacy did have an alter ego of sorts, though this was never medically proven. At one time, Gacy had befriended – although it was never reciprocated – a police officer by the name of Jack Hanley, a detective with the hit-and-run unit of Cook County law enforcement. Gacy developed a fixation for this cop. Jack was all the things Gacy was not – muscular, commanding and a devoted hater of homosexuals. Jack Hanley was the punishing type of lawman that Gacy both admired and feared. He became a kind of obsession figure for Gacy, an alter ego – and, later, a scapegoat.

It has been claimed that, when John started drinking or taking drugs, it seemed that his alter ego Mad Jack would take over and do things that Gacy would never do sober. Gacy would eventually confess to police that when he couldn't really remember the crimes – exactly what he had done with some of the bodies before he buried them under his house – it was because Jack had been in charge. However, this explanation does not fit with the John Gacy whom we have met so far, because we find a man who was trawling for sex with young men when he married for the first time, a man who was committing serious sexual offences long before he met Jack Hanley.

We have come to know an individual who used his role as the manager of several fried-chicken outlets to procure young boys, and he used the same technique and opportunity when working in politics and around the community. It is more than probable, though, that drugs and drink fuelled his sexual cravings.

Like so many serial murderers, Gacy never accepted the blame for his actions – it was always, without exception, the fault of 'Mad Jack', or the boys themselves.

There are many observers, including Dr Helen Morrison, who argue that John did not have a conscience. However, I contend that the 'good' John Gacy did have an honourable conscience, and the work and honours he gained working for the community are good testimony to this. Conversely, the 'bad' John Gacy had no conscience whatsoever; tragically, the 'bad' John Gacy prevailed during the last few years of his freedom. There would be no cure, and it stayed with him until the end of his days.

There is one final scenario which is terrifying in the extreme, one almost too awful for contemplation. Had John Gacy not served a ten-year prison term, and managed to emulate the achievements of his heroes, there is little doubt that he would have achieved high political office. The writing, as we have seen, was on the wall. He may have enjoyed a glittering political career. Had that been the case, Illinois might have enjoyed a mayor in John Gacy, or even a Governor. Inevitably, however, the bad John Gacy would eventually have prevailed and it seems that the people of Illinois escaped by the skin of their teeth.

Perhaps, however, the last word should go to William Kunkle, who said after Gacy's execution, 'He got a much easier death than any of his victims. In my opinion, he got an easier death than he deserved. But the important thing is he paid for his crimes with his life.'

On Thursday, 9 December 1994, I was invited to lecture on serial homicide by the Department of Criminal Justice Studies at Portsmouth University. Asked about the death sentence applied to John Gacy, I gave the same answer as William Kunkle, who said that he had had no qualms, 'none at all'.

This chapter is based on several visits by the author to Chicago and Des Plaines, Illinois; unique archive material; interviews with many of the principal police players; an interview with John Wayne Gacy at Menard, and a 63-minute police video of the exhumation of Gacy's victims from his crawlspace. The video has been released by the authorities and now available through www.newcriminologist.co.uk.

KENNETH ALESSIO BIANCHI

22 May 1951–

September 1996, Washington State Penitentiary, Walla Walla. My nerves are on edge. I am about to be locked into a small cubicle with a sado-sexual psychopath. Kenneth Bianchi is an exploitative homicidal maniac who ripped away the lives of some 15 young women including two little girls and dumped their bodies like so much trash.

I am about to get up close and very personal with this monster who has vowed to tear my face off. With a heavily pock-marked face, he is a powerful, dark-haired human predator with ink-black eyes which never blink; the cold, wet eyes of a Great White shark, soon to stare deep into my head with his evil tentacles of enquiring thought.

An arm's length away, a touch away now, Kenneth Bianchi does not smile as he walks into the room. He sits down and his breathing is shallow. I can almost hear his mind working like the ticking of a clock, even a bomb about to explode, for his hatred towards me radiates like red-hot coals.

Two long minutes pass. Not a word is said. Tick, tick, tick, tick. I lean back in my chair; I smile. 'You don't like me one bit, do you, Ken?'

There is no response and no movement from the man simmering a heartbeat away.

To break the ice, I rise to my feet and slowly walk around the table to him. I place my left hand on his shoulder. 'Hey, Ken,' I whisper. 'You are some miserable son-of-a-bitch. Come on, where is that fucking smile?'

Within a millisecond, a switch flicked inside his head. The tension seemed to wash out of him in an instant and a cruel smile slowly came to his thin mouth. It was this human contact, the physical touch and a dangerous up-close encounter – which could have played out either way – that now enabled me to have a 60-minute interview with 'The Hillside Strangler'.

When we parted, Ken stopped in his tracks, reeled around and snarled, 'Don't ever, *ever*, come near me again.'

I did – not once, but twice!

On the second occasion, as instructed by the guards who waited at the entrance of the tier, I slowly walked the yellow line down the Special Housing Unit (SHU). Cross the line and the spittle, excreta and urine from angry inmates will cover you. I stopped at cell number 8. Ken was lying on his bunk, headphones on, watching TV. I walked to his cell door and called his name. He stirred. He ignored me. Then he flew at the bars in a frenzy.

'Nice house you have here, Ken,' I said, smiling. Then I stepped away.

Third time, it was yard time. Bitterly cold, wet and windy at the Pen. Bianchi saw me watching him as he walked during exercise. This time mute, he turned up his collar, pulled his cap down over his eyes, and I would never see him again.

One girl was killed and, when she was dead, she was put inside the bedroom blindfolded. I took her girlfriend [Sonja] into the bedroom and raped and buggered her before killing her. She screamed for her mom, and the last thing she saw was the face of her dead friend lying under the sheets next to her.

Kenneth Bianchi to the author at interview, on the murder of 14-year-old Sonja Johnson

After four years of continual correspondence with Bianchi – who is also known as one of the evil Hillside Stranglers – I was finally granted a rare interview with him. The meeting took place at the notoriously tough Washington State Penitentiary (WSP) at Walla Walla – a medium-size city that squats in dry flatlands just a stone's throw from the Washington–Oregon border in the south-east corner of the state. Walla Walla, incidentally, is an ancient Indian name for 'Water Water'.

At the first visit, which was held in a small locked cubicle, Bianchi lost his temper, threatening to smash my skull into the wall before he calmed down. I then visited him and peered through the bars of his cell and he went berserk.

Bianchi stands around five feet eleven inches tall, and he is extremely well built. A tough exercise regime has toned his muscles to perfection; with a washboard stomach and powerful shoulders, today, well into his fifties, he is a fine specimen of a man. Ken's once rich, black mane of hair is thinning and turning grey; however, he still has the drop-dead handsome looks that the women always found so attractive. But it is his eyes that one finds fascinating, if not disturbing. They are small and jet-black. They are the eyes of a Great White shark; unblinking, devoid of any emotion whatsoever, they glitter with distilled evil. When one looks into Bianchi's eyes, I kid you not, you are looking into the abyss and that abyss is looking straight back at you.

ONE

Liar, Liar...

KENNETH Alessio Bianchi was born on Friday, 22 May 1951, in Rochester, New York. He was the last of four children to Florence King, an attractive, precocious 17-year-old 'go-go' dancer. She dumped him like an unwanted puppy shortly after giving birth. Kenneth never knew his genetic father, so, throughout his life, he suffered the social stigma of knowing he was a bastard.

Within weeks of his birth, Ken was fostered out to an elderly woman who had little time for him, so she farmed him out to a number of her friends and neighbours.

Every child has a need to be noticed, understood, taken seriously and respected by its mother and, as Dr Alice Miller says in her book *The Drama of Being a Child*, 'In the first few weeks and months of its life, the child needs to have its mother at its disposal, must be able to use her, and to be mirrored by her.' Therefore, it would be fair to say that, during this crucial period, Kenneth did not enjoy the benefits of having a mother. In fact, he did not have anyone to give him this vital attention. Indeed, it was quite the opposite, for he was shuffled from home to home, with each minder exhibiting different reactions towards him, ranging from short-term curiosity to unwelcome nuisance. So, in this respect alone, and in much the same way as so many other serial murderers, from day one, Ken was being emotionally deprived and damaged.

Italian immigrants Frances Bianchi and her husband, Nicholas, a manual labourer at the American Brake-Shoe foundry in Rochester, adopted Ken at the age of three months. He was to be their only child.

Born in 1918, Frances had wanted a child since her late teens, but she could not conceive. Time dragged by and, now aged 32, the only option open to her was that of adoption, to which her husband somewhat reluctantly agreed. Unfortunately, Frances was a hypochondriac and emotionally insecure; furthermore, she suffered frequent bouts of depression. Nonetheless, she was successfully able to conceal much of this under a veil of overt assertiveness, which manifested itself in an over-solicitous and totalitarian style.

In order to survive emotionally, Frances was capable of 'splitting off' from her weaker self. She used denial and repression, which broadly speaking means, when one is not happy with a situation, one puts the conscious thought out of one's mind. This was her mental defence mechanism, a vital requirement as her husband further aggravated the family's weak infrastructure with his inveterate gambling and losing the better part of his wages to the bookies.

Although a hard worker and a loyal spouse, Nicholas was weak-willed. And, as a direct result of him not being able to pay off his gambling debts, the family was always on the move because loan sharks threatened to shoot him if he didn't pay up. This confused package of mental and financial instability spilled into the Bianchi home on a daily basis, and it was Frances who felt it the worst with her paranoia soon rubbing off on her adopted son.

If Frances Bianchi deserved anything from this unsettled and worrying existence, she needed security, and she wrongly reasoned that she would be better off if there was someone who really needed her and, in turn, she would satisfy her maternal instincts by having a child. However, Frances wanted a child for all the wrong reasons, and Ken was to become an object at her disposal, an object which could be controlled, manipulated and become totally reliant and centred on her. The security that she couldn't find in her married life could be found in her adopted boy, she thought. Therefore, Ken would have to pay a very high price, and he was forced to give Frances his undivided admiration and full attention during the years to follow if he were to survive psychologically himself. A hint of these troubles surfaced just a year later.

Ken's adoption-agency records reveal that, although he was a 'sturdily built baby with bluish eyes and wavy brown hair, appearing happy, contented and alert', Mrs Bianchi was described as being 'over-solicitous'. A footnote added that Nicholas Bianchi was 'quiet, unassuming, but very friendly, able to control his incessant stuttering, which has troubled him since childhood, only when Kenneth is around him'.

In 1953, with loan sharks forever chasing Mr Bianchi for his gambling debts, the family were forced to leave their home on Saratoga Avenue in Rochester, New York, and move to Glide Street where they kept a low profile. The loan sharks soon caught up with them, so a year later they moved to Los Angeles where they stayed with Frances's sister, Jennifer Buono.

By now, Ken had developed asthma.

While in California, Ken attended the Century Park School, where, aged five, he suffered the first of two bad falls. He tripped while running up a flight of concrete steps, cracking open his head, then, a month later, he fell headlong from playground equipment, hitting a number of steel rungs and breaking his nose when he hit the floor.

After this accident, he started wetting his pants during the daytime. He developed a facial tic, which was apparent when he was stressed, and he was significantly accident-prone; choosing to run rather than walk, he was always falling over.

During their time in California, Nicholas Bianchi managed to save some money, which he used to pay off his gambling debts, so the family decided it was now safe to return to Rochester. Ken's asthma had all but disappeared, although his mother noticed that her boy had become withdrawn. He would retire to the attic where he spent hours gazing vacantly at the trains as they passed the house. Then, as might be expected, Nicholas started running up large gambling debts again.

The family's stay at 529 Lyell Avenue – in the red-light district where serial killer Arthur Shawcross trawled for victims – was short-lived. According to Ken, 'In 1958 we moved to a pink-painted house on Wildwood Drive, then in 1959 to 60, Villa Street, then on to Campbell Street,' and, all the while, Kenneth was changing not only any friends he had made, but schools as well.

In 1960, the nine-year-old was seen briefly at the Strong Memorial Hospital Clinic in Rochester. His appointment was prompted by a complaint from the Society of Prevention of Cruelty to Children. In a nutshell, this issue was based on school and adoption-agency evidence suggesting that the lad was not being properly cared for and, of course, there was every reason to believe this was the case. The report – published here for the first time – which followed Ken's visit, claimed:

Kenneth is a very anxious lad who has many phobias and counter-phobias. He uses repression and reaction formation. He is very dependent upon his mother. She has dominated him, and indulged him in terms of her own needs. He is anxious, protective, and this clinging control has made him ambivalent. But he represses his hostile aggression, and is increasingly dependent upon her.

Report on the care of the young Kenneth Bianchi

Therefore, as far back as nine years old, there appear to be significant indications that Kenneth Bianchi was made up of two opposing sets of attitudes and emotions. Echoing the psychopathology of his neurotic mother, he, like John Gacy, was mentally splitting in two. Undeniably, he had for years been the victim of a subtle form of child abuse and, unless something changed, he would be emotionally scarred for life.

But nothing did change. Indeed, matters became worse when, in 1961, two doctors at the DePaul Psychiatric Clinic in Rochester saw Ken again. On this occasion, the complaint came from the Monsignor at Ken's school because of his continual absenteeism. The facial tics and the enuresis (wetting himself) were also cause for concern, as was the asthma, which had returned with a vengeance. Doctors Dowling and Sullivan strongly recommended treatment for the lad, although, after two visits to the clinic, Mrs Bianchi bluntly told the doctors that she didn't see the need for any more treatment. She refused to let the doctors see Ken again and, in doing so, Frances placed her adopted son in great peril.

In June 1965, tragedy struck when Nicholas Bianchi died at work following a massive heart-attack. He was on the telephone to Frances when it happened, and he collapsed with the handset clutched tightly in his hand.

Later that year, Frances and Ken moved house yet again, and once more he was uprooted from his school, moving to the McQuaid Jesuit High School in the same city.

In his unpublished manuscript, Kenneth Bianchi devoted just half a page to the subject of his father, whom he says he 'adored'; however, over five pages contain explicit details of his early sexual experiences, and this is all rather sinister for a convicted serial killer who is intent on proving his innocence for a string of sexually related homicides, which include the rape, buggery, torture and murder of two little girls.

Nevertheless, the following is Ken's account and, although some may find this shocking, it is significant that this beast refers to young girls, aged around ten, as 'women'. He also claims to have been sexually active since the age of 11:

While my hormones increased, it was not until my sophomore year when I had my first sexual experience with a partner. It was when I was about eleven years old when I had my first solo experience. My first love was blonde, thin build, and easy to speak with. She had a cute way of flirting, head tipped a bit. A beautiful smile across her face. She smelled divine, as women do.

Our first sexual encounter was at her home, with her parents and sister away. It was brief and I was so nervous my hands shook. I tried my best to be patient and gentle as I assumed a man would be. I'm certain I was hurried and, with a touch of experience, I wore no protection, which she had insisted on. When we finished, I just held her. It was the most beautiful and memorable experience I'd had up to that point in my life.

Kenneth Bianchi on his early sexual experiences

In fact, the girlfriend in question was just nine years old, but this did not prevent Ken adding that she was not his steady girlfriend. 'We coupled for a week or so,' he claimed, 'but her heart belonged to several other guys in the neighborhood. She and I had sexual relations twice more before ending our relationship.' Warming to his theme, Bianchi admitted that he had 'scholastic problems', because his real interest was always the female sex: 'I was crazy about girls … I dated different women on a regular basis. Romance is wonderful, life was my opiate, women were my fix. I could easily be distracted from my studies by the right woman.'

With equal clarity, Kenneth Bianchi also remembered Sue Davis, a young girl from his school who was junior to him, it seems, who invited him to her home where there was a swimming pool. And, at this point in his writing, Bianchi launches into a more complete quasi-erotic explanation of a problem that occurred during that very same swimming session, and it bothers him some 40 years later:

> She was a little chubby. She had a spinal problem, and was bubbly and full-figured. We were in the pool, and I reached out to hug her. She turned and my hand brushed against her breast. I wasn't disappointed, but it was unintentional. We broke up after that. She thought I had touched her breast without her permission. That allegation upset me.
>
> *Kenneth Bianchi on Sue Davis*

Sue Davis was eleven years old, and Bianchi did more than touch her breast, he touched just about everything else. So, it is clear from the pen of the killer himself that, by the age of 18, the oldest girl he had had sex with was 14, and the youngest – at least three of them – were aged nine.

In 1970, Ken resumed his studies and set his sights on joining a police academy. He enrolled at college, and now aged 19 he was living with his adoptive mother at 105 Glenda Park.

With only a decent showing in Geography, in all other subjects Ken struggled abysmally, so it is not surprising to learn that Ken not only failed his degree, but he was also deemed to be totally unsuitable to become a police officer. He was, however, offered the more menial job of jail deputy, a position he promptly turned down while all of his fellow students were joining the police academy left, right and centre. Ken was now a laughing stock and he didn't like it one bit. But Kenneth's narcissistic obsessions were to have further, far wider-reaching and more dangerous implications than anyone could have predicted around this low point in his life, as we will soon see.

Ken's failure at college had been a severe blow to his over-inflated self-esteem, for he had convinced himself and promised his mother that he would become a police officer. When this dream was shattered, so was his ego, so he took to petty thieving and was soon being dismissed from every part-time job he took.

Ken did, however, have something in common with one small group of people, that sub-culture of society called 'emerging serial killers', for he was a pathological liar. Telling lies was his way of making himself seem cleverer than he actually was. Kenneth could not allow himself to be seen as inferior in the eyes of his peers, and looking back at him as he was then it is clear that this 'Billy Liar' suffered from a manifest grandiosity – and he still does to this day.

Upon leaving school in 1971, Bianchi married an extremely attractive girl called Brenda Beck. He took a part-time job at the 'Two Guys' store, and he furthered his education at the Rochester Monroe Community College where he reviewed plays and films for the college newspaper, *The Monroe Discipline*. Ken's enthusiasm then faltered; consequently, he failed to complete many of the classes, which included Psychology, in which he drew an 'incomplete'. However, Psychology was a subject he would return to under somewhat less than honest circumstances eight years later.

At the same time as Ken's academic efforts were tottering on the edge of a cliff, his personal life suddenly collapsed around him when his wife caught him in bed with another woman called Janice Tuschong. Brenda threw him out on to the street where he became the subject of much ridicule amongst the few friends that he had.

Brenda has never given interviews, although, in 1994, Frances Bianchi (now Piccione) broke her silence, telling me, 'Ken was a blatant liar. You'd catch him doing something, ask him why he did it, he'd tell you, "I didn't do it." I'd catch him in lies, and he would deny everything. And, in the end, you felt like you were the crazy one, and not him. He is such a smooth liar. He tells such lies that you believe him. You really believe what he says until you prove it for yourself.'

So, Bianchi needed to be admired for something he was not. This was his way of compensating for his shortcomings. He *had* to excel in everything he undertook; after all, this was what his mother had drummed into him, expected of him and, like all grandiose people, woe betide if something fails them. When that happens, a bout of severe depression is imminent and, in Ken's case, the catastrophe was immediate and lethal.

The collapse of Bianchi's self-esteem during this period of his life proved just how precariously his self-esteem had been hanging by a thread, for nothing genuine that could ever have given him strength, or support, had been allowed to develop inside his mind. As Dr Alice Miller says, 'The grandiose person is never really free. First, because he is so excessively dependent on admiration from others; and second, because his self-respect is dependent on qualities, functions and achievements that can suddenly fail.'

With Bianchi they did fail, and looking back through his history we can see that his relationships, and efforts to succeed, hung in the air on a very fine thread indeed. His self-esteem and grandiosity – his entire psychopathological infrastructure – were crumbling away like weathered cement. Then, when Ken's unstable support mechanism eventually failed, it required just one more adverse influence to knock his house down.

At the very time Bianchi's desperate attempts at becoming a police officer were foundering like a ship in a hurricane, his marriage lay in tatters, too. And, as soon as he became involved with Janice Tuschong, he messed that relationship up as well. Then, out of the blue, a number of horrific child murders shook his hometown of Rochester. These killings took place within a mile radius of Ken's front door, and he soon found himself being interviewed as a suspect in the killings. The media dubbed the cases 'The Alphabet Murders' or 'Double Initial Murders', because each victim's Christian name began with the same letter as the surname.

The first murder, that of ten-year-old Carmen Colon, was on Tuesday, 16 November 1971. Her body was found at Churchville, and this event took place within days of Bianchi learning of his third set of failed exam results, and of him being kicked out of the marital home.

There was a gap of 17 months before the murderer struck again. The murder of 11-year-old Wanda Walkowitz coincided almost to the day of Bianchi being thrown out of Janice Tuschong's apartment in April, because she had caught him sleeping with one Donna Duranso.

Bianchi's affair with Donna collapsed in November 1973 and, a day later, the Monday after Thanksgiving recess, 11-year-old Michelle Maenza went missing. Two days later, her body was found fully clothed along a lonely road in Macedon, Wayne County.

All three girls had been raped, then strangled to death. There were other links between the murders as well: all lived in rundown neighbourhoods; all were walking alone when they were snatched from the streets; all were from broken homes – their fathers gone, the mothers on welfare; all had eaten a small meal just before they met their deaths; all had white cat hair attached to their clothing; and each girl was last seen alive in the company of a young, white male, who was driving a white saloon car. The description of the car and the man matched Bianchi perfectly.

All three children were streetwise. They had been warned by their mothers not to speak to strangers, therefore, investigators reasoned that whoever had abducted them might have been disguised as a police officer, or even a clergyman.

Of course, there were other suspects in the frame, and one man committed suicide before the police arrived to interview him. Post-mortem blood tests, though, proved that this man – Miguel Colon, the uncle of Carmen whom FBI profiler Robert Hazelwood thought fitted the bill – could not have been the killer because the culprit was a non-secretor, an individual of blood group A, B or AB who does not secrete the antigens characteristic of these blood groups in bodily fluids (such as saliva, semen, etc). Bianchi is a non-secretor, a group making up just 20 per cent of the US population.

During his interview with Rochester homicide cops, Bianchi was as plausible as ever. A natural-born liar, well able to sell ice cream to Eskimos, he convinced the officers that he had watertight alibis for the three murders in question. However, he refused, as was his legal right in those days, to give body fluid samples, which would have confirmed that he was a non-secretor. Then, amazingly, even more so as Mrs Bianchi owned a white cat, and he drove a white car, suspicion fell away, and no one checked to confirm the veracity of Ken's alibis.

The author has since carried out research on these three murders, and quickly learned after speaking to the providers of the alibis in question, including Janice Tuschong, that Ken's claims were not worth the paper they were written on. And this poses some intriguing questions. Why did Ken lie about his alibis, and why would he refuse to give body fluid samples?

When he was questioned by the author at the Washington State Penitentiary, Ken confirmed that his mother had owned a white cat during the time of the murders, that he did, indeed, own a white car, and he argued that it was not in his interests to give bodily fluids, but that he had been telling the truth about his alibis.

Ken also says that he has been ruled out as a suspect in the 'Double Initial Murders', when this is not the case. When I visited the Rochester Police, Captain Lynde Johnston claimed that Bianchi has always been in the frame.

Frances (Bianchi) Piccione told me in 1992, 'It seemed that, whenever Ken had a fight with a girlfriend, or had a problem, he went out and killed someone. I even told the police the same thing.'

Bianchi's early life shows that he is atypical of the serial-murderer type in psychological make-up. He was superficially attractive to women, although, when his partners looked deeper, they found that he was transparent, immature, unfaithful and a pathological liar. Such men might seem to have many female friends, but they are unable to form or sustain any meaningful, lasting relationships. Deep down, they have formed a growing dislike, even a rage towards women in general.

There is no doubt that Ken felt that the world was stacked against him. He sat for hours, asking himself why, if he were so clever, which in a bigoted way he thought he was, he had failed, when all around him were enjoying success. And, like so many of his breed, it is not what Kenneth says or does that is so important, but what he will *not* say, or patently avoids saying, which is vital when trying to find the reason why he turned into such an abhorrent killer.

For instance, Bianchi has always claimed that he is a secretor, therefore he could never have been involved in other well-documented murders. Indeed, he went further by stating in countless letters that he can produce his medical notes to support this claim. However, when pressed to supply these documents, Bianchi avoided the subject by saying, 'Actually, I am not sure if I am a secretor, or non-secretor. I just don't know.'

In a search for the facts about his claim, the author contacted the FBI, who released a document dated Wednesday, 2 June 1982. In it, Agent Robert Beams, a specialist in blood grouping and body fluids, confirmed that, after taking samples from Bianchi, he was able to say that Bianchi was a non-secretor. More to the point, a recent discovery was made in Bianchi's cell. He has had a copy of that very same document, and it has been in his possession for decades.

Quite obviously, Ken believes that everyone in the world is a mug, except himself!

No account of Kenneth Bianchi's life and crimes would be complete without mention of his adoptive cousin and accomplice, Angelo Buono, who lived in Los Angeles.

With a population well in excess of 5 million, LA is the third-largest city in the USA. It also has one of the highest murder rates, per capita, in the western world.

Ten miles north of LA is the sprawling suburb of Glendale where, in 1975, Kenneth Bianchi alighted from a coach at the Eagle Rock

Plaza terminal minus his worldly possessions. His two suitcases had been lost during the gruelling trip from Rochester and he wouldn't retrieve them for several days. And meeting Ken at the terminal was his adoptive cousin, Angelo Buono, known variously by his cronies as 'The Italian Stallion' and 'The Buzzard'.

Buono's background offers some clues to his subsequent dysfunctional, violent and sadistic adult life: his mother and father had violent rows and split when he was very young; his mother found it almost impossible to make ends meet, and young Angelo was sucked into petty crime while still at school. His childhood idol was a rapist called Caryl Chessman, who lulled victims into trusting him by impersonating a cop.

Angelo spent some time in prison, had six kids by several mothers, all of whom ended up on the receiving end of his violent temper, and he bragged of abusing a 14-year-old girl 'to break her in'. Interestingly, his business, an auto-upholstery workshop, lent him an air of respectability, as he was a skilled technician, numbering Frank Sinatra and other stars among his clients.

One of Ken's first priorities upon arriving in Los Angeles was to find a job to help him pay his way with Angelo, and he managed to land himself employment as a real-estate customer services clerk with California Land Title (Cal Land). Ken had learned of the vacancy through Buono's female bank manager who put in a good word for him when he applied for the position. Then, at the firm's 1977 New Year's Eve party, he met Kelli Kae Boyd who worked at the company's head office in Universal City.

A stunning brunette with large brown eyes, she fell for Bianchi's smooth approach, and they dated for a month before she decided to end the relationship because of Ken's immaturity and insecurity. 'He was very possessive, and he always wanted to know where I was going, who I was doing it with, and I didn't really like that very well,' she later told Detective McNeill of the Bellingham Police Department.

With enough cash now to find a place of his own, Ken left Buono's place and rented rooms at Tamarind Apartments, and no sooner had he slammed the door shut than he picked up the phone and started wooing Kelli again. As was his practice with previous girlfriends, he sent her bunches of flowers and, before long, he was treating her at the most expensive restaurants he could afford. They moved in under the same roof and, at the beginning of May 1977, she announced that she was pregnant with his child.

Life with Kenneth was always going to be a rough ride. The couple argued frequently, and more than once Kelli turned him out. Each time, he returned to Angelo's place where he slept on the floor, or he would call his mother who mediated reconciliation. Throughout all this, Kelli still worked at Cal Land, although she was heavily pregnant.

Bianchi earned considerably less than Kelli and, although he had now been promoted to Assistant Title Officer, he decided to earn a little more cash on the side. He would become Dr Bianchi with a doctorate in Psychology, and here, published for the first time, is his account of why he formed this bogus service:

People in California are big on widow dressing. Joining the *Psychology Today* book club, I took in books to decorate my shelves. I was introduced to Dr Weingarten, and I asked him if I could rent part of his offices at night. I sounded literate, and he accepted me on the reference of a mutual friend. There was no extraordinary effort to fool the doctor, and if he'd asked me just some basic questions about psychology, he would have seen right through me. Placing ads in *The Los Angeles Times*, I received credentials from other psychologists and students applying for a job with me. A diploma replacement service supplied more decorations for my walls and shelves. Also, I had several basic psychology books from back east. I knew I was doing wrong, but I took every precaution to not harm anyone.

Kenneth Bianchi on his qualifications

So, now we find our 'Dr Bianchi' obtaining genuine diplomas by sleight of hand from students who applied for a post with him and, as soon as they dropped into his mailbox, he substituted his own name. To add further authenticity to the phoney venture, he forged letters from various well-known institutions, who thanked Dr Bianchi for his 'generosity', and for the 'small cash donations, and his valuable time in giving such enlightening lectures'. Of course, all of this was a figment of his overactive and crooked imagination. He then told Kelli that he had earned his Psychology degree way back in Rochester, and that he was helping two colleagues, one of whom was the unwitting Dr Weingarten, with their overload of patients. But then, like all of Bianchi's schemes, it fell apart.

During a visit to California to see her son, Frances could not fail to notice the many fraudulent diplomas which he had displayed in his apartment as well as his office. She was not impressed, and she berated Ken, threatening to expose him as a cheat. However, the warning went unheeded. Ken continued to pour money into advertising until his funds dried up. Patients failed to materialise, and he dumped the fabricated sideshow when Kelli heard the truth from his mother. And, yet again, Kelli Boyd threw Kenneth on to the streets. This time she had had enough.

But Ken had another ace up his sleeve. He told the gullible Kelli that he had cancer of the lung, and begged her to take him back. In a statement to the police, she later said, 'Those days were very fretful for me. I took time off work to be with him. He had appointments at the hospital, and I drove him there to make sure he was OK. But he made me wait in the car. He had many bad ways, and very good ways. He was bad at paying the bills, and he was always skipping off work. On balance, I loved him, and I didn't want him to die without seeing our child. Yet, all the time, he was lying to me about the cancer. Then he got dismissed from work for having drugs in his desk drawer. That's when I kicked him out for good.'

Poor old Ken was now falling apart like a cheap suit. The guy who was so bent he couldn't lie straight in bed had lost his job with Cal Land, his bogus counselling service had flopped, Kelli was heavily pregnant, he had no home and the bills were mounting daily. So, apart from wrecking his own life, he was destroying Kelli's, and perhaps she made the wisest move of her life by moving in with her brother at 200 East Palmer, the day after Thanksgiving 1977. Within a week, she moved again, this time to Adelaide Avenue. Shortly thereafter, she travelled north to Bellingham, Washington State, where her parents put a secure roof over her head. Sadly, however, a dormant serial killer would follow in her tracks.

A week after Kelli left him, Ken, who was never one to allow grass to grow under his feet, bounced back when he was introduced to a drop-dead gorgeous blonde at a party. Just turned 16, Sabra Hannan was an aspiring model with all the physical attributes to match her ambitions. For his part, Bianchi was loveless and penniless, and Angelo was sick and tired of handing out cash to his immature cousin, so, within minutes of meeting Sabra, the quick-thinking Ken came up with another scam which would raise money, and also please Angelo into the bargain.

After placing a drink in her hand, Ken slipped his arm around Sabra's waist and he gently eased her to another room where he explained that she was the most beautiful woman he had ever seen. He told her that he had friends in the movie business, and that she could easily earn $500 a week from the outset, and this figure would rise when she became better known.

That night, Sabra, now a little the worse for drink, was lured to The Buzzard's nest, and Buono's eyes lit up when he saw the slim-figured, busty teenager. As the hours drifted by, Sabra fell asleep, totally unaware of the scheming cousins who were whispering quietly in another room.

This time, Ken had come up with a great idea. The two men would force Sabra into prostitution and, before the week was out, she was left under no illusion that they would kill her if she attempted to leave. By then, she was already their sex slave and soon-to-be hooker.

Fearful for her life, Sabra was now coerced into introducing her friend, 15-year-old Becky Spears, to the cousins. She, too, was forced into prostitution, and every night both men sodomised the girls to the degree that the young women had to wear tampons in their rectums to stop the bleeding. Then life for the girls took an unexpected turn for the better.

After a fortnight of this living hell, Becky was summoned to a wealthy lawyer's apartment for sex. On her arrival, she looked so downhearted her client asked her how she had become involved in prostitution. With tears flooding down her face, she explained that Buono and Bianchi subjected her and Sabra to degrading sex acts and sadistic cruelty. She said that the two men had threatened to track them down and kill them if they ran away.

To his credit, the lawyer acted immediately. He drove Becky to the airport where he bought her a ticket to her home in Arizona and, just before she boarded the aircraft, he stuffed a large wad of notes into her pocket. Then, he kissed her on the cheek and said goodbye.

As might be expected, Angelo went ballistic when his youngest hooker failed to return home, so he made several threatening phone calls to the lawyer, stammering, 'Give me her fuckin' address, or I'll fuckin' shoot you.' Through his real-estate contacts, Bianchi obtained the lawyer's address then placed an ad in a local paper, advertising the luxurious property and its entire contents for sale. However, these were the types of threats which the attorney could easily deal with, for among his clientele was the local Chapter of the Hell's Angels, and he asked them to pay Mr Buono a visit.

Fitting new mats into a customer's car, Angelo was still fuming with rage when he was tapped smartly on the shoulder. At first, he ignored the leather-clad bikers, which was not exactly the diplomatic thing to do. Then, as one biker produced a sawn-off, pump-action shotgun, the largest of the group, six-foot-four-inch, 350-pound 'Tiny', reached through the car window and extracted the struggling Buono by his shirtfront. 'Do we have your attention, Mr Buono?' he asked.

Unfortunately, there is no record of the discussion that followed; unsurprisingly, the cousins didn't bother the lawyer again, and the remaining girl was allowed to go free.

This incident was certainly the crucial turning point which led the perverted Buono to become a serial murderer. Word of his humiliation flashed around the neighbourhood like a bush fire. He lost face with his cronies, and the intensely macho crook was outraged that he had been shown to be a weakling in front of Bianchi. At Henry's, Buono's favourite eaterie, regular customers and staff alike sniggered behind his back. It was rumoured out loud that 'The Italian Stallion' could no longer control his women.

When the author questioned Bianchi about his role in the stable of hookers, he denied that he ever touched the girls. He added that a man called JJ was a partner with Buono and himself, and that he was only the driver and responsible for collecting the cash of which he might receive a small percentage.

After his arrest many years later, Bianchi was interviewed by Sergeant Frank Salerno of the LAPD about the call-girl service. The following transcript has never been published before:

Salerno:	What was the financial arrangement for the call-out service? You guys obviously were going to get something out of what the girls made.
Bianchi:	The girls would be working for JJ, completely, and the girls would have to pay Angelo… I can't remember the exact percentage because it varied.
Salerno:	So, it was coming out of the girls' take?
Bianchi:	Right, and it would go to Angelo.
Salerno:	Strictly to Angelo.
Bianchi:	Yeah, and then Angelo would, you know, give me what I…

Salerno: What? What would he give you?

Bianchi: It varied. It just depended on what the girls got. Sometimes if the girls got only, came home with only $20, there would be no take or very little take and I wouldn't get anything, you know, it would just be a pass situation. Sometimes the girls would come home with like $100–$200.

Salerno: What would you get out of that?

Bianchi: I would probably end up with about $20–$30 out of that.

Salerno: Out of $100 or out of $200?

Bianchi: Out of about $200.

Salerno: What would the girls end up with?

Bianchi: The remainder. Probably about $140.

Salerno: And Angelo would get $20 or $30?

Bianchi: Right, about the same.

Salerno: So, in essence, you and Angelo were still partners in … an out-call service or something along that line?

Bianchi: Right.

TWO

Police Make a Killing

WITH the slave girls gone, Buono's pimping income dried up so the two men had to find more teenage girls. They tried to abduct one girl then suddenly realised she was the daughter of a famous actor. Snatching her from the streets was far too risky. Eventually, they found a young woman and installed her in Susan's former bedroom. They also bought a 'trick list' from a prostitute named Deborah Noble with names of men who frequented prostitutes. However, the truth was quite the opposite, because it was a list of men who wanted to visit one particular good-time girl in her own apartment. To make matters worse, this prostitute already had a pimp, and she had no intention of going into business with the likes of Buono and Bianchi. The list was useless; the dirty duo had slipped up yet again and, to explain the effect this rip-off had upon the two men, Bianchi wrote in a letter, 'We went off in search of the vendor, madder then hell.'

The police have always maintained that Bianchi and Buono never found the seller of this list, and that an acquaintance of the seller, Yolanda Washington, was the first victim in the Hillside Strangling series. However, Bianchi told me that this was not the case. Ken argues that Laura Collins had sold them the phoney list, and that is why she was the first to die.

Also of some interest is the fact that when the Hillside Strangler task force was assembled in December 1977, Laura Collins's name was erased from the victims' list, and it was not until January 1978 that the then Assistant Chief of Police, Darryl Gates, publicly indicated that Laura was indeed a victim of the strangler.

Laura Collins, 26 years old, was last seen alive just after noon at Ventura Freeway and Lankershim Boulevard, on Sunday, 4 September 1977. Her partially clothed body was found near the Forest Lawn exit slip-road off the Ventura Freeway, Burbank, at 10.30am on Friday, 9 September. She had been strangled, and this homicide became the blueprint for all of the subsequent killings.

At 1.34pm on Monday, 18 October 1977, a naked body was found perversely sprawled on its stomach alongside Forest Lawn Drive, close to the famous cemetery of the same name, and just south of the Ventura Freeway. Lying in a crucifixion position, with the right hand crooked over, the legs apart, it appeared that she had been dragged from a vehicle by two men and dropped near a pile of broken road-surfacing concrete just a yard from her head. Behind the body was a yellow 'No Trespassing or Loitering' sign.

Tall and leggy, the black woman was immediately identified by Vice officers as Yolanda Washington, a particularly attractive 19-year-old, who had almond-shaped eyes and medium-length black hair. She was a part-time bar waitress and hooker who was known to have touted for business with Laura Collins.

Enquiries soon established that Yolanda had last been seen alive just before midnight the previous day as she solicited for business at Vista and Sunset Boulevards. On a good night, she could earn over $300, which helped her support her 30-month-old daughter Tameika.

The autopsy showed that she'd had sex with two men shortly before death – one of whom was a non-secretor. With her killer kneeling over her, she had been strangled with a piece of cloth while she was lying down. There were marks around her wrists, and Yolanda had been anally raped, too.

Bianchi confirmed this to me, saying that he had killed her in the back seat of his car and had removed a turquoise ring from her finger which he later gave to Kelli Boyd.

Just after midnight on Monday, 31 October 1977, a white female was abducted from the Hollywood area of Howard and Wilcox. Unattractive, with medium-length reddish-brown hair, 15-year-old Judith 'Judy' Ann Miller lived in a ramshackle hotel, which was her base as a part-time hooker. From trailer-park stock, her mother was wanted in connection with a welfare fraud, and her father had jumped bail for a similar offence.

It was a pretty grim sight that Hallowe'en morning at Alta Terrace and La Crescenta. The naked body lay close to the kerb in a middle-class residential area, covered by a tarpaulin by a property owner to shield the corpse from the children in the neighbourhood. The bruises on her neck showed that she had been strangled. She had ligature marks on both wrists and ankles as well. Insects feasted on her pale skin. On her eyelid was a small piece of light-coloured fluff that Sergeant Frank Salerno of the Los Angeles County Sheriff's Department saved for the forensic experts, and it did not appear that she had been murdered at this location.

The coroner determined that she had been strangled to death around midnight, some six hours before she was found. It was also clear that she had been raped and sodomised.

Bianchi says that Judy had been taken back to Buono's house where she had been raped. Bianchi sodomised her, then strangled her. He finished her off by suffocating his victim with a plastic supermarket bag. 'She involuntarily urinated after death, just as Washington had done,' Bianchi claimed, with an evil grin playing across his mouth. 'We made her go into the washroom before we killed her to stop it happening, but it didn't work. She was tied by the arms, legs and neck to our special chair in Angelo's bedroom. She didn't like dying one bit.'

A white waitress at the Healthfair Restaurant near Hollywood and Vine, and part-time prostitute, 21-year-old Teresa 'Terri' (aka 'Lissa') Kastin became the stranglers' fourth victim. Moderately attractive, with a Roman nose and bushy dark hair, Terri was stopped by Bianchi and Buono, who were posing as police officers, at 9.15pm on Saturday, 5 November 1977. They ordered her into their black-over-white sedan and, like Miller, she was taken back to Buono's home for what Bianchi called 'questioning'. There, she was tied down into the special chair, and her striped sweater and short skirt were cut off with scissors. The two men were repelled because she had hairy legs, and Bianchi was reduced to raping her with a root-beer bottle as he throttled her. When she kicked out in her death throes, Buono sat on her legs, shouting, 'Die, you cunt, die.' Terri was allowed to suck in lungfuls of air many times before she lost consciousness for the last time.

At 1.15am the next day, Terri's body was found at Chevy Chase and Linda Vista. Identification was made swiftly after a news broadcast reported the murder and Terri's father telephoned the police reporting his daughter as missing.

At autopsy, no semen was present in the vagina or anus, which supported Bianchi's confession that neither of the two men had physically raped this victim.

Jill Barcombe was an 18-year-old white hooker who had moved to Hollywood following a string of prostitution convictions in New York. She was last seen alive at Pico and Ocean Boulevards at around 7.00pm on Wednesday, 9 November 1977. She was found naked and strangled at 5.50am the following morning at Franklin Canyon Drive and Mulholland. Jill had put up a fierce fight for her life, as severe head trauma was present.

A 28-year-old aspiring actress and part-time model with a real 'wow' factor, Jane King was rated by the 'Hollywood set' as a stunning blonde bombshell who had literally exploded on the scene when she was just 16. Over the years, Jane had raised the eyebrows of every hot-blooded male and film producer who saw her. She was also a Scientology student and a follower of L Ron Hubbard's work on Dianetics, the eradication of negative thought and energy to lead a more fulfilled life. Police claimed that she was a part-time hooker, although this was incorrect.

Jane was last seen alive outside 9500 Lemona, at 10.10pm on Wednesday, 9 November 1977. Posing as police officers, Buono and Bianchi cruised up, arrested her on suspicion of prostitution and took her back to Angelo's home where she was dragged screaming through the living/dining area into the east bedroom where she was stripped naked. Bianchi confessed that they 'were delighted to find her pubis was shaven'. However, because she struggled while she was being raped, the two men decided to teach her a lesson. A plastic bag was placed over her head while Bianchi sodomised her. Jane pleaded desperately for her life during a four-hour period of terror before she was allowed to suffocate to death as Bianchi climaxed.

Jane's naked body was found on a bed of dead leaves in undergrowth at the Los Feliz exit slip-road of the Golden State Freeway on Wednesday, 23 November. She lay on her back, legs open, with the right knee drawn up.

The murders of Sonja Johnson and Dolores 'Dolly' Cepeda, and the violence and brutality they suffered, shocked everyone involved in the case. Aged 14 and 12, they were two innocent little girls who happened to be in the wrong place at the wrong time. Judge Roger Boren – former prosecutor at Bianchi and Buono's trial in LA – told me, 'Angelo Buono and Kenneth Bianchi followed the girls on a bus as they travelled from a shopping mall, and apparently used some police ruse that they were being arrested. They took these two young girls to Angelo Buono's house and did with them what they did with the other victims – tortured them and strangled them to death.

'They took the girls to a hillside overlooking one of the largest freeways in Los Angeles and discarded their bodies. That particular hillside was used by many people to discard trash. There were couches, mattresses… things of that sort had been thrown down that hillside. And these two bodies had been discarded in a like manner. In fact, they were not discovered for two weeks.'

The 14-year-old Sonja and 12-year-old Dolly were both pupils at the Saint Ignatius School. They were last seen alive on Sunday, 13 November 1977, boarding a bus at the Eagle Plaza stop, which was just a quarter-of-a-mile from Angelo's home. They followed the vehicle and, when the girls disembarked near their home, again, posing as a police officer, Bianchi approached the girls and accused them of shoplifting. They were taken 'downtown' and interviewed in Angelo's house. Sonja was raped and murdered in a bedroom by Buono, while Dolly sat outside with Bianchi.

'Where's my friend?' asked the girl when Buono came out alone.

'Oh, don't worry,' said Bianchi, 'you'll be seeing her in a minute.'

The last thing Dolly saw was the dead face of Sonja on the bed beside her as Bianchi raped and sodomised her.

Children playing on a rubbish tip at Landa and Stadium Way found the girls' naked bodies at 4.00pm on Sunday, 20 November.

The scenes-of-crime photographs showed Dolly and Sonja sprawled out among the discarded beer bottles and tin cans. Sonja rested almost on her right side, her left hand tucked up under her breasts, the hand nudging her chin. The right arm, hand gripped tight in a death spasm, was outstretched and underneath her right side. The legs were almost straight, the left foot draped over the neck of Dolly who was on her stomach; her torso slightly crooked and leaning to the right of her legs, which were parted. Dolly's left arm was also tucked underneath her body, her hand covering her mouth as if to stifle a scream. The right arm, bent at the elbow, was outstretched. There were a set of human bite marks on her left buttock.

When one sees such terrible things, only then can one understand the true, evil nature of Kenneth Bianchi and Angelo Buono.

The public were just outraged that we, as law enforcement officers, could not do anything to stop these brutal murders. Especially the single women in this city who went to work at nights, going to the markets, going to see their families. They were petrified.

Detective Richard Crotsley, LAPD, to the
author at interview

Like Jane King, 17-year-old Kathleen 'Kathy' Robinson was another attractive blonde who was well known around the hotspots of Hollywood. Her flowing blonde hair caught the attention of the Hillside Stranglers at 9.30pm on Wednesday, 16 November 1977. She was walking towards her car which was parked near Pico and Ocean Boulevard, when Buono and Bianchi drew up alongside her. Flashing a phoney police badge, they ordered her into their car. She was found fully clothed, strangled, with her throat cut, at Burnside and Curson, at 8.30am the next day.

A quiet young woman, 20-year-old Kristina Weckler was an honours student at the Pasadena Art Centre of Design. She lived at Tamarind Apartments, 800 Garfield, Glendale. This was the same apartment block where Bianchi had once resided, and he knew the young woman and had pestered her for a date. Kristina, who knew that Ken was living with the pregnant Kelli Boyd, rejected his advances.

Kristina's naked body was found at Ranon's Way and Nawona on Sunday, 20 November. Detective Sergeant Bob Grogan immediately noticed the ligature marks on her wrists, ankles and neck. When he turned her over, blood oozed from her rectum. The bruises on her breasts were obvious. Oddly enough, there were two puncture marks on her arm, but no signs of the needle tracks that indicate a drug addict.

Bianchi told me that, at around 6.00pm on Saturday, 19 November, he knocked on Kristina's door, telling her that he was now a police officer, and that someone had crashed into her car parked outside. Once in the lot, she was bundled into his car and driven to Buono's home where they tried to kill her using a new method. They had intended to inject Kristina with caustic cleaning fluid; however, when this barbaric method of murder failed, they covered her head with a plastic bag and piped coal gas into her lungs. Bianchi raped Kristina, ejaculating into her during the moment she convulsed in death. She died as the result of strangulation by ligature.

The truth, however, was slightly different. Bianchi told police that he had knocked on Kristina's door and had asked her if she wanted to go to a party. At first, Kristina said that she was tired. But Bianchi was insistent and she soon took up the offer, slipping on a pair of brown loafers, a beige, long-sleeved blouse and a skirt, and followed Bianchi to his car, in which Buono was sitting.

They arrived at the murder house at about 12.30am. It was obviously deserted and the men said that the other guests would soon arrive. Within minutes, they were killing her. Using the method described above, the terrified and totally compliant Kristina took over an hour to die.

Describing how Buono injected the poor girl, Bianchi told police:

He [Buono] suggested that… he said, 'How about just injecting air into her? The air bubble would probably kill her.' I said, 'Oh, you want to try something different. Whatever.'

We both walked back into the dining room, put the chair back at the dining-room table. He grabbed her underwear and her socks and he went back into the room and set the needle down on the bed… at one end of the bed and he said, 'Come on, now, we're going to stand up,' and we both helped her up. He said, 'Sit down here,' and he sat on the edge of the bed and he helped her get her clothes on, her underwear and socks, he said, 'OK, now, come on. Stand up.' And he helped her stand up and we walked her to the open part of the room at the bottom of the bed and set her down on the floor, face up. He took the needle, took the cap off of it, he pulled back the plunger and he told me, he said, 'Hold her legs.' I held her legs, he crouched down. He's on her left side. He stuck the needle in her neck [left side] and pushed the plunger in and pulled it out.

He did it a couple of times. She flinched and made a murmuring sound and he stood up and he said, 'Let go of her legs,' and he walked towards me and pushed me lightly back towards the doorway and he says, 'Just stand here and see what happens.' So I stood there for about five to ten minutes. Nothing happened. He says, 'What I should do is put something in the needle. Stay here. I'll be right back.' He went into the kitchen area. When he came back there was a blue solution, some kind of blue solution, in the needle.

He injected her and said, 'Help me to get her up.' We helped her to her feet and she was still shaking. Walked her into the kitchen and walked her into the front where his stove was being put in, or the connection was, and lied her down on the floor. He stood up and started to walk away from her and he indicated to me to walk away with him, he had to talk to me. We walked into the dining room, and in the dining room he said, 'What I'll do is put a bag over her head,' he says, 'I'll use the twine; I'll cut off a piece of twine, so we can make a seal on the bag,' he says, 'and the pipe, the bendable pipe is long enough,' he says, 'stick that under the bag and when I tell you, turn the gas on and when I tell you, turn the gas off.'

After we'd had a little discussion in the dining room, we walked back into the kitchen. Kristina Weckler's lying on the floor in this direction, in front the fixture. Angelo is standing here to her left side. She's still shaking really bad, probably from that blue stuff that was injected into her. He put the bag over her head and there was no unusual movement when he did that. He told me to get the pipe and stick the pipe under the bag, which I did. He then wrapped the twine a couple of times around her neck and pulled it tight and said, 'OK, go ahead. Turn it on.' I turned on the gas, the bag inflated. He said, 'Turn off the gas.' I turned off the gas, and he waited until it deflated. Turned it on again. We repeated this probably about four or five times.

Finally, it was obvious that she had stopped breathing, so he said to take the tubing out, which I did... put the tubing back and made sure the valve was turned off all the way. He took the rope off of her and the bag off her head. He took out his keys and rolled her over and I held her shoulders while he rolled her over and unlocked the handcuffs. I took off the tape and gag from her mouth and took the blindfold off and he removed her pants and underwear. We both walked into the dining room and put everything into a paper bag. He then got the roll of tape and taped up the bag. I walked to the back door. He walked to the dumpster. Moved a few things around and tossed the bag in there. Put things on top of the bag. He came back in, asked me for the keys to my car. He said, 'I'll open up the trunk.' When he got through opening up the trunk, he walked to the street, looked around and came back again... then we dumped her off.

Kenneth Bianchi at police interview

A promising lead in the hunt for the killers came on Monday, 28 November 1977, the day after a student and trainee secretary disappeared from 9500 Lemona, Sepulveda, in the San Fernando Valley. The father of 18-year-old Lauren Rae Wagner found her car parked, with the driver's door open and the interior light on, near his house and directly in front of the home of an elderly woman called Beulah Stofer. Mrs Stofer told police how she had seen the young redhead abducted by two men. They were driving a black-over-white sedan, and first she thought that it had been a police car.

At 7.30am the following day, a driver on his way to work found a naked body at 1200 Cliff Drive in the Mount Washington area. Lauren was lying on her back, her left arm outstretched, her left lower leg just touching the road. Her mass of rich, red hair framed her pretty face, and her eyes were peacefully closed. Strangely, it looked as though she had burns on her palms. Like the unusual puncture marks on Kristina Weckler's arms, it looked as though the killers were experimenting – possibly with methods of torture. There was also something else that was different – a shiny track of some sticky liquid, which had attracted a convoy of ants. If this substance was semen or saliva, there was the possibility that the killer's blood type could be determined. Tests on semen found on the earlier victims had revealed nothing.

Bianchi told the author that, back at Buono's house, Lauren pretended to enjoy being raped in the desperate hope that her attackers would allow her to live. However, they tried to electrocute the woman by attaching live electrical wires to the palms of her hands, but this only caused extreme pain and superficial burns. Bianchi then raped her, and Buono strangled Lauren to death with a ligature.

The two killers now realised that they had been seen by Mrs Stofer, so they obtained her telephone number, and called her from a kiosk in the Hollywood Library in North Ivar Street, where they subjected her to death threats. Undeterred, though, she was able to furnish police with an excellent description which matched Bianchi and Buono in every respect.

On Monday, 14 December 1977, police were called to a vacant lot on a steep slope at 2006 N. Alvarado Street, where they arrived at 7.03am. The sun had just come up, and it was a clear day with very few clouds in the sky. Rampart Divisional Patrol Unit 2-A-47, consisting of officers Lewis and Akeson, had responded to a radio call alerting them to a dead body lying by the road, which ran through the floor of the canyon splitting Lakeshore Drive and Alvarado.

When homicide detectives Oakes and Richard Crotsley arrived, they noticed that the tall, blonde victim was lying on her back in the now usual spread-eagle position, and that post-mortem lividity had started to form in her toes. The young woman was Caucasian, and in her twenties. There were ligature marks around both wrists, ankles and her neck. On her left forearm she had a tattoo – a square 'cross' with four dots within its border. On the right ankle was a second tattoo of faint design bearing the name 'Kim'. With no other identification to be found, she was labelled as 'Jane Doe #112', and the stranglers' penultimate victim was on her way to the morgue.

Using documents furnished by the LAPD, and confirming this with Bianchi himself, it is now possible to plot the victim's last hours in some detail. She turned out to be Kimberley 'Kim' (aka 'Donna') Diane Martin and, for the first time, using this previously unpublished material, we can see the cunning of the Hillside Stranglers as they entrapped their victim.

At precisely 8.30pm, on Tuesday, 13 December 1977, the phone of 'Climax Nude Modelling', 1815 Serrano Avenue, rang, and Michelle Elaine Rodriguez answered it. The call came from a man who gave the name 'Mike Ryan' (Kenneth Bianchi), and below is the transcript of that recorded conversation:

Rodriguez:	Hello, modelling service.
Bianchi:	Hello, yes. Can you get me a girl?
Rodriguez:	That depends where you are located, sir.
Bianchi:	I'm in Hollywood.
Rodriguez:	That will be no problem. I can have a girl with you in about 15 minutes.
Bianchi:	How much does it cost?
Rodriguez:	$40 for a modelling service.
Bianchi:	OK. My wife has left town for the first time in two years, so I would like you to send me a pretty

blonde model if you could. Possibly wearing black stockings and a dress.

Rodriguez: That will be no problem, sir. May I have your name?

Bianchi: Michael Ryan.

Rodriguez: And could you spell your last name, please?

Bianchi: R-Y-A-N.

Rodriguez: May I have your phone number?

Bianchi: 462-9794.

Rodriguez: Sir, that is a payphone.

(Once again, Bianchi was using the kiosk in the Hollywood Library in North Ivar Street.)

Bianchi: Ha, ha, ha. You know it's funny. A lot of people seem to think that this is a payphone. It must be a digit in the number or something.

Rodriguez: That must be what it is. The reason I thought it was a payphone is that the fourth digit of the number is a '9', it's a payphone.

Bianchi: That must be it, or the fact that you hear my TV in the background. Would you like me to turn it off? (The 'television noise' was the customers' conversations who were using the library.)

Rodriguez: Oh, no. I'll verify it.

Bianchi: All right.

Rodriguez: And what is your address, sir?

Bianchi: 1950 Tamarind.

Rodriguez: Sir, could you spell that for me?

Bianchi: T-A-M-A-R-I-N-D.

Rodriguez: Is this a house, or an apartment?

Bianchi: This is an apartment. Number 114.

Rodriguez: Sir. How are you going to pay?

Bianchi: Cash.

Rodriguez: May I ask where you found our advertisement?

| Bianchi: | The Freep. (A local free paper.) |
| Rodriguez: | OK, sir. I'll have a girl out to you shortly. |

This was end of the first conversation, and Michelle then rang the operator to verify the number. She always followed this practice to ensure she didn't send a girl out to a prank call. First, she asked the operator if the number was a payphone. If it was, under normal circumstances, the operator would confirm it; however, if it was a private number, the operator would advise the caller that she could not give out that information. But, on this rare occasion, Bianchi had luck on his side. On this occasion, the operator spoke to her supervisor, and she came back to Michelle, saying, 'No. My supervisor won't allow me to give out that information.' Of course, Michelle understood this to mean that her client had booked one of the girls from a private address – which it wasn't – and therefore the call was good. She phoned 'Mr Ryan' back, and he picked up the handset immediately 'as if he was waiting for the call', Michelle later told the police. Unwittingly, Michelle had now sealed the fate of Kimberley Martin.

Bianchi:	Hello.
Rodriguez:	Hello. Michael?
Bianchi:	Yes.
Rodriguez:	This is just the modelling agency calling to verify your call.
Bianchi:	OK. Thank you. How much longer will it take before the girl will call me?
Rodriguez:	Very shortly.
Bianchi:	OK. Thank you. Goodbye.

Michelle then phoned Kimberley Martin who worked under the name of 'Donna'.

Rodriguez:	I have a call. It's a cash call out in Hollywood in an apartment. Do you want it?
Kimberley:	Yeah. Give me the information.
Rodriguez:	Michael Ryan. Phone number 462-9794. 1950 Tamarind, Hollywood. Cash. Apartment 114. Sounds like a good call to me. It's an apartment. It's near your location, but always be careful and make sure he's not a cop.
Kimberley:	Sounds good to me. I'll give him a call.
Rodriguez:	Phone me and let me know whether you'll go on it?
Kimberley:	OK. Goodbye.

Kimberley Martin called her prospective client, then she rang the agency back.

Kimberley:	Sounds good to me. I'm going right on it.
Rodriguez:	Call me when you get there. Goodbye.

The distance from the library on Ivar Street to 1950 North Tamarind Avenue is nearly a mile, taking an average of five minutes to drive. Bianchi was seen sitting on the library steps by a witness at around 9.00pm, then he suddenly stood up and walked off. Buono was picking him up.

At around 9.05pm, Kimberley left her apartment, and it took Kim 15 minutes to drive the 3.8 miles to Tamarind, where she parked up and walked into the lobby, where several people saw her at 9.25pm. Shortly thereafter, residents heard a woman screaming, 'Please don't kill me,' but all of them thought that this was a domestic dispute. Minutes later, though, they found the contents of a woman's handbag strewn along a hallway.

Bianchi claims that he and Buono dragged the woman out through a rear entrance and into the underground car park where they had left their car. They drove her to Buono's home, where she was tortured, raped and killed. 'We killed her because she was fuckin' useless in bed,' he explained to me.

THREE

The Truth Will Out

EVEN though 84 officers were assigned to the Hillside Strangler investigation, the general public now thought that the police were helpless, and they were about right. With some 10,000 leads to follow up, thousands of fingerprints to be processed and a reward of $140,000 posted for information that would lead to the Hillside Strangler's arrest, the task force were no nearer catching the killers than they were on day one.

After press headlines suggested that the killers were posing as police officers, the public trusted no one, and it was even suggested that two renegade policemen might be running amok on some kind of sick vendetta. It had got to the point where nobody could be certain of the true identity of a man wearing a uniform, or waving a silver badge, and citizens were simply not stopping when requested by any cop, uniformed or not. So the police implemented a new policy which allowed motorists to drive to a police station with a flashing patrol car following them, and this prompt action partially put people's minds at rest.

Nothing happened on the murders during the month of January, possibly because Angelo Buono's mother was in the hospital with a terminal illness. But in February of 1978, the last of the Hillside Stranglings murders in Los Angeles occurred when Cindy Hudspeth's body was found up in the mountains above Glendale on the Angeles Crest Highway.

Judge Roger Boren, former prosecutor at Bianchi and Buono's trial in LA, to the author at interview

On Friday, 17 February 1978, the crew of an Angeles National Forest helicopter spotted an orange Datsun car, which was parked precariously close to a ravine by the Angeles Crest Highway. Upon opening the trunk, police found the body of 20-year-old Cindy Lee Hudspeth, a brunette who worked as a telephonist. She was also employed as a part-time waitress at the Robin Hood Inn, a restaurant frequented by Angelo Buono.

In his statement to police, Bianchi claimed that he had arrived at Buono's auto-upholstery shop where he found Cindy's car parked outside. 'She had called to enquire if Angelo could make new mats for her,' he said. The two men spread-eagled Cindy on a bed, hog-tied her, then raped and strangled her for almost two hours. Then, with the dead body in the trunk, Bianchi drove her car, closely followed by Buono in another vehicle, to the ravine where they tried to push the Datsun over the edge. It rolled 50 feet then stopped, but by then the killers had fled.

Cindy's naked body was found about 30 feet down the incline. Her arms were by her side, her legs apart.

The murder of Cindy proved to be the last of the Hillside Stranglings, for after a heated argument with Bianchi, during which Buono pointed a loaded revolver at Ken's head and told him to 'F-f-f-ff-fuck off', Bianchi packed his bags and left Los Angeles. Buono went back to refurbishing cars and did not kill again, while Ken scooted north to Bellingham, leaving 13 dead bodies, countless broken lives and a mountain of debt behind in his wake. His new hunting ground awaited him.

Well… Mr Bianchi? He was … a wannabe-cop. He wanted to be a police officer. He tried in his hometown of Rochester to be a reserve. He moved to California, got involved down there, wanted to be a deputy police officer in Los Angeles. He actually got into their ride-along programme.

Because of his ability to con, he talked a security agency into thinking he was really hot stuff, so they made him a captain in their organisation. He became friends with several Bellingham police officers, and he took the test, the examination for the Bellingham Police Department.

Scenes-of-crime officer Robert Knudsen, Bellingham PD,
to the author at interview

The small, seaport city of Bellingham has a population of about 60,000, and it lies 20 miles due south of the Canadian border, on the north-west seaboard of Washington State. Bellingham is the gateway to the Mount Baker recreational area, which looks over one of the most magnificent vistas in the area – the pine-clad slopes of San Juan, the Vancouver Islands and the Strait of Juan de Fuca.

When I visited Bellingham in 1996, the place was wrapped in an icy coat, a typical winter in those parts, and my thoughts travelled back in time to January 1979, when the weather was similar, but laced with the cold chill of murder. Violent crime in this neck of the woods was such a rarity in those days that, when Chief of Police Terry Mangan was informed one Friday morning that two young women had been reported as 'missing under suspicious circumstances', his first thought was that they had left town for an early vacation without telling anyone.

Co-eds 22-year-old Karen Mandic and her roommate 27-year-old Diane Wilder both studied at the Western Washington University, and several friends were concerned about their welfare.

Chief Mangan was a former Roman Catholic priest whose close friend Sister Carmel Marie once ran the Saint Ignatius School in Los Angeles. She had introduced Terry Mangan to the bookkeeper of her diocese, one Tony Johnson. In November 1977, when the Hillside Stranglings were at their peak, Mangan had read in a paper that Johnson's 14-year-old daughter, Sonja, had become one of the victims. Now, however, in January 1979, and following an amazing string of tragic circumstances and coincidences, Mangan would secure the arrest of one of the Los Angeles killers, 1,050 miles north of Tinsel Town, and in his own backyard.

Karen Mandic was a beautiful student with long, blonde hair. She had last been seen alive at 7.00pm on Thursday, 11 January, when leaving the Fred Myer department store on Interstate 5, where she worked as a part-time cashier. Earlier in the week, she had told two friends, Steve Hardwick and Bill Bryant, that a man who had recently asked her for a date had offered her a house-sitting job for that Thursday evening, and it paid $100 an hour. In fact, he had asked her out several times, and his name was Kenneth Bianchi.

Ken, who by now was back living with Kelli and his son Ryan, had previously worked at Fred Myer as a security guard, and he was now employed as a security officer with the Whatcom Security Agency (WSA), a local company that provided mobile and static security patrols throughout a 50-mile radius of Bellingham. Ken had pledged Karen to secrecy; nevertheless, she was thrilled with the opportunity to earn some extra cash.

Upon learning of the offer to Karen, Steve Hardwick was suspicious from the outset. Karen, however, would have none of it, insisting that everything was OK. She explained that the house, owned by a Dr Catlow, was in an upper-class area, that the doctor was going on vacation with his family, that the alarm was not working, and that she had asked a friend called Diane Wilder along for company. It was easy money, she told Hardwick. All they had to do was wait until the burglar-alarm-repair people turned up later in the evening, and then she could return to Fred Myer and cash up. Besides, Bianchi worked for WSA; it was a highly regarded firm, and even Hardwick knew that.

Hardwick, who could smell a latrine rat from miles away, was still highly suspicious, so he pressed Karen further. 'Don't worry,' she snapped back, 'it's only for two hours, and I'll be back to finish up at the store by 9.00pm. Everything will be OK. I'm taking Diane with me. Besides, Ken has given my name to the insurance company who are paying the bill. I can't change anything now.'

When Karen failed to return to Fred Myer later in the evening, the manager telephoned Hardwick, who immediately drove to Dr Catlow's house at 334 Bayside, where the split-level property appeared deserted. Although he could not recall Bianchi's name, Hardwick did remember WSA, so he telephoned the night dispatcher, Wendy Whitton, and requested any information on the Bayside account. Wendy, who was not authorised to reveal details of her employer's business, promised the anxious Hardwick that she would call the firm's co-owner, Randy Moa, and, as soon as she did, alarm bells started to ring.

Moa and his partner, Joe Parker, had just completed a somewhat belated security check on Bianchi's résumé and, in doing so, they had spoken to one Susan Bird, an attractive woman who lived locally. Susan had been shocked to hear that Bianchi had obtained work in the security business because he had recently suggested to her that, because of her stunning figure, she would make a good prostitute, and he could become her pimp. Susan was even more concerned because she knew that Ken had applied to the Bellingham Police Department for a job as a cop.

At first, Moa and Parker didn't believe Susan Bird, so she put them in touch with a girlfriend called Annie Kinneberg. Annie and her pal, Margie Lager, confirmed what Susan Bird had said, relating that Bianchi had also wanted to photograph lesbian models for clients that he said he had back in LA. 'He's a kinky bastard,' Annie explained. 'He's living with a woman called Kelli, and they have a little boy. That guy is real weird, you know.'

Upon receiving the call from Wendy Whitton, Moa sprang into action. First, he radioed Steve Adams, and ordered the night patrol officer to check out the Bayside address himself. Unfortunately, Steve went to the wrong address, 302 Bayside, where he knocked up the bleary-eyed owners who knew nothing at all. Then, having realised his mistake, he called the office, and waited in his truck until the police turned up.

In another effort to solve the problem, Moa telephoned Bianchi at home. Ken denied all knowledge of the house-sitting job. He also denied knowing anyone called Diane Wilder or Karen Mandic, adding to his protestations of innocence by claiming that he had been to a Sheriff's Reserve first-aid meeting that evening.

Moa was now not only confused but also becoming increasingly alarmed, so, in an effort to clear up matters, he summoned Bianchi to the firm's office. Then Moa contacted the instructor of the Sheriff's Reserve to confirm what Bianchi had told him, and learned that Ken had been lying. Ken had failed to turn up for the class, so Moa then rang the Bellingham Police Department.

Upon their arrival at WSA, the cops asked Ken if he knew the two young women. Initially, Ken flatly denied the suggestion, then realising that he was painting himself into a corner, he backtracked, saying, 'Maybe Karen.' A gut feeling told the officers that Bianchi was lying because he wouldn't look them straight in the eye. He appeared shifty and nervous, too. However, with little evidence to take him into custody, Bianchi was allowed to return home.

At 6.00am that morning, Bill Bryant, who was a university-campus cop, obtained a key to Karen's apartment. By the telephone, written in red ink, was a message in Diane's handwriting. It read: 'Karen. Ken B called. Phone 733-2884.' Picking up the scrap of paper, Bill decided to call the number. It turned out to be WSA, and, lo and behold, it was Bianchi who answered the phone. 'I know your voice,' said Bryant. 'You called Karen's apartment on Tuesday, and I told you that she wasn't in.' Once again, Ken denied knowing Karen Mandic, adding that anyone could be using his name.

Bryant then called his father, who was also a police officer, and he, in turn, called the Bellingham Police Department who re-interviewed Bianchi later in the morning. Officers Geddes and Page confronted him with the note, and Ken reacted angrily. 'I'd sure like to know who has been using my name,' he snapped. 'I'm well known. I was in the newspaper when I left Fred Myer to come here in charge of operations.'

Nevertheless, even though Bianchi was now the chief suspect for the girls' abduction, the officers could do little more than allow him to carry on with his work, despite the evidence mounting against him.

They were told to lay face down and then they were separated, tied up and, individually, one by one, untied, undressed and I had sex with them. Then they were both dressed again. Then I killed them separately. I believe, ah, Diana Wilder was first and Karen Mandic second. Then they were carried out and put in the back of the car and driven to the cul-de-sac.

Kenneth Bianchi confessing to the author at interview

At 4.40pm the same day, Karen's green Mercury Bobcat was found. Just a mile from the Bayside address, in a cul-de-sac in Willow Drive, the vehicle contained the fully clothed bodies of Karen Mandic and Diane Wilder. At autopsy, it was determined that both young women had been raped and strangled with a ligature.

The car was locked; however, the passenger door was only on the first catch and so I had no trouble getting into the vehicle that way. I opened both doors, and took a closer look, and the bodies of two young ladies had been tossed in like two sacks of potatoes, one thrown on top of the other.

Scenes-of-crime officer Robert Knudsen, Bellingham PD,
to the author at interview

With this grim discovery, an order went out for Bianchi's immediate arrest, but first they needed the help of Randy Moa. Knowing that he might be armed, and considered dangerous, Moa radioed Ken in his truck, instructing his unwitting employee to check out a disused guard shack at the south terminal, a remote area of the docks, and, moments after he arrived, Detective Terry Wight, who was brandishing a pistol, arrested him.

With Bianchi now in custody, the investigation moved up a gear and, while police broke the tragic news to Karen's father, Detectives Nolte and McNeill, and Field Investigator Moore, conducted a thorough search of Bianchi's home, where in the bedroom they picked up a pair of blue uniform trousers. The crotch had been ripped and Kelli confirmed that these were the trousers that her common-law husband had been wearing the previous evening. She also pointed to a red, plaid shirt, and there was an identical one lying underneath it. Kelli said that Ken had been wearing one of those shirts the night before, and fibres, identical in every respect to those of these shirts, were later found in Dr Catlow's home. The officers also took possession of a pair of cowboy boots, and they soon matched the sole tread pattern with imprints found both at Willow Drive and Bayside.

Hanging in the bedroom closet was a .357 calibre, a Highway Patrolman's revolver, complete with a standard Sam Browne belt and holster. Again, in the same closet, Nolte discovered a shoulder holster and several cameras. The firearm was licensed and in extremely good condition. The cameras and photographic equipment were of professional quality, and this added veracity to the claims of Susan Bird, Annie Kinneberg and Margie Lager that Bianchi wanted to photograph them.

The officers now turned their attention to Kelli's dressing table, where they found a quantity of jewellery and seven watches. Kelli explained that Ken had given her most of these items as presents – in fact, these had been taken from former Hillside Strangler victims. They were his trophies from the crimes.

Bianchi's home was now searched from top to bottom. In the basement, officers found several thousand dollars' worth of brand new tools, all in their original boxes without price tags or sales receipts. It was soon discovered that this treasure trove had been stolen from Fred Myer when Ken had worked there as a security guard.

However, the stash of stolen goods didn't end with the tools, for on one shelf there was a large quantity of medical supplies, enough to supply a doctor's surgery. Ken had stolen it all from the Verdugo Hills Hospital in Los Angeles. And, when Detective Moore made the mistake of prising open a cupboard, he was literally buried under scores of tins of crabmeat that tumbled out. Ken had taken the horde from a cold storage company where Whatcom Security had assigned him as a guard. Finally, a box full of brand-new jackets and touch-tone telephones was opened. These had been stolen from the Uniflite Corporation, whose offices were at the dock's south terminal.

But this merely proved that Bianchi was a thief, not a murderer, and at this stage there wasn't the merest hint that he had been involved in the Hillside Stranglings.

Both of Bianchi's motor vehicles had now been impounded at Bellingham Police Station, where Detective Knudsen waited for Kelli Boyd to arrive before he could search them. At 2.00am on Saturday, 13 January, though, he started looking for clues on Karen's 'Bobcat'. Crawling underneath the car, Knudsen noted that the gasoline tank had a fresh dent on the driver's side. It appeared from the angle of the damage that this was a 'back-up' dent and, later that day, the investigator found paint on a dislodged rock in the driveway of 334 Bayside. This evidence was solid proof that, at some time, the 'Bobcat' had been on Dr Catlow's property.

When Kelli eventually arrived at the car pound, Knudsen went through Ken's beaten-up VW with a toothcomb and, in the front passenger footwell, a brown leather attaché case was discovered. Tipping the contents of the case on to a table, officers found that every document tied a 'Dr Bianchi' to a psychiatric counselling service in Los Angeles. Taken together, these were unusual items to say the least, so Nolte and Knudsen took stock. It seemed that they might have captured a double-murderer, sex pervert, thief, bent security guard-cum-pseudo cop and psychiatrist all in one hit.

Nolte was cautious and he decided to make further enquiries. He called the LAPD. 'We've got a real fruit under arrest here in Bellingham,' he explained. 'We got him in on suspicion of two homicides, an' rape. Do you know the name "Kenneth Alessio Bianchi"?'

Within the hour, the LAPD called back. 'Sure,' said the breathless voice, 'we got a Bianchi, KA, on our list. He applied to join the Force; he even had a ride-along in a squad car. Yeah, his name has come up several times during the Hillside Strangler investigation, but, ya see, no one has gotten around to speaking with him yet. We can wire you an ID FIT of our suspects if you need it.'

One face from the printout was Bianchi to a tee.

At the time of his arrest, Ken had been in possession of a large bunch of keys, which were now in a police property box. Detective Nolte had overhead Randy Moa saying that a ring of keys, along with several client account cards for the southside district of Bellingham, were missing from the office, so Nolte went to the property box and retrieved them, and Moa identified them as belonging to those accounts for which Bianchi was solely responsible. One key in particular fitted Dr Catlow's front door. Indeed, the account card was tied to this key, and this proved that Bianchi had had access to the Bayside address.

With the very real prospect of them having arrested a cold-blooded serial killer dawning upon them, the police then searched Ken's Whatcom Security Agency pick-up, call sign 5. However, the only item of note recovered from Bianchi's truck was a striped towel. Tests later proved that it was stained with the semen of a non-secretor and, as we now know, this fitted Bianchi exactly.

On Monday, 15 January 1979, Nolte and his colleagues searched Karen Mandic's apartment for the second time. In a drawer, Nolte found a business card in Ken's name indicating that he was the self-styled 'Captain Kenneth A Bianchi' of Whatcom Security. Nolte spoke to Randy Moa who reported that no such 'Captain' title had been authorised by his company.

A few days later, police carried out a thorough search of the South Terminal area where Bianchi had been arrested. Here, they found a coat belonging to Diane Wilder and, in one of the pockets, were the keys to Karen's car. Obviously, as the two young women couldn't have dropped the coat off at the South Terminal, their killer must have done so. The noose was tightening around Bianchi's neck.

It was now crucial for the police to establish Bianchi's movements for the relevant times in question because, if he produced a solid alibi to say he couldn't have committed the murders, the police would have been back at square one.

Kelli Boyd was positive that Ken had arrived home on Thursday evening at about 10.30pm. She told the cops that she noticed that he had ripped the seat of his denim trousers, which she thought was 'kinda comical', but she was surprised when he threw the garment into a bin. She had retrieved the trousers because she thought that the cloth might come in useful as her mother was making a rug, and she needed all the denim she could lay her hands on. Kelli also recalled that Ken had been sweating profusely when he walked through the door, and this was unusual. 'He smelled kinda strange,' she said.

When Kelli was asked about a little gold Italian 'Good Luck' horn on a chain, which had been found on her dressing table, she explained that it had been a gift from Kenneth way back in Los Angeles. Later, this item of jewellery proved to be identical to one belonging to the murdered Yolanda Washington.

With Kelli placing Bianchi at home around 10.30pm on the night of the murders, the police looked elsewhere for witnesses who might have seen him out and about, and first they spoke to a Mrs McNeill who lived at 327 Bayside, and almost opposite Dr Catlow's home. She reported that, at around 9.30am on Thursday, 11 January, she had seen a yellow WSA pick-up truck enter Dr Catlow's drive. At noon, she saw an identical vehicle enter and leave the property and, at around 7.00pm, or shortly thereafter, she heard a vehicle enter the drive but did not see it. When questioned about the sound of the engine, Mrs McNeill said that it had sounded like the vehicle that had made the earlier visits.

On Saturday, 13 January, a vital witness came forward in the form of Raymond Spees, who claimed that, during the late evening of the murders, he had been to church. Between 10.00 and 10.30pm, he said that he was returning to his home past the cul-de-sac where the bodies were found in Karen's car. As he passed the cul-de-sac entrance, a vehicle came out rapidly, and he had to swerve to avoid it. Spees described the vehicle as a yellow WSA pick-up truck with a flashing light bar on the driver's cab. Spees was positive about this identification because he knew the firm, and noted its emblem on the cab door. Spees also noticed that the driver was shielding his face with his hand.

With overwhelming evidence mounting against him, Bianchi consistently refused to admit guilt, and then he asked for legal representation. Attorney Dean Brett advised his new client not to talk to the officers again without him present and, initially, Ken found Brett 'a shining example of an energetic champion of justice'. This flowery accolade was withdrawn a week later after he started to sum up his predicament. Ken was furious that Kelli had held a yard sale to dispose of his property, and then he accused her of having an affair with Dean Brett. Ken was also worried about the lies he had told police about his movements during the time of the murders. He had told officers that he had attended a Sheriff's Reserve meeting, and this was blatantly false. In the years to follow, he wrote to me with a pathetic excuse for telling the lie:

> I hate confrontations. People only have their whereabouts checked when they are suspected of doing something wrong. So, knowing I hadn't done anything wrong, and nothing to hide, I had given the original, short answer, about going to the Sheriff's Reserve class. That was simpler than the longer, true explanation. Besides, if I had killed the girls, I would have remembered it. I didn't, and that's what I kept telling the police.
>
> *Kenneth Bianchi*

Poor old Ken! This is yet another example of deep-seated, psychopathic denial, and it is illustrative of Bianchi's thinking process around the time of the murders and, indeed, his warped thought processes today. Of course the 'true explanation' to which he refers is that he had just raped and strangled two innocent young women. Now, that would have taken some explaining away.

FOUR

Acting Up

WHEN Bianchi was charged with the two counts of murder, he pleaded 'not guilty'. An 'Affidavit of Probable Cause' set out the allegations in detail, and this was the first opportunity for Bianchi and his legal team to study the case presented by the state. It was also the chance for Ken to embark on the first of his many 'fly-specking' exercises, where he examines everything in minute detail, for which he has become notorious ever since.

The main thrust of the prosecution was to file for the death penalty, but there was a plea-bargain offer on the table; if Bianchi pleaded guilty, the State wouldn't press for the death penalty, and Bianchi would live. This somewhat rocked Bianchi's boat, for he had no intention of simply throwing his hands in the air and admitting guilt. Dean Brett, however, was quick to point out that protestations of innocence would no longer wash; besides, the lie-detector test to which he had submitted had failed him. Nevertheless, Bianchi tore up the plea-bargain offer, and he returned to his cell to sulk.

In the United States, the moratorium on capital punishment was lifted in 1976, and Brett was anxious that his client would not be the first killer to be hanged in Washington State, so he attempted to mitigate Ken's culpability for the Bellingham murders by suggesting that he should plead 'not guilty by reason of insanity' (NGI). To this end, Dean Brett felt obliged to inform Ken of the horrors of death by hanging, going on to paint a morbid and terrifying picture of this form of execution. 'Most go to the gallows screaming,' he told the white-faced Ken. 'Some collapse and have to be strapped to a board. An' hanging is goddamn painful if it don't work out right.'

'That meeting scared me straight,' Bianchi wrote in a letter. 'I was in a corner not of my own making, an' I had nowhere to run or hide.'

So now confronted with the stark choice between death or a life behind bars, Bianchi reluctantly agreed to plead NGI.

With their client's permission in their pocket, Ken's legal team employed the services of John Johnson, an investigative social worker, who started to probe Bianchi's history right back to day one. Johnson was an excellent researcher, and before much time had passed he reported back to Bianchi and Brett. It was good news, for it was suggested to Ken that he might have been abused as a child and this would have unhinged his mind. In fact, the defence team went even further. Ken's failure in having remembered killing the co-eds could be due to some form of amnesia. Therefore, with this information now at hand, there was the possibility of Ken receiving a reduced custodial sentence with a specific period before parole or, better still, his time could be served in a psychiatric institution where the silver-tongued killer could work his ticket to freedom, as so many killers do.

Talking to this author, Dean Brett denied any such attorney/client manipulation, although it is certain that he advised his client to undergo a series of hypnosis sessions, which Bianchi called 'the modern version of the rubber cosh'. And then Ken seized on what he thought was a great idea. He would invent a multiple-personality disorder!

Although the medical profession had been aware of the enigmas of the multiple-personality disorder (MPD) since the early 19th century, the general public learned of the illness largely through the 1957 film *The Three Faces of Eve*, which was based on the book of the same name written by two psychiatrists.

MPD seems to be caused by severe psychological traumas in childhood, such as sexual abuse or extreme cruelty, and these experiences can be so painful that the victim literally blots them out. In later life, a violent shock can reactivate the trauma, causing the 'everyday' personality to blank out.

The most remarkable case of MPD in recent years was that of Billy Milligan. In 1977, he was arrested in Columbus, Ohio, for rape. Billy later declared to a social worker that he was not Billy but 'David', and subsequent examinations by psychiatrists made it clear that Milligan was a genuine MPD case.

Sexually abused in childhood by his stepfather, Billy had become another personality to escape the misery. Eventually, he split into 23 separate personalities, including a lesbian, a suave Englishman who also spoke Arabic, an electronics expert and a Serbo-Croat. (It has never been explained how Milligan came to speak Serbo-Croat.) Nevertheless, all these personalities were so distinctive that only a remarkable actor could have simulated them. It was later discovered that the lesbian personality committed the rape, and another of the personalities had turned Billy in to the police. And it is now thought that the Milligan case – much publicised in the late 1970s – may have given Bianchi the idea of pretending to be a 'multiple'.

Ken had indeed watched *The Three Faces of Eve* while he was in custody. He had even read the book, and it is known from his custody records that he also saw the movie *Sybil*, which concerned another multiple-personality disorder. So the whole idea of MPD was a gift from the gods, and Bianchi rubbed his hands with glee.

Kenneth Bianchi was sitting in his cell beaming with delight as his attorney arranged the first of many hypnosis sessions. Once again, the killer was playing centre stage, and the immediate follow-up came about when forensic psychiatrist Dr Donald T Lunde recommended that Ken accept a course of hypnosis under the expert supervision of a Dr John Watkins. Dr Lunde reasoned that, if anyone could find a genuine MPD, then it had to be Watkins.

On Wednesday, 23 March 1979, Dr John Watkins, a specialist in multiple personalities and hypnosis from the University of Montana, was brought in to perform the first of many sessions with Ken. By now, Bianchi was more than eager to co-operate and, within minutes, it appeared that he was in a trance. He started speaking in a strange, low voice, introducing himself as 'Steve Walker'. This 'Steve' came across as a highly unpleasant character with a sneering laugh. He told those present that he hated Ken. 'Ken doesn't know how to handle women,' he said. 'You gotta treat 'em rough. Boy, did I fix that turkey. I got him in so much trouble, he'll never get out.'

Dr Watkins believed that what he was witnessing was indeed a genuine multiple personality, and he bought Ken's performance hook, line and sinker. With little prompting, 'Steve' turned to the Los Angeles murders, describing how Ken had walked in on Angelo Buono while he was murdering a girl. At this point, 'Steve' admitted he had taken over Ken's personality, and had turned Ken into Angelo's willing accomplice for all the Hillside Stranglings.

'Are you Ken?' asked Dr Watkins.

'Do I look like Ken? Killing a broad doesn't make any difference to me. Killing any fuckin' body doesn't make any difference to me. Angelo is my kind of man. There should be more people like Angelo in the world. I hate Ken,' snarled Bianchi in response.

To Watkins, at least, it seemed perfectly clear that Kenneth Bianchi was made up of two opposing personalities – the loving father, kind friend and hard worker who made up Ken, and the vicious rapist, sadist-cum-serial murderer who made up 'Steve Walker'.

Watkins firmly believed that Ken had subconsciously invented 'Steve' as a repository for all his hateful feelings towards his adoptive mother, Frances. And, in this way, Ken could remain a loving, devoted son, the affectionate guy that almost everyone knew and liked, while 'Steve', who was apparently unknown to Ken, would periodically emerge to wreak terrible vengeance on young women. Yes, Kenneth Bianchi had done his homework very well.

Word soon leaked out that Bianchi was 'coughing' to the LA murders, and that he had implicated his accomplice, Angelo Buono, so LA task force detectives rushed to Bellingham and sat outside Ken's cell door in anticipation of what might happen next. However, dissatisfied with this not quite Oscar-winning performance, Bianchi expanded on his scheme and, knowing that the inquisitive police would read his prison diary, on Wednesday, 18 April 1979, he penned a note for them to read:

If this person is more real than just my dream, and if this is the same person haunting me, which is more likely, this person could have been responsible for the uncontrollable violence in my life, the instigator of the lies I've done. The blank spots, amnesia, I can't account for, and the deaths of the girls, all the ones in California, and the two here. But if he is in me, then he killed them using me – why can't I remember for sure? I want to know if this is so – what if?

Kenneth Bianchi in his prison diary

To be absolutely sure of his diagnosis of multiple personalities, Watkins also administered the Rorschach inkblot test to check out both Ken and 'Steve', the results of which appeared to support his overall hypothesis – both tests differed and were consistent with two personalities – so he reported back to Dean Brett, saying, 'It is one of the clearest cases of Dissociative Reaction and Multiple personality I have diagnosed in over 40 years.'

Somewhat condescendingly, Bianchi would later write, while shooting himself in the foot, 'Dr Watkins is a kind, soft-spoken, honest behavioural expert who was caught up in the excitement of the moment. When all the hypnosis sessions stopped, the MPD never appeared again.'

But the damage had been done and a leak prompted *Time* magazine to pronounce: 'BIANCHI – A MULTIPLE PERSONALITY'. These headlines so outraged Judge Kurtze that he decided to appoint a panel of experts to evaluate Bianchi, and the judge summoned Dr Watkins and Professor Donald T Lunde to act for the defence. Doctors Ralph Allison and Charles Moffett represented the court, and Doctors Martin Orne and Saul Faerstein acted for the State, in an effort to sort, as the police suggested, 'the bullshit from the bullshit'.

Fortunately for Dr Watkins, he had an ally in the judge's camp with Ralph Allison, who was also the author of a famous book called *Minds in Many Pieces*. Dr Allison's credentials were impeccable and, under apparent hypnosis, Ken, through 'Steve', claimed, 'I fuckin' killed those broads… those fuckin' cunts. That blonde-haired cunt, and the brunette cunt.'

'Here in Bellingham?' asked Allison incredulously, while gripping the arms of his chair.

'That's right.'

'Why?'

''Cause I hate fuckin' cunts.'

After that short exchange, Dr Allison pressed his subject about the murder of Yolanda Washington in Los Angeles, and 'Steve' piped up again. 'She was a hooker. Angelo went out and picked her up. I was waiting on the street. He drove round to where I was. I got in the car. We got on the freeway. I fucked her and killed her. We dumped the body off and that was it. Nothin' to it.'

In apparently regressing Ken back to his childhood at around the age of nine, Dr Allison found an environment filled with pain and suffering, which, he thought, had spawned Ken's 'Steve' alter ego. Under the so-called hypnosis, Ken claimed to have met Steve while he was hiding under his bed. 'Mommie was hitting me so bad, I met Stevie,' he whined in a childlike voice.

Dr Allison was now in his professional element, and probed a little deeper. 'How did you first meet him?' he asked quietly.

'I closed my eyes. I was crying so hard,' Bianchi whimpered. 'All of a sudden he was there. He said "Hi" to me. He told me I was his friend. I felt really good that I had a friend I could talk to.'

Outside in the corridor, police officers rolled their eyes towards the heavens, while others stuck their fingers down their throats. Detective Terry Wight popped a mint into his mouth and remarked, 'That fucker is blowin' smoke in our yard. He's either fuckin' innocent or he's a damn good actor.' And he was right on the money. This was going to be a red-ball case, weeks of unpaid overtime and little sleep, just to get Bianchi into court. With a bit of luck, they might get a judge who suffered from insomnia, and a jury with at least one brain between them, but the cops also reasoned that, even if the judicial train did manage to haul itself into the right station, the shrinks would say that he was nuts, and he would end up doing the rounds of psychiatric interviews long after even they were dead.

Of all the experts who were summoned to evaluate Bianchi, Professor Donald T Lunde, MA, MD, was perhaps the most qualified. A clinical associate professor of Psychiatry and Behavioural Science, and Lecturer at Stanford University, he is the author of *The Die Song, Murder and Madness* and *Fundamentals of Human Sexuality*. He is also a member of the American Academy of Psychiatry and the Law. Therefore, it might not seem unreasonable to infer that Professor Lunde would provide a correct assessment of Kenneth Bianchi's state of mind. However, in all fairness, he did not, and he later agreed with me on this point, all of which goes to show that even the finest psychiatrists in the world, of which Professor Lunde is one, can be manipulated and conned by a cunning and murderous psychopath.

Lunde began his report, dated Monday, 23 July 1979, by

explaining how he had formed his evaluation of Bianchi, and on what sources he had based his diagnosis. His four-month study included three short sessions with the subject which took place on 11, 12 and 13 July. He had read some 3,000 pages of police documents, witness statements, medical and psychiatric reports and school records. He also gained access to the information compiled by Dean Brett, John Johnson and the DA's Office, he reviewed the audiotape and videotape interviews, and read transcripts of examinations performed by his colleagues. Donald Lunde even interviewed Kelli Boyd, along with dozens of other people who knew Bianchi, although Mrs Bianchi refused to speak to him.

With factual accuracy and not educated guesswork, Lunde started by making a glaring error when he reported that Ken had been fostered for the initial 11 months of his life, when it had only been three months.

Mistake number two came when he misread the DePaul Clinic evaluations by stating that Mrs Bianchi had blamed her husband for being unable to have children, when she had said no such thing. And he compounded this error by saying that Nicholas Bianchi was 'overshadowed and overpowered' by his wife, when this was not so.

Professor Lunde also gave the wrong dates for Kenneth's schooling, and he was fundamentally inaccurate when he claimed that Ken's enuresis problems were psychosomatic in origin when they were physiological.

Professor Lunde suggested that Bianchi's mental condition was of a 'dissociative reaction, with extreme stress bordering on psychosis'. In his report, the professor wrote:

This condition (Dissociative Reaction) has been present since at least the age of nine years, and is manifested by periods during which the defendant acts without awareness of his actions, and for which he subsequently has amnesia. During some of these periods, the incredible amount of unconscious (repressed) hostility towards women present in this man surfaces. The best demonstration of what I have just described is seen in some of the videotapes, which were made while Bianchi was under hypnosis, and emerged as a quite different personality calling himself 'Steve Walker'.

Professor Donald T Lunde

It was debatable, said Professor Lunde, whether Bianchi represented a true case of multiple personality, as he felt Bianchi could have been capable of faking his symptoms given the wealth of literature in his possession and the fact that he had tried unsuccessfully to pass himself off as a medical expert. But Professor Lunde went on to conclude that 'Bianchi is not psychologically sophisticated enough, nor is he intelligent enough to have constructed such an elaborate history which gives him the mental defence if he were subsequently charged with a crime.

'Furthermore, one would have to assume that Bianchi began plotting his strategy for these crimes and his defence at about age nine, since this is when the first documented symptoms of his mental disturbance occurred.'

Professor Lunde could not contemplate for a moment that Ken had literally coached himself on multiple-personality disorder simply by watching a few movies and reading a book in his cell, or that the crooked idea had only entered his head as he considered his fate at the end of a hangman's rope. The professor had completely under-estimated the cunning of Bianchi, who is the greatest cock-and-bull storyteller since the beginning of time.

But this was not quite the end of the matter as far as Professor Lunde was concerned, because, while stating that Bianchi was mentally competent to stand his trial, he reported that, in his opinion, Ken was indeed suffering from Dissociative Reaction:

It [Dissociative Reaction] has affected him in such a manner that he would have been unable to perceive the nature and quality of the acts with which he has been charged. It is my opinion that the defendant did not have a moral sense of right and wrong, but was aware that what he was doing was against the law, and for this reason, precautions were taken to avoid incriminating evidence.

Professor Donald T Lunde

So, Professor Lunde believed that Bianchi was only taken over by 'Steve' when he needed to rape and murder, and at no other time, which turns out to be highly convenient for a defendant facing the death penalty. But, although Ken had no moral sense of right and wrong, conversely, Bianchi knew that, when he was committing his heinous crimes, and undertaking the careful pre-planning, the murders themselves and the elaborate cover-ups, that he was in fact breaking the law.

Having studied the case file, and having interviewed Bianchi for some eight hours, Dr Moffett felt it wiser to sit on the fence, believing Bianchi to be 'psychotic and probably schizophrenic', which did nothing to endear him to Dr Allison, who was effectively on the same team. However, Moffett still plunged into the same trap as Watkins, Allison and Lunde, in believing that Bianchi had genuinely been hypnotised.

Having now sown the seed of a multiple personality in the minds of three eminent psychiatrists, with a fourth leaning towards a different diagnosis altogether, Ken had only to sit back and watch with amusement as the experts argued the toss about his state of mind, for each psychiatrist who examined him was predisposed to stake a claim on being correct.

By co-operating with the psychiatrists, Ken pleased them, and they are the first to agree on this point. When Ken tried to ram normality down their throats, it was a successful and calculated attempt to prop up their beliefs that he really had been hypnotised; therefore, any words that fell from his lips had to be the truth. Dr

Moffett, like Lunde and Watkins, firmly believed that Ken had been hypnotised, which led him to conclude that 'Steve' was the result of an 'ego, or an identity split' rather than the 'different personality' which his colleagues had now agreed upon. Moffett added, 'Is this so different from a patient hearing the voice of Satan and struggle against alien control?'

In believing that 'Steve' existed as a 'split' rather than an entirely 'separate' personality, Dr Moffett missed another vital observation which would have proved Bianchi to be a bare-faced liar, for Ken was delighting in reliving his wicked crimes in all their gory detail, safe in the knowledge that this was coming from 'Steve'. Safe, too, in the knowledge that he could confess without blame being apportioned to him personally. He was suckering the doctors; he was playing the starring role to a well-established and well-intentioned audience who could make him internationally famous. Ken had struggled all his life to be someone and, at last, he had almost achieved his goal.

Dr Moffett's diagnosis, actually, wasn't wildly off the mark, having claimed that Ken was suffering from 'delusional grandiosity', but added, 'Ken lives on the brink of regressed and infantile terror. He literally wakens in his cell at night, hiding under his bed in nameless terror.'

Ken did wake from his sleep, and he did hide under his cell bed. However, not unlike the phoney notes he penned in his jail diary, that were sure to find their way to the attention of the authorities, these nocturnal activities were feigned sideshows to arouse the attention of his guards, to further bolster his act, and to substantiate the façade of his vulnerability.

Dr Moffett eventually concluded in his summary to Judge Kurtze, 'He [Bianchi] intellectually knows right from wrong. The combination of his grandiose alter ego, and his dissociation, and his lack of awareness of the violent aspects of his own being, would not permit him to effectively control and govern his actions.'

When Doctor Orne from the Department of Psychiatry at the

Pennsylvania Medical School arrived in Bellingham, he fired a single salvo, and blew not only his colleagues, but also Bianchi, out of the water in a flash of brilliance. Aware of the benefits to Bianchi if he succeeded in faking a multiple-personality disorder, Dr Orne decided to analyse, not so much Ken's personality, but the assumption of multiple personality itself. This was a unique move, a lateral test to see whether Bianchi had been really hypnotised at all, for Dr Orne figured that, if this man could fake a multiple-personality disorder, then he could easily fake hypnosis. In Dr Orne, Bianchi was about to meet his nemesis.

Before attempting to hypnotise Bianchi, Dr Orne mentioned in passing, and deliberately almost out of Ken's hearing, that it was rare in the case of multiple personalities for there to be just two personalities. Bianchi overheard the doctor, and, shortly after he entered a phoney trance, out came 'Billy', who amounted to personality number three. Minutes later, Dr Orne asked 'Billy' to sit back and talk to his lawyer who wasn't present in the room, but, on this occasion, Ken overplayed his part. Of course, 'Billy' had no lawyer at all, but this did not stop Ken from leaning across the table and shaking the invisible attorney's hand. Then Dr Orne had Dean Brett walk into the room. Bianchi, or 'Billy', immediately shifted his attention to the visible lawyer, asking, 'How can I see him in two places?' This behaviour proved beyond a shadow of a doubt that Bianchi was faking hypnosis and, following a few other tests, it was shown that Bianchi was faking MPD, too.

So, at long last, Ken had come unstuck and he was now exposed as the faker he really was. And the entire fabrication completely collapsed when a detective recalled seeing the name of 'Steve Walker' among the documents found in Ken's attaché case. Steve Walker, it transpired, was the real psychology student who had unwittingly furnished Bianchi with his diploma – the very same item that Ken had altered to suit his own ends – back in Los Angeles. Checkmate.

After pleading guilty to seven murders, which included the

Bellingham slayings, Kenneth Alessio Bianchi was sentenced on Friday, 19 October 1979. Three days later, Angelo Buono was arrested in Los Angeles, and he was charged with ten murders. On April Fool's Day 1984, Buono was sentenced. A plea bargain meant that neither would face the death penalty if they gave evidence. Of course, 'Steve' and 'Billy' never again surfaced, but someone else did, and she was a beautiful, part-time actress and writer. Her name is Veronica Wallace Lynn Compton.

FIVE

Femme Fatale

Let's deal with our mutual friend, Bianchi. Ken's not stupid. Ken is the slickest criminal I've ever met in all of my years, and I've met a few criminals. But, without doubt, Ken is the master of them all. He is very circumspect … that's where his brilliance lies, in his ability to premeditate things, and to protect himself. He is very good at that.

Veronica Compton, in conversation with the author

WHILE held in custody at the Los Angeles County Jail during Buono's trial, Ken almost engineered his freedom when a young actress and budding screenplay writer fell in love with him. 'VerLyn' was a statuesque beauty with sultry, raven hair. She had a figure that made most men – and many women – drool and, as one woman observed, 'VerLyn has a figure that most women would die for.' Indeed, even after serving 15 years in prison – she has since been released – Veronica is still an extremely beautiful woman.

Veronica was, and still is, highly intelligent, too, but it would be fair to add that she has never fully applied her many abilities to any studies or goals and, around the time of the Hillside Stranglings, she was deeply hooked into a downward spiral of cocaine and sexual perversion, the latter of which would become her downfall.

In the waning days of 1979–80, Veronica was into sadomasochism, practising as a dominatrix. She was partying every night, heavily dependent on the cocaine high that fuelled her fantasies and fed her enormous bisexual appetite for whipping the flesh of LA's movers and shakers.

When I met Veronica at the Western Washington Correctional Center for Women (WWCCW) in Gig Harbor, she explained, 'In those days, I was inexorably slipping deeper and deeper into the nether world of the leather and the lash scene. The more lurid, the more wickedly cruel the fantasy, the better.'

She also explained that she had had aspirations of becoming an actress and a screenplay writer. In fact, she had penned a number of frantic, blood-dripping fiction pieces, which were far too extreme for any mainstream publisher to commission. One of those stories was called *The Mutilated Cutter*, concerning a female serial killer who injected semen into her victim's vaginas to make police think that a man was the murderer.

The Los Angeles trial of Bianchi and Buono was in full swing at this time, so Veronica wrote to the handsome Ken, asking him to help her research *The Mutilated Cutter*. Within a short space of time, they were meeting frequently in the county jail, and Veronica fell in love with Bianchi, who had now convinced her that he was an innocent man.

Week after week, they shared fantasies and intimate love letters and, quick to take any advantage that came his way, with the plot of *The Mutilated Cutter* appealing to him, Ken persuaded VerLyn to carry out her literary plot in real life – in Bellingham, of all places. This, he said, would prove that the Hillside Strangler was still at large. 'If you can do this, I will be let out of prison and be free to marry you,' he told her.

The first and most important part of the scheme was to obtain Bianchi's semen and smuggle it out of jail. Bianchi soon solved that problem when he cut the finger from a stolen kitchen rubber glove. He masturbated into it and then tied the open end with the cord from a string of rosary beads, which he had acquired from a visiting Roman Catholic priest. He then stuffed the small package into the spine of a law book, which had been loaned to him by Veronica, and, when she called to visit him a week later, she walked out of the jail with the book tucked under her arm.

With the first part of the plot completed, they now had to establish alibis for the times of the Los Angeles murders, for even Bianchi could not be in two places at once and, if he could prove that he was elsewhere when the murders took place, he reasoned that he would be home and dry.

To achieve this difficult feat of establishing alibis, Veronica travelled out of state, staying at hotels, where she granted sexual favours to the staff in return for blank bar tabs and backdated receipts for rooms Ken had never used; and it proved easy. She forged Ken's signature on these documents, but, to add even further credence to the plan, she stole gas-station receipt books and filled them in. The idea was that, in the weeks to follow, she would miraculously uncover this 'new evidence', present it to the police and hope that this would ensure her lover's release from prison.

In 1980, and now completely under Ken's hypnotic spell, VerLyn flew to Seattle, and from there she drove up to Bellingham, where she befriended a young woman called Kim Breed in a bar. In an audiotape she sent to me, Veronica's exact words were:

The task would be settled in mere hours. The victim would fit the needed requisites. I would arrive in Bellingham, Washington, on a Fall afternoon. Another woman's body would be discovered

FACE TO FACE WITH SERIAL KILLERS

shortly afterwards. The method of killing would be familiar to the Whatcom County Homicide team. Their worst nightmare would be relived; a serial killer had apparently returned to town to continue the reign of terror he had enjoyed only 20 months previously. What they were not to know was that this individual was not a serial killer, neither was it a man.

The peculiar murder tools remained undisturbed in the luggage I retrieved from the airport conveyor. There were no suspicious glances; and, with a small pillow under my clothes, I was just another pregnant woman, dressed perhaps a bit too 'California', with my long, blonde hair held back with a silk scarf, a muslin dress and designer sunglasses, more suited to a beach-side patio than gloomy Washington. Still, even with the clothes, I could hardly qualify as anyone noteworthy.

My purse contained plenty of cash and a cache of narcotics; both would be essential in my work ahead. A taxi took me to my destination, a small motel off the town's main boulevard. I signed the register with a fabricated name, the same one as I had used for my plane tickets, to keep my real identity a secret. Without taking off my gloves, I picked up the room key, and said, 'Thank you,' in my best-affected Southern drawl. It, like everything about me, was a performance. A creation. A fiction.

The motel room was standard, but it held everything necessary for my purpose. There was a queen-size bed, a mirrored vanity area and a small bathroom. Still keeping my gloves on, I unpacked the one suitcase, and arranged the items in a vanity drawer. I carefully laid out two pieces of rope, one with a pre-tied noose, the other loose, to be used to tie the victim's wrists.

Satisfied with my organisation of the items, I started the ritual of medications – tranquillisers, cocaine and alcohol, to be taken as he [Bianchi] had directed. Finishing with them, and with my addictions sated for the moment, I felt hopeful that the

148

hallucinations would be kept at bay, so I settled into tending the blonde wig and adjusting the padding that made my flat stomach give the appearance of pregnancy under my dress. All part of the fictitious creature partly of my making and partly of Ken's.

Veronica Compton

During her first evening in Bellingham, VerLyn met Kim Breed in a local bar. After a few drinks, VerLyn invited Kim back to her motel room. Once there, she slipped the noose over the unsuspecting woman's head, then tried to tie her wrists. However, Kim Breed was a martial-arts expert, so she athletically threw her assailant over her head, and rushed into the street, leaving Veronica dazed and scared on the bedroom floor. When she recovered, Veronica fled back to Los Angeles with the police in hot pursuit, having traced her airline ticket.

When she was arrested and returned to Bellingham, she knew that she was in a serious predicament. In this conservative town, where wearing a garter belt was considered 'kinky', and drug addicts thought to be the curse of the nation, VerLyn was about to stand her trial with the odds a million-to-one in favour of a guilty verdict. Subsequently, Veronica was sentenced to 15 years for trying to duplicate a Kenneth Bianchi murder in an effort to free one of the most hated men in American criminal history. Only recently, and after one escape bid in which she climbed under the wire and almost got clean away, Veronica is a free woman, married and living near Seattle.

Kenneth Alessio Bianchi arrived at the Shelton Reception Center in January 1985, and was furious that his file had 'Sexual Psychopath' over the cover, with the words 'Child Killer' underneath. This file was supposed to remain out of the sight of other inmates, but, by the time Ken arrived at his cell, the prison grapevine had ensured that his true identity was known throughout the Pen. Now he had a price on his head, as everyone wanted the kudos of having murdered one of the infamous Hillside Stranglers.

In February 1985, Bianchi was taken to the Washington State Penitentiary at Walla Walla, where he was immediately placed in 'Punitive Segregation'. Known as 'The Hole' in prison parlance, Ken was confined here for almost two years, living in terror of his life. During this period, he had the gall to apply for parole, while reasoning that, if this failed, he would turn to God to see if the Almighty could help him out.

William B Matthews, a 63-year-old former communications technician who doubled as a Christian visitor, recalls meeting Bianchi shortly after his arrival at Walla Walla, saying, 'I remember it was a time of duress for Ken. He told me that urine had been thrown over him several times, and faeces thrown at him once by other inmates. I might explain that Ken gave his life to Christ during the first week of his stay at WSP. I wish that it was possible to convey what it was like when I walked through that filthy tier called "The Hole", and to see this man, Ken, with so much joy and peace within himself.'

So, wily Kenneth Bianchi was up to his old tricks yet again, this time by flicking a switch and becoming a devoted servant of God almost overnight. And delighted he would have been, for with the threat of murder around every corner, it goes without saying that he would have been very pleased to see the friendly, if not naïve, face of William B Matthews staring at him through the cell bars.

In support of Bianchi's somewhat premature parole application, which was scheduled for 17 December 1985, residents of Walla Walla, Gordon and Dorothy Otter, wrote to the Board of Prison Terms and Paroles on 16 August, stating: 'From our observations of Mr Bianchi, we feel that he is sincere and a dedicated Christian man, who has a very positive attitude. He is always pleasant, takes an active part in the religious services, and he is concerned about the welfare of others.'

The Otters' intentions may have been good, but it seems that they failed to grasp the fact that the main reason inmates attend religious services is to get out of their cells for a few minutes, grab a decent biscuit, enjoy a cup of coffee – with sugar – and suck up to any do-gooders who might be inclined to influence parole hearings in their favour. Kenneth was no exception, and the Otters fell for it. Unfortunately, the Otters had also failed to appreciate the true extent of Ken's concern for the 'welfare of others', which did not extend to the many women and children that he had raped and murdered over the years. The more obvious fact that Ken hadn't been within a mile of a church in his life didn't concern the Otters at all.

On the very same day that the Otters' letter arrived at the parole office, a reference from Pastor Dick Jewett, of the Stateline Seventh-Day Adventist Church in Milton-Freewater, Oregon, dropped through the parole board's letterbox. It read,

I am filing this reference on behalf of Ken. He is a member in good standing of my church. I have baptised Ken myself and, after extensive interviews, I have satisfied my mind as to his sincerity. He is an active member and regular attendee at our services on the prison campus. His attitude and conduct at the present time is exemplary.

Pastor Dick Jewett

It was obvious that Ken had been very busy indeed, especially when parole officials opened yet another letter which had been sent by a Mr and Mrs Black:

We had the privilege of witnessing Ken Bianchi make a commitment to the Lord in Baptism. Ken appears to be very sincere, devoted and earnest. His views are conservative, but he never fails to look at both sides. He has always been polite and sensitive concerning this. He wants to attend college, which shows he has goals. My husband and I have been involved in the Prison Ministry just over two years. We have written and talked to many prisoners. From these experiences we have learned to be fair judges of character. It is obvious to us that Kenneth Bianchi truly loves the Lord and his behaviour and attitude strongly proves it.

Mr and Mrs Black

Another letter of recommendation was received from Father Frederick Ellsworth, a well-meaning priest from the Christ the Healer Orthodox Mission, saying, 'Ken is open, willing to share and quite responsive. I have two young daughters, and I would even welcome him into my home. He would fit in well with my family and his writing has been a highlight.'

And the icing on the cake came from one Bruce Zicari from Penfield, New York, a tax consultant. Bruce declared, 'I would certainly like to reiterate my confidence and high regard for Kenneth Bianchi, and I am certain that he has the capabilities to be successful at whatever field of endeavour he might choose.'

Of course, Bianchi's endeavours in the field of sado-sexual serial homicide had been highly successful. Fortunately, however, none of this impressed the parole panel who rejected Bianchi's application out of hand. So Ken settled down to his studies, and he started by attending a Saturday-morning computer class, and in doing so he was paving his way to participate in regular college programmes. For the time being, Bianchi would put God on the back burner, but not before offering some enlightenment in a letter to me:

I have academically completed a Ministerial training programme given by the Evangelical Theological Seminary, and I am blessed to have been ordained by a Full Gospel Church back in 1986. My faith had taken an exploratory course with independent studies in Eastern religions, Earth religions, Judaism and Biblical archaeology. I even mailed out, free of charge, a written homily entitled Word on the Word. I ceased doing it because it became too expensive. I would not, and cannot, accept donation.

Kenneth Bianchi in a letter to the author

Well, Ken *is* being a little economical with the truth here, for, after speaking to prison officials, I learned that he raked in as much cash as he could before the Department of Corrections stopped him from running his own 'Save Ken Bianchi' campaign. And, it also transpires that, for years, Bianchi's church had sent him quarterly newsletters detailing forthcoming religious events. They addressed correspondence to none other than 'Reverend K Bianchi'. This, however, did not last long, for, when James Blodgett, a new, tough, no-nonsense prison administrator took over, Bianchi's ordination certificate and letters were confiscated.

But Ken keeps on trying – or trying, at least, to pull the wool over everyone's eyes. In June 1988, he received his 'Associate in Arts Degree'. In truth, he cannot draw a straight line, paying more able inmates to draw fine pencil pictures which he then signs as his own, making a few bucks into the bargain.

Then, on Thursday, 21 September 1989, Ken Bianchi married Shirlee Joyce in the prison chapel. Shirlee, who was a pen pal, met him for the first time and spent just two hours with the killer the day before the ceremony where he wore an immaculate tuxedo. She wore a white wedding dress and veil, and the guests included representatives of both families.

The following day, prison records show that Ken refused to work, claiming, 'You must be joking. It's the day after my fuckin' wedding.' This caused Officer Estes to give Bianchi an infraction. Shortly afterwards, Officer Grudzinski overhead Bianchi threatening to 'fuckin' get Estes' at the first opportunity. This loose remark, although probably made in the heat of the moment, resulted in Bianchi being disciplined and thrown again into The Hole. He lost his job in the law library – a rare privilege amongst the several thousand inmates – and the opportunity to consummate his marriage during a 23-hour session with Shirlee in the Combo Area of the penitentiary.

Shirlee divorced Ken in 1993.

In October 1989, our man received a 'Bachelor of Science in Law Degree', and since then he has earned a 'Juris Doctor Degree'. At the time of writing, he is a Member of the National Bar Association. It could be argued that Bianchi knows as much about the law as anyone, and he does, for, in 1992, Bianchi sued a playing-card manufacturer for $8.5 million.

Eclipse Enterprises Inc, of Forestville, California, had launched 10 million of its 'True Crime' collector's cards in July the same year. This incurred the wrath of Bianchi, who argued that his face, which was number 106 in the 110 card line-up, was causing him irreparable harm, and affecting his appeal process. 'They appropriated my face to make money. They breached my copyright,' he griped in a letter.

Eclipse fought the case and, in a landmark decision, the judge ruled in their favour. Nevertheless, the cost of defending the action brought Eclipse to bankruptcy. A former partner in the firm, Katherine Yronwode, explained to me, 'Bianchi was part and parcel of my company's collapse. The cost of defending the case caused the break-up of my marriage, and everything I had worked for 20 years to achieve came to nothing. I cannot say what I think of Bianchi. I just can't say.'

In 1995, I saw the Hillside Strangler in the flesh for the last time. He was lying on the bunk of cell number 12 in the Special Housing Unit, where he is kept for his own protection. The very sight of me peering through the bars of his cage infuriated him. He went berserk, and immediately threatened to sue the Department of Corrections for allowing me to violate his civil rights. This threat was not hot air. For a start, it brought down a mountain of paperwork for the DOC to deal with and, with his appeal against the

Bellingham convictions – Petition C95-0934 – filed on 11 June 1995, in the pipeline, we have not heard the last of Kenneth Bianchi.

Over years of cumulative experience, professionals know that the majority of psychopaths – or 'sociopaths' or 'antisocial personalities', as they are also called – lie, manipulate, deny and deceive to avoid taking responsibility for their crimes. Dr Richard Kraus is quoted in the late Jack Olsen's book *The Misbegotten Son* as saying in reference to psychopaths:

> Their robotic cruelty reflected dehumanization, stunted conscience, and inability to empathize. They are usually smooth, verbose, glossy, neat, artificial – both controlled and controlling. Behind a 'mask of insanity', they lived superficial and often destructive lives.
>
> *Dr Richard Kraus*

Kenneth Bianchi is all of these things and more, so one might categorise him as an exploitative, displaced, sadist serial killer.

He is exploitative in that his sexual behaviour was that of a man always on the prowl for women to exploit sexually, to force women to submit sexually with no care about the victim's welfare.

He is displaced in that his sexual behaviour was an expression of anger and rage, the cumulative backlog of experienced and imagined insults from the many people he had met over the years, all of which continually chipped away at his self-esteem and fragile ego. It was his mother who said, 'It seemed that, whenever Ken had a fight with a girlfriend, or had problems, he went out and killed someone.'

And, of course, Bianchi was a sexual sadist. With Angelo Buono, another perverted individual cast from the same mould, both men were able to enjoy their sadistic tendencies to the full and this made them extremely dangerous creatures indeed.

It goes without saying that Bianchi did suffer a form of psychological child abuse during his formative years, and there can be no doubt that this damaged him. Many believe, as I do, that this is no mitigation for his heinous crimes.

By his own admission, he was having sex with young girls before his teenage years, whom he refers to as 'women'. It is also known that he masturbates at the thought of having sex with pre-teen girls and his murder victims even today.

Throughout his life, Ken carried the social stigma of being a bastard, and perhaps there is some truth in the fact that Kenneth Bianchi really wanted to be someone special, to be able to prove his worth, not only to himself, but also to his adoptive mother who had all but drained him of emotion for some 16 years. But therein lies the rub, for everything he set his hand to – with the exception of serial murder and rape – he failed at dismally. Whether it was love or work, he was a born loser.

As for Ken's fake multiple-personality disorder, the invention of 'Steve' and 'Billy', these were really only another two in a long list of alter egos, for, by the time of his arrest in Bellingham, he had already consciously invented several other false identities – Dr Bianchi, Captain Bianchi, the fake cop, the terminal cancer patient, the phoney film producer – all of which he put in place to compensate for his secret but self-acknowledged inadequacies. And, without these phoney alter egos propping up his self-esteem, he would have crumbled mentally.

But has he learned from all of this? Unfortunately not, for his fascination for alternative identities continues to this day. He has legally adopted a couple of squeaky clean, new names, with a good, old-fashioned Italian ring about them – 'Anthony D'Amato', meaning 'of the beloved', and then 'Nicholas Fontana'. Of course, we shouldn't forget the 'Reverend Kenneth Bianchi'.

Like most serial murderers, Bianchi is an excellent example of the antisocial personality. He is a liar through and through. He will deny guilt to suit himself and, when the cards are stacked against him, he will lie again and again at the drop of a hat to suit the circumstances.

In fact, one rather gets the impression that Ken does not know the meaning of the word 'truth'.

Today, as he appeals against his convictions for the murders of Karen Mandic and Diane Wilder, he appears to have forgotten that he gave police details of the murders that only the killer would know. Nevertheless, he has recently concocted a risible scenario whereby a former staff member at the Whatcom Security Agency conspired with Karen's two boyfriends, not only to murder the two co-eds, but to shift blame on to himself. Yes, it is true that Kenneth Alessio Bianchi does actually exist in a world where elephants fly.

Angelo Buono died from a heart condition at the Calapatria State Prison on Saturday, 21 September 2002. He was 64.

This chapter is based upon two years' continual correspondence with Kenneth Bianchi, his adoptive mother Frances and Veronica Wallace Compton; unrestricted interview access to Bianchi at WSP Walla Walla by the WDC and the assistance of police and the judiciary in Los Angeles, Rochester, NY and Bellingham, WA. The complete Bianchi interview transcripts, and files, are available from www.newcriminologist.co.uk

WILLIAM GEORGE HEIRENS

15 November 1928 –

In simple language the question is this: In what circumstances are we justified in convicting a fellow citizen of murder when no one saw that murder committed and the prisoner denies his guilt? The answer lies in the phrase 'circumstantial evidence'.

Judge Christmas Humphreys, MA, LLB (Cantab) of the Inner Temple, Judge and Barrister-at-Law, 1931

In 1670, French trader Pierre Moreau built a cabin on the site where the Chicago River empties into Lake Michigan. The area was called 'Chickagou' ('bad smell') by the Pottawatomie Indians because of the skunk cabbage that choked the bogs draining into the river.

The Chicago case of William Heirens *has* to be the quintessential serial-killer whodunnit mystery of all time. In investigative terms, the case rivals anything penned by Agatha Christie and, in its shock-inducing horror, exceeds anything dreamed up by Stephen King.

For women generally, there must surely be few scenarios more terrifying than finding yourself waking from sleep, alone in your own bed, to find a knife-wielding, sex-crazed psychopath in the room with you. The intruder is oblivious to your pleas for help, and there is nowhere to hide from the evil monster who is advancing threateningly towards you. For two women and a little girl, this nightmare was one from which there would be no merciful awakening.

Centre stage, as in all well-executed murder stories, is our main character. His name is William Heirens. Around him are scattered the brutally murdered corpses of two Chicago women and a strawberry-blonde-haired, six-year-old schoolgirl. The two women are drenched in blood; they are discovered soon after their deaths. But the schoolgirl vanished from her bedroom in the dead of night. She was discovered, dismembered, a few hours later. The evil spectre visiting a slumbering child's bedroom defied all known police investigative techniques in gangster-war-torn Chicago half a century ago, and continues to baffle the FBI even today.

Each victim was sound asleep in her own bed. A muffled noise, maybe a strange smell, someone, or something, roused them from their slumbers. Then terror struck at their hearts. There was no defence.

The two dead women were carefully washed, their wounds dressed as if by some caring nurse after a diabolical operation. The little girl? Dismembered and quartered, her remains dropped into filthy, rat-infested sewers. The killer was, as crime history claims, William Heirens.

Maybe, just maybe, history has got it wrong.

Perhaps a little overweight, with quizzical yet understanding eyes, inmate #C06103 William George Heirens cut a grandfatherly figure as he walked slowly and uncertainly into the interview room to meet me several years ago. I interviewed him for a TV series called *The*

Serial Killers and warmed to the elderly man from the outset. He is a softly spoken 'Mr Nice Guy', and you will have an opportunity to make up your own mind as to whether one of the world's most maligned serial killers is really guilty of his alleged crimes.

He was calm and shook my hand warmly. Bill did not smile. Here was a man who was at peace with himself, I thought. A person who knew that, despite the fact that he could walk out of the open prison at almost any time, he would never live as a free man again. This much he is resigned to. There were no bars keeping Bill Heirens caged, just the blacktopped roads and open fields that encircle the Vienna Correctional Center, Illinois... and the fact that his face is probably known to every US citizen, many of whom would kill him in an instant for the horrific murders he committed nearly sixty years ago.

The Vienna Correctional Center is a Level-6 minimum-security facility that houses adult male offenders. The facility opened in 1965 and is located in southern Illinois adjacent to the Shawnee National Forest in Johnson County. Since my interview with him, Bill has been transferred to the Dixon Correctional Center, which caters for the needs of elderly and psychiatric patients. Its Special Treatment Center (STC) is designated medium-security and houses both mentally ill and developmentally disabled inmates.

ONE

Daylight Robberies

'Ah, my parents were in the flower business. And, ah, it was in the years of the Depression and, um, they eventually lost the business.'

William Heirens to the author

WILLIAM Heirens was born on Thursday, 15 November 1928, to parents Margaret and George Heirens, in Evanston Hospital, Chicago. It was a difficult birth – 50 hours of labour, sweat and tears brought the world 8 pounds 10 ounces of red-faced infant, and none of it fat, a troubled start in life and perhaps a harbinger of what was to follow.

The couple's marriage wasn't necessarily in trouble, although far from happy, and always teetering on the edges of poverty, the coming Depression made matters worse. Mr Heirens's meagre paycheques, earned as an odd-job labourer, often went to treat

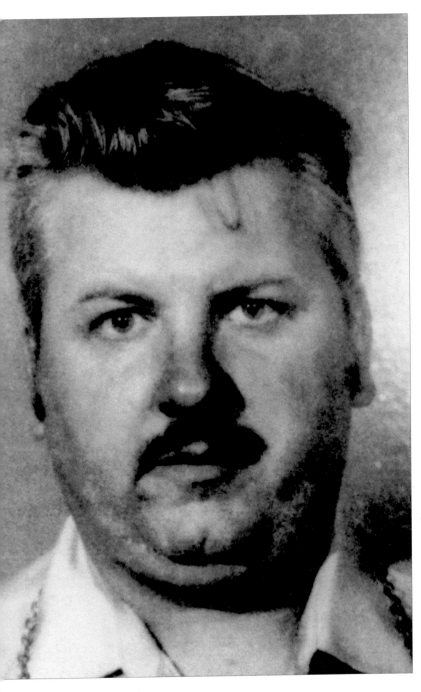
John Wayne Gacy in 1978.

Police bring out another body from John Wayne Gacy's house in December 1978.

Kenneth Bianchi in November 1978. A little under a year later, he would be sentenced to life in prison.

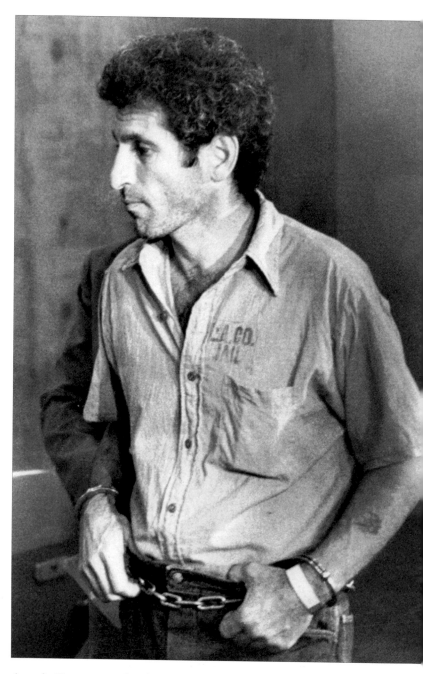

Angelo Buono, cousin of Kenneth Bianchi, about to be arraigned at Los Angeles Criminal Court Building in October 1979.

Top: Members of the Los Angeles Police Hillside Strangler task force investigate the car containing the body of 20-year-old Cindy Lee Hudspeth in February 1978.

Bottom: Eagle Rock Plaza was the site of the November 1977 abduction of Dolly Cepeda and Sonja Johnson. Both girls were killed by the Hillside Stranglers.

Having been found guilty of murder in 1945, William Heirens stands in his cell in the Cook County Jail in Chicago.

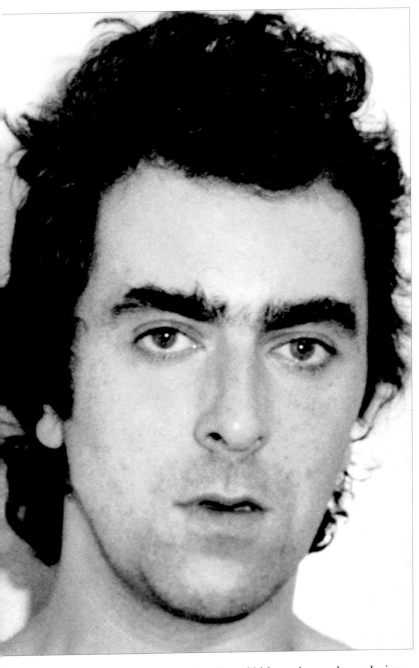

John Cannan in 1989. He was found guilty of kidnapping and murdering Shirley Banks.

Suzy Lamplugh disappeared in summer 1986. Convicted murderer John Cannan was linked to the case.

himself and his pals at the local bowling alleys. Money, or the lack thereof, continued to be the source of all family problems to come.

William's childhood, for all practical purposes, and despite the domestic problems, was normal enough. He was a restless boy, mischievous. Because his mother was forced to help provide income, he and his younger brother Jere, born three years after him, were often left at home with babysitters who found them a handful. One afternoon, their mother returned from her job at the bakery to find the parlour draperies charred and a section of the carpet burned. A science experiment had gone wrong.

On another occasion, Mrs Heirens found her son on the top of the garage roof, cardboard wings strapped to his arms, on the point of doing an impersonation of a pterodactyl about to leap from a cliff. She shrieked and the would-be birdman was discouraged from attempting his solo flight.

Friends remember Bill Heirens as a curious boy who liked toying with chemistry sets, taking things apart and putting them back together. Basically a loner, he would potter for hours. His mother recalled that he liked to work on model aeroplanes, fix old clocks, tinker with mechanical things, and draw. 'Some of our friends commented on Bill's ability to do such work with care and precision,' she said. 'They thought his drawings of airplanes and ships were especially good, and they predicted interesting things for him in the future.'

So while Bill's formative years seemed normal enough, it was particularly the violent arguments between mother and father over money that he would later recall.

Jere seemed to be able to cope with it… I couldn't. As long as I could remember, money was the source of all arguments. Mom would get into one of those screaming harangues that would make me grit my teeth. Dad would fight back, but in a low tone. I guess Mom figured she would lose an argument if she didn't make more noise. I became conscious of money when I was small. It became the 'root of all evil' – evil if you didn't have it… Ours was not a very happy home.

William Heirens

Bill would fly from his home at 714 Grace Street and take to the streets, going on long walks, staying away, anywhere to avoid listening to his parents' squabbles, and that is when he took to burgling.

According to Bill Heirens, he started thieving while he was delivering groceries after school in the seventh grade:

I had to collect money from customers. On one occasion, I accidentally short-changed myself by one dollar and knew that I would have to make it up when I returned to the grocery store. While making a delivery in an apartment building, I noticed some bills lying loose inside an open door and I went in and took one to replace the dollar I had lost. I was surprised how easy it was.

William Heirens

Robbing houses, apartments and stores, he found it exciting, an outlet for the tensions that had dammed up daily at home. The dangers he felt thrilled him and proved to be an antidote to help him overcome – forget – his personal travails. Except for the occasional cash he stole, he never robbed for money, and never tried to pawn off the objects he took – cameras, radios, jewellery – he didn't know any fences on whom to unload the merchandise, or even cared to find them. For Bill, the reward was in the sensations he was able to conjure up from the act, a buzz of excitement, as well as a warm feeling of security.

In an interview with author Dolores Kennedy, Heirens explained his *modus operandi*, which differed from season to season:

In the winter, I chose early evening between 5.00 and 6.00pm because it grew dark early and I could tell whether or not anyone was home. Often, especially in the winter, I burglarised the lakefront area. I would walk around the building, check the windows, ring the front bell and, if no one answered, go to the back door. I would enter through the window off the porch and then chain or double-lock the front door so I couldn't be surprised.

William Heirens

In the summer months, Heirens robbed mostly apartment hotels, he told Kennedy, gaining access through the buzzer then following a random hallway to possible luck. 'Tenants often left their doors open to catch the cross draft. I could look into the room to see if there was anything of value. Fire escapes were a last resort because there was too much exposure.'

Author Lucy Freeman, in researching Heirens's *modus operandi* for her book *Before I Kill More* determines that, at times, Heirens proved something of a Houdini. She quotes Earl R Downes, who was in charge of the robbery investigations at the time:

That kid was like a monkey... Back in '42, he used a narrow board to span a five-foot area from a third-floor porch to reach a third-floor bathroom window at 837 Belle Plain. He crawled across the narrow board while 30 feet below him was a cement sidewalk – death if he fell...

The same holds true for the time he lowered himself over a roof to a third-floor apartment at 3933 Pine Grove, something like a human fly. Or the time he climbed up a wire mesh-covered English basement window to grasp the window ledge and then pull himself up into the first-floor apartment at 3744 Pine Grove. How he got a foothold in the wire meshing is beyond imagination...

Earl R Downes in Before I Kill More, *Lucy Freeman*

Most of what Bill stole he stashed in an unused storage shed on the roof of a nearby apartment building. In no time, the shed bulged with women's furs, men's suits, radios, utensils... and guns. Heirens admitted he liked guns, they fascinated him; his father had been a security guard at one time and he loved to study the unloaded object, to investigate the mechanical gadgetry of it. In those days, many residents owned a gun for protection against home invaders. While pilfering private homes he would occasionally find one in the dining-room bureau or in the bedroom dresser and steal it. At age 13, just before grade school commencement exercises, he encountered his first run-in with the law, involving a stolen .25 calibre automatic.

Had he stolen only money then Bill's burglaries would have been more understandable. But, insatiably, he stole clothing, guns, jewellery, radios, cameras and made no attempt to sell any of the objects he took. 'I was not very sophisticated,' he recalls. 'I just didn't know how to get rid of things, so I kept them.'

On Sunday, 1 June 1941, a policeman stopped a suspicious-looking teenage Heirens in a park and, on frisking him, uncovered the weapon on his person. The lad explained that he had just found it on the ground, but the officer didn't believe his story. He escorted the boy to the Delinquents Home where he was locked up until his hearing, some three weeks later. In that period, Bill Heirens admitted to 11 burglaries and to being the procurer of the stolen goods that the police had found in his rooftop hideaway. The juvenile courts sentenced him to the Catholic-run Gibault School for Wayward Boys in Terre Haute, Indiana.

Upon his release the following June, Heirens returned to burglary, and was arrested again. At the nearest police station, a policeman beat him during his interrogation, but the boy admitted to his mother, 'It was the punishment I deserved.'

This time, a judge ordered him sent him to St Bede's Academy, a detention centre run by the Benedictine Monks on the banks of the

Illinois River in Peru, Illinois. In its care, he proved to be an excellent student and a team player, earning top grades and excelling at sports.

Heirens's scholastic average was so high that he was urged to take a test for admittance into a special learning programme offered by the University of Chicago. He was notified that he had been accepted, and was urged to start classes the following term, 1945, skipping his senior year in high school. He would have been only 16 years old. This achievement pleased his professors and his mother, who figured her son had finally outgrown his insurgent ways.

But Heirens's need to steal was too great. His parents still argued incessantly, and William sought peace of mind the only way he knew how, by psychologically blanketing his problems with pulsating colour. The robberies represented to him a fantasy, a daydream of freedom, as a highwayman of old would experience on the open country road.

'It later became obvious that Bill only stole when he was spending substantial time at home,' Dolores Kennedy writes in her book *Bill Heirens: His Day in Court*. She quotes him as saying that, when he was away at boarding school, 'I wasn't even tempted. Then I would go home, and the tensions would build, and I would find myself burglarising to ease them.'

In the meantime, Heirens had begun classes at the university, majoring in electrical engineering. He commuted at first, his father dropping him off and picking him up from Hyde Park on his way to and from the steel mills. But then Heirens decided to board at Gates Hall, near his classes. His parents could not afford the tuition nor the dorm costs, so the student grabbed whatever jobs he could find. He worked several evenings a week at the Orchestra Hall downtown as an usher and at university functions. For a while, all went well.

By the second year, Heirens's grades had begun to slip. He had discovered girls – and they had discovered his smiling face and dark, wavy hair – and he began a series of romantic flings. His favourite date was attractive blonde fellow-student JoAnn Slama, who lived in the campus area. When not on a date, he and his roommate Joe Costello spent leisure hours discussing philosophy and playing games instead of attending to homework.

And then, of course, there were the burglaries. They continued without interruption as, Heirens admitted, a means to supplement his college costs. Hitting unwatched wallets and purses in homes and hotels in the campus area, Heirens was able to 'save' enough to buy two $500 US Savings Bonds. Through underground channels, aided by university chums, he also garnered stolen War Bonds that, once the owners' names could be scratched off with a surgical scalpel, were worth $7,000. These he kept in a worn suitcase beneath his dorm cot, beside the surgical equipment that he had managed to steal as well.

On the muggy afternoon of Wednesday, 26 June 1946, Heirens left his dormitory and walked in the direction of the Howard Street 'El' (elevated) station. His ultimate destination was the post office in suburban Skokie, immediately north of the city. He knew the area well and had used the post office many times to cash cheques. Today, he found himself low on available funds and spontaneously had decided to cash at least one of the bonds. College debts were due and, besides, he had promised to take JoAnn to the movies the following night. As he boarded the El, the two $500 bonds were tucked into the fold of his wallet. In the inside of his coat, he secreted an old pocket revolver, all seven chambers loaded. He later claimed that he wasn't even certain the gun worked; it was there for show, providing a comfort factor while carrying large sums of money.

Bill Heirens's life was about to change forever.

If it was a knife, I would carry a heavy-duty knife, 'cos I use it for prying – sometimes I would carry a screwdriver. Once in a while I would carry a gun... not so often.

William Heirens to the author at interview

Arriving at the post office at 3.00pm, he discovered it locked and dark. A sign he had never noticed before in the window announced that the place closed after noon during summer months. Angered at having taken the long, hot trip for nothing, and realising that he would have no cash for the eagerly anticipated date with his girl, he turned to what had worked so well before in times of need – burglary.

The Wayne Manor apartments at 6928 Wayne Avenue were familiar to Bill. He had memorised the layout of the six-storey building, which had been his target several times before, and his *modus operandi* remained the same. He opened the front door and pressed the buzzer panel. When a woman answered, Heirens recalls, 'I would talk gibberish. In those days, communication in such buildings was through brass tubes and, by the time the sound got to the receiving end, it was hard to tell what was being said. Since they couldn't understand me and I kept ringing the bell, they would simply buzz me in.'

He rode the passenger elevator to a chosen floor, then paced the hallway until he spotted an open doorway. On the third floor, he found one. From his angle, he could see a wallet resting on a cabinet. Scanning the empty living room, he entered, took the wallet and walked to the end of the hallway to examine the contents. It contained an oversized one-dollar bill which he thought might be a collector's item. As Heirens returned the wallet to the room, he was spotted by the adjacent neighbour Richard O'Gorman, who testified later, 'I saw a man enter the Pera apartment and went back out and re-enter again. So I said to my wife, "You better go over and see if Mrs Pera is home."

'With that, she crossed the hall and she come face to face with William Heirens as he was coming out the door. She hollered at the time to Mrs Pera, "Do you know somebody was in your apartment?" Mrs Joanne Pera hollered, "No."'

Heirens, startled at the outcry, tore down the stairwell with O'Gorman in hot pursuit, and soon janitor Francis Hanley joined in. Heirens whipped out his gun and threatened the two men. Not until he rounded the nearest intersection and darted down a private gangway did Heirens realise he had probably lost the two men. Wheezing, but afraid they might be circling the block roundabout, he climbed the wooden fire escape behind 1320 Farwell Avenue to gain a better vantage point of the alley beyond.

Describing the chase, Heirens recalled, 'I decided that my best chance was to get out of sight as quickly as possible, I ran into the back passageway of a two-storey dwelling. At the rear of the building, I climbed the stairs quickly. On the second floor, the kitchen door was open behind the screen door. I sat in a chair on the porch panting. A woman came to the door and asked me what I wanted, so I made up a story about heart trouble and needing a rest. To keep her occupied, I asked for a glass of water.'

Although she knew nothing of the attempted burglary, Mrs Pauline Willett was suspicious. She beckoned Heirens to sit down while she prepared his drink, then, after slipping the door catch shut, she telephoned the Rogers Park Police Station.

Officers Tiffin Constant and William Owens responded. When Heirens saw their approach through the yard, he attempted to run. Seeing that the officers had blocked both ends of the staircase, however, the boy knew he was trapped. There was no safe way down. Both policemen neared him from opposite ends. Above them, on the landing and frustrated, Heirens saw no alternative but to turn with gun in hand toward the closest officer, Constant. The officer ducked, but when the fugitive started away, the cop charged. A tangle ensued.

So I took the gun I had. So I threw it at him, and he ducked the gun and the gun fell to the mid-landing. And I jumped from where I was standing, down on top of him and knocked the gun out of his hand, and we were wrestling on the mid-landing. Then someone came up from behind and hit me over the head with some flowerpots they had found on the back porch.

William Heirens to the author at interview

In the meantime, an off-duty patrolman named Abner Cunningham had witnessed the mêlée and joined it. He was on his way home from the beach with his wife and children; clad only in his bathing trunks and a T-shirt he had seen Heirens point the gun at O'Gorman and Hanley.

The suspect later said that he had not intended to fire it, only to scare Constant out of the way so that he might escape. If this were the case, he had done the worst thing anyone could have done to a policeman on a sweltering June day when tempers needed little to push them over the edge. Cunningham was the first to reach the struggling duo, so he grabbed three adobe clay flower pots and dropped them one at a time on to Heirens's head.

I started getting into trouble when I was 13, and that was burglarising. I got arrested and sent off to a boarding school. And, when I came back, I got in the same trouble again. They would catch you for burglaries and ask you questions about burglaries. Then, if you say 'yes', then you're gonna get convicted on burglary. So it is better to keep your mouth shut entirely. So, whatever questions they asked me, I wasn't answering any of them.

William Heirens to the author during interview in prison

Bill Heirens began house-breaking and stealing women's clothing at a young age and carried a firearm; indeed, when police searched his home in Chicago, they found a horde of hidden weapons After a spell in a reform school where he impressed the authorities with his above-average intelligence, he enrolled at Chicago University.

While studying there, Heirens continued to commit crimes, then on Tuesday, 5 June 1945, it was alleged that he entered an apartment where Josephine Ross lay asleep. He cut her throat and stabbed frenziedly at her body.

In December of the same year, he allegedly attacked another

woman in her home, shooting her twice and sticking a bread knife into her neck. He left a message scrawled in lipstick on the wall: 'For heaven's sake catch me before I kill more. I cannot control myself.'

But did he leave that message?

Without a Clue

IN January 1945, six-year-old Suzanne Degnan was abducted from her home in the dead of night. A ransom note was left demanding $20,000 for her return. However, by the time it was found, her body had already been dismembered in a nearby basement and her body parts had been dropped into the sewers through gratings in the street.

Heirens was caught a few months later when an alert apartment caretaker spotted an intruder and raised the alarm. At first, Bill denied the killings, insisting that George Murman, his alter ego, committed them. Still only a teenager, Heirens was judged insane and given three consecutive life sentences with the recommendation that he never be paroled.

But there is a problem here, for William Heirens has proclaimed his innocence from the day his life sentences were passed, and it was for this reason I wanted to interview the man whose crimes brought a tidal wave of shock and revulsion which swept across the USA and halfway around the globe.

Yes, I live with this every day I breathe air and my heart beats. I know that I will never be released from prison because of what people think and say. I have nothing to gain or lose by saying, to you, or anyone, that I am guilty or innocent because it will not make a difference to my life. I will never be free. Christopher, I did not murder little Suzanne, or anyone. It is not inside me to do these things and it never was.

William Heirens to the author at Vienna Correctional Center
in a TV interview

At 43, Josephine Alice Ross's life, with each day adding to the tedium, was inexorably passing her by. She had been married three times, two ending in divorce and the third in her husband's death. Her home was an apartment at 510 North Kenmore Avenue, two blocks east of the Lawrence Wilson driveway and Lake Michigan. North Kenmore runs from north to south and is in the Edgewater district of Chicago.

The apartment was a small place, a mere three rooms which she shared with her daughters respectively from her first two marriages, 21-year-old Mary Jane Blanchard and 17-year-old Jacqueline Miller. For the true-crime aficionados, all of the locations mentioned still exist today.

Choosing not to work for the past ten years, Josephine's *modus vivendi* was a dull existence grinding slowly to a halt. She spent most of her time making short forays to the local stores, visiting cinemas, having her fortune read – the day before her murder she received a favourable reading – and fighting her last husband's insurance company for a $1,500 policy they said wasn't valid, claiming that Herbert Ross had falsified his medical records.

Josephine had grand plans had the cash been paid. She had dreamed of opening a restaurant with the money but, financially, things looked bleak. Short of funds, she had set her eyes on a way out of the mess; she planned to marry again and had set her sights on Oscar Nordmark, a truck driver. For Josephine, a fourth marriage was the Last Chance Saloon.

Tuesday, 5 June 1945 dawned and it would prove to become a hot day; not even a cool breeze whispering across the vast expanse of Lake Michigan would bring relief. Kids from the deprived areas on the south side would play among the gushing fire hydrants and their parents would sweat out the day just sitting on their stoops.

Josephine fixed breakfast for her two daughters; Mary Jane left for work at 7.00am, and Jacqueline departed the fifth-floor apartment at 9.30am, after which Josephine, with little to do, returned to her bed. Her body was discovered at 1.30pm that afternoon when Jacqueline came home for lunch, as she usually did.

Jacqueline was met with a gruesome scenario when she opened the door and realised that something was terribly wrong. Her home had been ransacked. Confused, and slowly succumbing to raw terror, she rushed to her mother's bedroom where she found a horrendous sight. Mrs Ross was sprawled across her bed, her throat gashed by multiple stabbings, her head wrapped in a red dress and secured by a silk stocking. Blood had sprayed across the room on to the walls, the drapes, the furniture and a radiator, and a massive stain drenched the mattress dark red. The sitting room where mother and daughters had spent hundreds of happy hours was spattered with the life force of Josephine Ross. In the adjoining bathroom, several articles of the dead woman's clothing and undergarments lay in a pool of bloody water in the tub. Only a few dollars were missing from the premises.

Jacqueline was severely shocked. Almost fainting, she reeled across the room to the door, threw it open and screamed and screamed.

When the police arrived, they discovered five inches of bloody water in the bath. A bloodstained housecoat lay on the floor, and two towels appeared to have been used to mop up spilled water. A roll of adhesive tape lay to one side, and an officer picked up a bra with the straps torn, or cut away. The unfortunate victim had been stabbed four times, and adhesive tape was wrapped around the deep cuts on her neck.

Scenes-of-crime technicians found no suspicious fingerprints. The murderer had either worn gloves or wiped any dabs clean. Josephine's fiancé, Oscar Nordmark, had an airtight alibi, and the police were stumped.

Two witnesses – the building's custodian and a fellow tenant – both described an unfamiliar, swarthy, dark-haired male in a white sweater and dark trousers whom they had seen, seemingly without purpose, wandering through the building earlier. Janitor Elmer Nelson estimated the dark-haired, dark-skinned stranger to weigh about 190 pounds and said he was wearing a light sweater. He had spotted the man descending the fire escape around noon.

Lodger Bernice Folkman, who also had an apartment on the fifth floor, described the man as 'slender, wearing a white sweater and dark trousers'. The stranger's back was turned and Bernice could not see his face. Neither witness appears to have approximated the stranger's age.

Eight weeks after the incident, the trail had gone cold. Police Captain Frank Reynolds, who had more murders in his jurisdiction than his officers could cope with, blandly admitted that the Chicago Police Department had drawn a blank on motive and culprit, but that the investigation would, of course, continue.

Looking back on this murder today, we can say that this was an 'opportunist' and 'disorganised' killing. It was committed by a man who entered the apartment block and, after wandering around the floors at his leisure, happened upon the unlocked door of Josephine's rooms. The principal motive was probably one of financial gain because the killer had rifled through the drawers searching for money or valuables. No doubt his victim had disturbed him, so he killed her in what can only be described as a frenzied attack to avoid recognition. But what else can we glean from the murder itself?

Although there was no evidence of physical sexual assault, clearly there was a sexual element after the killing, for, having stabbed his victim to death, he attempted to 'dress' the fatal injuries with adhesive tape, and covered the head with a red skirt which he secured tightly with a stocking. In the bathroom were the mutilated bra, a housecoat and, in the bloodstained water, were several items of Josephine's underwear.

At an address less than a ten-minute walk south-west from Josephine Ross's apartment lived petite, brown-haired Frances Brown. She shared room 611 on the sixth floor at the Pine Grove Apartment Building on North Pine Grove Avenue with roommate Viola Butler.

During the evening of Monday, 10 December 1945, she had been for dinner with friends and, upon arriving home at about 9.30pm, she was told by the night desk clerk that a man had entered the foyer earlier enquiring about her. When informed that she was out, he left without leaving a name. According to the clerk later, Frances seemed to have been expecting the caller and seemed not at all surprised or concerned that a man had been asking after her.

Roommate Viola Butler was spending the evening at a friend's house and, uncharacteristically, Frances was now alone. Before retiring to her bed, Frances telephoned her mother in Richmond and the conversation centred around visiting her mother for Christmas. She showered and went to bed.

At around 9.00am the following morning, housemaid Martha Engels grew curious as to why Frances's radio was making so much noise. Putting aside her duties for a moment, she walked to the door of room 611 and found it ajar, so she peeked in. The sight, almost identical to the one witnessed by Jacqueline Ross, would live with Martha for the rest of her life. The bed was splattered with blood and a trail of it led to the bathroom where Martha found Frances draped over the bathtub, her head wrapped in her pyjamas. A ten-inch bread knife belonging to the victim was rammed into her neck with such force it protruded through the opposite side. There was a stab to the chest, and a .38 calibre bullet hole had penetrated her skull. Another bullet had entered her shoulder. Not unlike the Ross homicide, Frances's head was wrapped in towels, and towels had been used to mop up the bloodstained water on the bathroom floor.

Within moments, a distraught Engels had rushed to the front desk and summoned the police, who arrived shortly afterwards. It was clear that the apartment had been ransacked – just like the Ross murder – yet nothing of much value had been stolen, not even a wristwatch which lay in plain sight. However, this time the killer had left a message written in bright-red lipstick on the living-room wall – 'For heaven's sake catch me before I kill more. I cannot control myself.'

And, this time, the killer had left a bloody fingerprint. It was found several days after the murder on the bathroom-door jamb.

George Weinberg, a neighbour, had heard what sounded like gunshots around 4.00am. The night clerk, John Dedrick, told police that, at about the same time, a man had emerged from the elevator looking very nervous. He fumbled at the front door and left. He was described as about 35–40 years old, five feet six or seven inches and weighing about 140 pounds. Police determined that he had entered Miss Brown's apartment via the fire escape and climbed through the victim's bathroom window, which was open.

As later events would testify, William Heirens, at the young age of 17, could hardly be described as looking like a 30- to 45-year-old man! The desk clerk would later be unable to identify the youth, Heirens, as the person who had called earlier in the evening seeking Frances Brown; indeed, there would be no physical evidence to prove that Bill Heirens had been in the apartment, with the exception of the bloody fingerprint and the writing on the wall.

The fingerprint evidence and the handwriting, as now revealed by Dolores Kennedy, is suspect in the extreme. Nevertheless, what we can suggest with more than a reasonable degree of certainty is that the killer of Josephine Ross and Frances Brown was the same man whose two victims were females living in apartment rooms not more than a few streets apart in the north district of Chicago.

The killer's *modus operandi* was identical in every respect – the man entered the apartment blocks, wandered around at his apparent leisure until he found either an unlocked door or climbed a fire escape to enter the premises. The man was intent on theft, or so it seemed. Upon being disturbed by his victims, he resorted to murder by stabbing and, in the Brown case, also shooting with an automatic pistol.

Post killing, the killer attempted to 'dress' his victims' fatal injuries with clothing and, in the Ross murder, adhesive tape. A bath was used to some effect in both incidents, and women's clothing, towels and undergarments featured throughout. Both women's heads were covered – a red skirt tied with a stocking in Josephine Ross's case, and a towel in Frances Brown's.

He [Heirens] took the body ... went through the same window that he came through ... went to a nearby basement ... chopped her up. He cut her into six individual pieces ... he decapitated her strawberry-blonde head ... he then took each one of those pieces and put them into a separate location. He took the head and put it in a sewer. He took each of the dismembered parts of that precious little girl and put them in catch basins around that same neighbourhood.

He went back to his dormitory. He did some studying. He was then back in class at the University of Chicago, for all the world to see, appearing as normal as he says he appears today – within hours of dismembering that little girl.

Attorney Thomas Epach to the author at interview

The scene for the next atrocity was set on the first floor of a lovely, well-established house on the corner of Thorndale and Kenmore

Avenue in the wealthy Edgewater section of northern Chicago. Sunday, 6 January 1946 had been busy for the Degnans who rented rooms from the owners, Mr and Mrs Flynn, who retained the second floor along with the attic room, which was used by their daughter, Mary Keegan, and her husband, Tom. The Degnans, who had recently moved from Washington, had been out all day, not returning until late, at which time Helen Degnan made sandwiches for both her daughters, Suzanne and Helen, and shuffled them off to bed. In the morning, both girls would return to the Catholic Sacred Heart Academy at 6250 North Sheridan Road, because the festive holidays had ended.

During the bitterly cold night, the only sounds the household heard were the momentary barking of a neighbour's dogs, a ordinary disturbance, and Cecelia Flynn heard some men talking suspiciously in the street at about 12.50am. Mrs Flynn thought the men were arguing with one saying, 'This is the best building around.' Mary Keegan was woken by the dogs at approximately the same time, while the maid, Ethel Hargrove, who slept directly above Suzanne Degnan's room, heard the dogs bark at about 12.50am, then Suzanne mutter, 'Oh, oh, I'm sleepy.'

At some time during the night, Mrs Degnan sat up in bed, waking her husband beside her in the process. She explained that she thought she had heard six-year-old Suzanne crying. The couple listened a few more minutes, heard nothing more, then went back to sleep.

At about 6.30 in the morning, Jim Degnan went to wake his daughters for school. He thought it odd that Suzanne's door was closed. The child was much too afraid to sleep in the dark so it was always left ajar to allow the hallway light to filter in. Peering in, he saw that her bedroom window was fully raised, the curtains billowing in the ice-cold breeze; the coverlet was neat and tidy and her pillow was smoothed over, although the girl was nowhere to be seen. The rest of the family scoured the quarters – closets, window seat, even outside on the fire escape – then woke their neighbours, the Flynns, and asked them to search their premises. Panic set in when it became apparent that Suzanne had disappeared. They would never see their blonde-haired daughter alive again.

It was about 7.30pm. It was school night so we went to bed earlier. An' my mother would come in and help us say our prayers, tuck us in, kiss us goodnight. Then usually Dad would come in and play games with us. Get us all riled up, so she would come back in and settle us down again.

Suzanne's window was darker because there were no lights from the garage as at my window the garage lit mine. And I assume that's why Heirens chose Suzanne's because no one could see her window.

My mother came into my room first and woke me and went into Suzanne's and saw the ransom note and knew that a crime had taken place.

I didn't know how… how graphic… how he mutilated her. I knew he strangled her and it was a while before I… I knew that he had cut up her body and put her into the various sewers around the neighbourhood. My parents tried to keep that from me because it was quite horrible.

Should he be released, he could harm another child. He could put another family through this, and I couldn't sleep at night if this did happen.

Betty Finn (sister of Suzanne Degnan) to the author
at interview

Because of the nature of the crime, a child's disappearance, and because of the heat it had been taking over unsolved crimes, the Chicago Police Department dug into this case with fervour. The new Police Commissioner, John C Prendergast, became personally involved. The apartment was soon swarming with as many as 45 police and detectives eager to unravel the disappearance of little Suzanne Degnan.

On the floor of the girl's bedroom they found what at first appeared to be a tattered, discarded paper resembling tissue covered with oil, but it turned out to be a ransom note. Probably blown from the bed by the wind, it read: 'Get $20,000 ready & waite for word. Do not notify FBI or police. Bills in $5's and $10's.' On the reverse was a warning: 'Burn this for her safty [sic].'

There were no suspicious fingerprints, and not a wet footprint on the carpet, but outside the apartment the police found what they thought was a second vital clue – a seven-foot-six-inch ladder that, when held upright, reached to the sill of Suzanne's window. The old and rickety ladder, police soon learned, had been stolen from a nursery several blocks away.

Upon being shown the ladder, Mr Degnan remembered that it had not been there when he had thrown out the Christmas tree the day before and, strangely, there were no marks on the side of the building or the windowsill to suggest that the ladder had been used as a means of entry.

Investigators spread throughout the area, searching, asking questions, hoping to find witnesses, then an anonymous telephone call suggested they check surrounding sewers. That evening, 7 January, detectives Lee O'Rourke and Harry Benoit did just that. Noticing that a sewer cover on nearby Winthrop Avenue looked misplaced, they shone their flashlight into the well and found what looked like the head of a golden-haired doll. But it was no doll's head. An alarm went out. Before the evening ended, the rest of Suzanne Degnan – her legs and torso – was found scattered in adjacent sewers. Her arms were found several weeks later. All of the body parts had been wrapped in rags then placed in bags. A basement washtub below an apartment off Winthrop Avenue – just two blocks from the Degnan home – proved to be the place of dismemberment. Blood, pieces of human flesh and blonde hairs were found in its drain. A monstrous butcher had been at work.

'Chicago's greatest manhunt, and perhaps one of the most intensive ever conducted in the nation, was on. Police had the task of trying to pluck the killer out of a city of four million,' wrote author Lucy Freeman. 'They worked around the clock, often driving their own cars and using their own time… Police worked day and night questioning suspects. They interviewed more than 800 persons suspected of the crime; gave lie detector tests to 170. The crime laboratory compared 7,000 sets of handwriting with the ransom note. A total of 5,250 were received from all over the world offering clues or theories; 3,153 were investigated.'

Police believed that the kidnapper-killer must have driven a car the few blocks to the place of dismemberment; carrying a heavy child through the streets would have attracted too much notice. After all, the streets were not exactly empty, even for night-time.

Witnesses had seen a woman in the locality carrying a large bundle in both her arms in the vicinity of the Degnan home. She got into what seemed to be a waiting car where a balding man sat behind the wheel.

Another witness saw a large, dark man carrying a shopping bag. But the phantom couple and the man with the bag were never identified.

Of more interest was a butcher called George Catraboni who was under arrest for some 13 murders, which included mutilation and decapitation killings in Cleveland, Ohio, and who had confessed to the Brown murder. He was removed from the suspect list because he had lied to police so often they could not believe a word he said. But was he now telling the truth?

In the interim, police had spent much time in the laundry basement where Suzanne had been cut up. There were six lockers belonging to the tenants who lived above. The locker of Mr and Mrs Frank Haeger had been broken into, and bags, which had contained the body parts in the sewers, and the rags, which had covered the limbs to stop body fluids from weakening the paper wrappings, had been stolen.

Mrs Freda Meyers, whose rooms were directly above the basement, told detectives that she had been restless during the early morning of 7 January. She had a nervous disposition, now even more so in the knowledge that a little girl had been hacked up just a few feet beneath her floorboards. She explained that at around 3.20am she made a cup of cocoa, before returning to bed ten minutes later, then she heard a sinister noise. There had been the sound of footsteps in the passageway leading from Winthrop Avenue east to the alley, the laundry room and her very bedroom.

Now gripped with anxiety, her first thought was to rouse her husband from his slumbers, but listening intently she thought better of it when the footsteps faded away. However, after calming herself down, the person returned and this pattern was repeated four or five times with the nocturnal visitor coming to the basement then leaving, the sounds of crunching boots fading into the night.

With the arms of petite Suzanne Degnan still missing, police started to try to reconstruct what had happened that fateful early morning, with little success. The time-window for the abduction and dismemberment was narrow – no more than three hours in total. Several members of the Flynn/Degnan household had heard the barking of dogs at around 12.55am, and men's voices had been heard outside and the maid had overheard Suzanne mutter, 'Oh, oh, I'm sleepy,' at approximately the same time. And, we recall that insomniac Mrs Meyers had heard the footsteps coming and going from the alleyway outside her bedroom from 3.40am onwards.

From this sketchy information, we may safely assume that Suzanne was most certainly abducted at around 12.55am. Probably being woken by the intruder, she muttered, 'Oh, oh, I'm sleepy,' before being strangled and spirited away to the basement at Winthrop Avenue where her body was dismembered from 3.40am thereafter.

At autopsy, dirt was found on the soles of Suzanne's feet; giving rise to the theory that the child had been removed from the building still alive and made to walk a short distance. However, the risk of the child screaming out loud as she was taken from her bed, forced through an open window and carried down a high ladder, was a risk that no kidnapper would consider, that is unless the child was silenced with a blow to the head or gagged.

The police were also puzzled about the absence of ladder marks against the wall of the house and upon the windowsill. Indeed, there was no evidence to show that the ladder, which was old and in a dangerous state, had been used at all. No impression on the ground existed that it had been propped up, even less that someone climbed up it and through the window which had been firmly shut and locked when Suzanne had gone to bed, but was open in the morning. The glass had not been broken, nor the latch forced and, to confuse matters totally, various officers suggested that under these circumstances the killer had entered the house by the back door of the apartment, entered Suzanne's room, killed her and left via the same route, leaving the window wide open and the unused ladder as a decoy.

Mr Degnan was asked if the back door had been locked, but he could not remember. And what was the significance of the stolen ladder being placed outside Suzanne's window? It would have been a hazardous exercise descending the steps carrying a child weighing 74 pounds, combined with the weight of the kidnapper; it was a task almost impossible for one person to carry out alone without the serious risk of a heavy fall. Casts of footprints in the ground by the ladder were taken by the police and enquiries in this direction came to nothing.

The ladder and the closed-then-open window – later, police said that it was open just a few inches – and any significance they may have had in the abduction of Suzanne Degnan was a mystery. The ransom note further confused the situation.

To begin with, the Chicago Crime Laboratory was unable to find a single fingerprint on the note, which was photographed several times before being sent to the FBI who had more sophisticated methods of fingerprint detection. The paper, upon which the note had been written, was a single sheet torn in half. Two partial palm prints were revealed, though they were far too incomplete to classify. But this did not prevent Thomas Lafferty of the identification bureau from later mistakenly identifying them 'as belonging to William Heirens'.

The police were also unable to decide whether the note had been written, then smeared with oil, in an attempt to disguise the handwriting, or if the paper had been tainted with oil before the words were written. Was the note a genuine attempt at blackmail, or was it a decoy – even an afterthought to confuse and mislead the police over the true motive for the crime? And had it been written prior to the murder, or afterwards?

Jim Degnan was not a rich man by any stretch of the imagination; in fact, he was often borrowing money from people less well off than himself. He held down a job with the Office of Price Administration (OPA) which had been created during the Second World War in order to issue ration cards and keep prices under control. Jim had been instrumental in setting up the organisation but now it was causing problems, particularly in the meat and dairy industries, where the black market was rife.

Although Jim had a few police friends, to say that he had a few enemies would be an understatement, so investigators considered this, too. He lived in rented rooms, and a blackmailer would have found much richer pickings from the hundreds of other suitable house owners elsewhere in the upmarket Edgewater district. Notwithstanding this, Jim went on local radio, pleading for his daughter's safe return, saying that he had burned the ransom note as ordered – which he had not – and that he would raise the money come hell or high water.

During the inquiry, a number of people came forward to assist the police where they could. Robert Freutal, who lived at 5959 Kenmore Avenue, left his home for work at about 3.00am on 7 January. He claimed he saw a man wearing a light coat exit from a 'slate-coloured car, probably a Ford or Chevrolet'. The vehicle was parked on the west side of Kenmore Avenue facing north and about 100 feet north of the Degnan home; the man looked as if he was carrying a bundle.

Miss Crawford, of 5900 Kenmore Avenue, told officers that, at about 3.30am that morning, she was sitting with a friend in a car on the west side of Kenmore Avenue, just south of Thorndale, when she noticed a grey-coloured sedan containing a man and a woman cruising up and down the street several times. Several taxi drivers spotted the same car.

Robert Reisner saw a dark-grey car parked on Thorndale with a bare-headed, heavy-set man behind the wheel, while Albert Johnson noticed a woman, carrying a bundle in both arms, enter a car parked on Thorndale Avenue, between Sheridan Road and Kenmore Avenue. The car was described as either a 1940 or '41 Ford four-door with a partial licence plate as '11' – the first two numbers for an Illinois plate. The time was approximately 2.00am.

None of the car drivers came forward to remove themselves as suspects and the identity of the 'mystery couple' remained unresolved until the police had another break. A milkman reported seeing 'the ladder in question' on top of a Hudson car early on Saturday and again on Sunday morning.

Certainly, the police felt that they were moving in the right direction and then, out of the blue, neighbours, and not the Degnans, told police that, several months earlier, two men had driven up to the Degnan house and attempted to force Suzanne into a car with them as she returned home for lunch. The child had screamed, neighbours were alerted and the men drove off.

This claim was highly significant for several neighbours independently verified the incident. It is also highly significant in that Mr Degnan didn't report the attempted abduction of his daughter to police; strangely, he didn't even bring the matter to the investigator's attention after Suzanne was abducted. His neighbours did that. And it is important because Heirens did not have the use of a car at the time, and he most certainly would not have had an accomplice

Working on all the various theories and available evidence, police were convinced that a vehicle had been used to take the child from her home to the laundry-room basement two blocks away. Even in the early hours of Monday morning, there were simply too many people about who would have noticed someone carrying a dead girl over their shoulder for two blocks. And, as Dolores Kennedy brightly says, 'They [the police] wondered about the "mystery couple" who had never come forth.'

The post-mortem examination showed that Suzanne Degnan had been strangled and she had not been sexually abused. Dr William D Nally, a toxicologist, reported to Coroner Brodie that a sharp knife had been used to dissect the girl and the expertise used could have only come from a butcher or a hunter. Dr Jerry Kearns, the coroner's expert, stated, 'The killer had to be an expert in cutting meat because the body was separated at the joints. Not even the average doctor could be so skilful. It had to be a meat cutter.'

Police Chief Storms told reporters, 'The killer was either a physician, a medical student, a very good butcher, an embalmer, or perhaps a livestock handler.'

Coroner Brodie added more weight by stating, as fact, 'It was a very clean job with absolutely no signs of hacking as would be evident if a dull tool was used. The bones were all intact, carefully wrenched from their sockets.'

William Heirens did not have the use of a motor vehicle. He never used an accomplice because he was very much a loner. He had no such medical knowledge or expertise, so from the post-mortem examination evidence alone, there is not a shred of physical evidence to suggest that it was he who had entered Suzanne's bedroom, took her away and dismembered the body.

On this evidence alone, William George Heirens was totally out of the frame, but someone killed Suzanne... so who did?

When looking at the evidence surrounding the Suzanne Degnan murder, there seems to be a great deal of doubt over one significant piece of evidence – the ladder. We know, or at least the police claim, that it was stolen. We know that it was old, in a bad state of disrepair, barely able to carry the weight of an adult, far less likely the combined weight of a 74-pound child *plus* an adult man struggling with the body. It would have been a hazardous if not almost suicidal venture at best and, without the help of an assistant – as any builder will testify – on the uneven and slippery ground beneath, a risk of extraordinary proportions.

We also know that there were no imprints in the ground to indicate that the ladder had been used for such exertions, or marks on the apartment's outer walls or the windowsill to show that it had ever been placed against it.

From this, it could be strongly suggested that the ladder was a red herring.

But if the ladder was a red herring, what of the note? This was a crucial item of evidence, yet it actually revealed little if anything at all, in terms of criminological value. The ransom demand was written on a scrappy piece of paper contaminated with oil – hardly the handiwork of a well-planned kidnap.

Today we can look once again at this ransom note in a more considered manner, and there is only one scenario in which it could have been penned – before the successful murder and abduction of Suzanne Degnan.

At first glance, there appears to have been a motive of financial gain; the premeditated kidnap of a child from her bed in the dead of night, and an intruder demanding an almost impossible $20,000 for her safe

FACE TO FACE WITH SERIAL KILLERS

return. It should also be remembered that there was an alleged attempted kidnap of the young girl some weeks beforehand, and the bid failed because she screamed and alerted neighbours. We also know, from the autopsy reports, that there was no sexual assault on this victim. We also know that Suzanne was dismembered and disposed of within a few hours of her abduction. All of these issues are undeniable facts.

This being said, are we being asked to believe, just for an instant, that the cold-blooded kidnappers – the police say that two people had to have been involved – used the ladder for such a dangerous form of entry and exit, strangled the girl in her warm bed, then wrote the note in a darkened room, tidied up the child's bed and made away with her, to hack her to pieces and dispose of the body parts just a few hours later? Or did the killers, having selected the victim, write the note beforehand?

If we are being invited to believe that the kidnap for ransom was 'genuine', then the note had to be written prior to the entry into the apartment because killers the world over flee the crime scene as soon as possible to avoid the slightest chance of being challenged there. An exception to this is the killer of Josephine Ross and Frances Brown, who attempted to patch up and dress his victims' injuries after they were dead.

All of this brings us to the most obvious conclusion – the ransom note, aimed at people who were patently unable to find the money – was, like the ladder, another red herring... unless the whole thing was dreamed up and carried out by the most bungling idiots on the planet

So, why two red herrings?

Taking all of this into account – the ladder and the ransom note; the police strenuously claiming that two people were involved, one of whom apparently had excellent butchery skills; and the use of a car – Bill Heirens must surely be removed from the equation completely.

Various witnesses – whom the police held great store by, because the Chief of Police issued a request for information on radio – claimed to have seen a heavy-set, grey-haired man and a woman driving around the neighbourhood circa the time of the murder. The man in no way resembled Heirens, who did not enjoy the company of women anyway. Nor did Heirens have the use of a car.

The milkman who reported that he saw 'the ladder in question' on top of a Hudson vehicle early on Saturday, and again on early Sunday, also removed Heirens as a suspect when he described the driver as 'heavy-set and dark-haired'.

The cars concerned alternated in colour between grey, dark grey and, for the Hudson, no colour at all. The makes varied between Ford, Chevrolet and Hudson. The occupants between single males or couples.

Something else to consider is the previous attempted abduction of Suzanne Degnan by two men, which was only brought to the police's attention by neighbours, not the child's parents, and in *no way* could these men be described as looking at all like William Heirens.

Could it have been that the murder of Suzanne Degnan had been someone known to the child? Police later received an anonymous message from Boston, Massachusetts, which stated:

Since it has been reported the child was heard to cry in objection to being awakened as still 'sleepy' – wouldn't it seem logical that if it were a total stranger, she would have screamed to her parents for help?

The attack upon the child was made by one who, in order to cover his crime of 'attack', was obliged to kill.

The ladder was just a 'blinder' made by the criminal, but never used. Arrest the closest male relative the child had, and you will be closer to solving the problem of kidnap.

Note to police

As in most cases of such magnitude, cranks claiming to have 'evidence' inevitably surface. The Degnan inquiry proved no exception and Jim Degnan was brought into the firing line.

A former associate of the bereaved father at the POA wrote:

Jim was always borrowing, from almost anyone, even from people whose income was substantially less than his. And he was not known as a good risk. Gossip had it that he 'was into' some of his associates for pretty big sums, as their salaries went, and that Jim indulged in some fancy borrowing to meet creditors' claims when pressed. Could Jim be in debt to anyone of unbalanced mind?

Former associate of Jim Degnan

The police questioned the father closely, and he had this to say:

I suppose I have, like anybody else, skeletons in the closet that would be incidents in your life that you would not be too keen to draw out and review, but from the bottom of my heart I can tell you I know of no incident in my life that would not bare full review in a thing like this.

I have made mistakes that presumably would cause prejudices. I have thought of all the places I have been and all the people I know, and the one thing that has been a tremendous degree of satisfaction to me is that no place I have ever been I can't go back and have a lot of friends. I suppose I have people who don't like me, but nobody that I know of that feuded [fought with me].

Jim Degnan to police

However, this heartfelt statement did not prevent the letters coming in. Even a human ear was posted to Helen Degnan, along with a threatening note. Police arrested suspects by the truckload, and each time the men were released.

On Friday, 11 January 1946, the remains of Suzanne Degnan were buried in a small white coffin.

On Saturday, 19 January, the girl's arms were discovered by electricity workers in a sewer near a Commonwealth Edison plant just south-west of Thorndale Avenue.

The investigation stalled, then ground to a halt. Crime-ridden Chicago had another three victims; another three homicides were unsolved.

Once arrested, Heirens confessed to reaching sexual climax during his housebreaking, and was judged insane, sentenced to three consecutive life terms, and was never to be released.

> Ah! The handwriting; the lipstick message on the wall, and the Degnan ransom note. They had their experts say that was mine.
>
> *William Heirens to the author*

The case of William George Heirens has been well documented over the decades since his incarceration; it has not been my intention to examine the case in detail here, but to clarify the salient points.

The truth as to Heirens's guilt or innocence is left to the reader; it is my considered opinion that there was not one iota of physical evidence linking Bill Heirens to any of the three murders. Thief he may have been… but murderer? Most certainly not.

This chapter is based upon case papers and the author's interviews with principal characters, including William Heirens.

JOHN DAVID GUISE CANNAN

20 February 1954–

I need, it seems, to ram it home to you once more. I have no knowledge of what happened to Suzy Lamplugh. I was not in London on the day of her disappearance. I am still willing to receive both Mr and Mrs Lamplugh here at the prison, not to tell them why, but to show them why I am not responsible for their daughter's disappearance. I am not willing to expose either myself or the Lamplugh family to further publicity and turn the thing into a comic opera. These matters should be private and confined only to Mr and Mrs Lamplugh, the Metropolitan Police, my solicitor and me. If they refuse to come and see me or write to me, then frankly I can only ask why this should be. If it was my daughter I would bulldoze the prison gate.

John Cannan to the author at interview

Handsome, debonair and entirely plausible, John Cannan was undoubtedly Britain's emerging Ted Bundy. He was a vicious armed robber, serial rapist and serial killer, and I spent three years corresponding with the man police now publicly confirmed as the killer of the London estate agent Suzy Lamplugh. I amassed hundreds of documents and police files, many of which are now solely in my possession. More recently, I consulted with the Metropolitan Police Serious Crimes Group as they reinvestigated the Suzy Lamplugh case.

The police now say publicly that Cannan is the only suspect in the murder of Suzy Lamplugh. But what more does Cannan know and why might he be living in fear of his life? And was there a conspiracy to kill Suzy because she knew too much?

This is an account of a human predator, prone to serial violence, an arch opportunist who trawled for victims in wine bars and car parks. The minds of such individuals are shaped by a variety of sociological, physiological and psychological factors and, while the 'nature versus nurture' debate continues within the criminological community, what is clear is that individuals such as John Cannan, Kenneth Bianchi and John Wayne Gacy do know the difference between right and wrong, but simply don't care.

Such predators are difficult to detect because their behaviour is masked with protective cunning. They merge into society and appear to all intents and purposes normal and well adjusted. Yet they are loners, restlessly roaming from place to place in search of opportunities to fulfil their lusts. It would seem that John David Guise Cannan is such an individual.

Nature endowed John with the good looks and easy charm of the 'ladykiller'. He conquered the hearts of beautiful women with seemingly little effort and enjoyed his powers to the full. But nature had infected her gifts with a fatal flaw which transformed him into a cold-blooded killer. He developed a destructive urge which he could not control.

John is currently serving a natural life sentence at Wakefield Prison for the murder of Shirley Banks, a newly married young woman who disappeared from Bristol in October 1987 and whose badly decomposed body was found in Somerset the following year. This murder, it has been claimed, was the high point of violence in his criminal career. What undoubtedly preceded it was a string of robberies, violent assaults, rapes and a conviction for murder, interspersed with a number of amorous affairs.

John displayed increasingly tense and violent behaviour in his normal relationships and reached a stage where he began to trawl for victims, and his adult life and the pattern of his behaviour bear all the hallmarks associated with cold-blooded killers. He was charismatic, mobile, opportunistic and a master manipulator. John has a narcissistic personality disorder. When he suffers rejection or humiliation, his mind turns to revenge and he seeks out the kind of satisfaction that is gained by inflicting pain on others. Like all such individuals, he blames other people's treatment of him for his plight, rather than either blaming himself or taking responsibility for his own inadequacies. In this state, he can be ruthless and is quite capable of justifying irresponsibility, unethical or illegal behaviour and his outrageous demands. Any contrary opinion is regarded as totally unfair, worthless or vindictive.

At the time of writing, it is generally agreed by law-enforcement officers that Shirley Banks may not have been his only murder victim. Cannan's name is now inextricably linked to the murder of Suzy Lamplugh and police have also named him as one of the suspects in their hunt for the killer of Sandra Court, both in 1986, although he has consistently denied murdering these young women.

And 'consistency' is the key to this man's mind. He consistently argues that he has some knowledge of both killings but he vehemently denies murder. But who would believe a man who has cried 'wolf' too many times for his own good? Police officers and psychologists claim that John Cannan is a sophisticated and consistent liar. The flipside of the coin, though, is that one does not have to be sophisticated to be able to tell the truth consistently or, more importantly, *believe* one is telling the truth. This is the enigma of John Cannan and, within this puzzle, is the answer to the riddle of Suzy Lamplugh's murder.

John regards himself as a wronged man, who, from the outset of his adult life, was let down by the people around him, and when things went wrong for him, he was victimised by the system. His conviction, he believes, was contrived by people in influential positions – the police, the judiciary, the media who needed a scapegoat.

I have sought to protect the feelings of the rape victims by not using their real names. Thus 'Sharon Major', 'Jean Bradford' and 'Donna Tucker' are pseudonyms for the three women who experienced brutal attacks. These are the only names which have been changed. Here I am at variance with John, who coldly maintains that, if these individuals made allegations against him, they should be publicly revealed. The other women who featured in John's life, with some exceptions, did so willingly and saw something of the better side of his character.

John Cannan, Shirley Banks, Suzy Lamplugh and Sandra Court have all been linked in the most tragic circumstances, but the truth concerning the parts they played in each other's lives remains obscure – the victims' voices have been stilled, and only the killer and his accomplices hold the answers.

Undoubtedly, John killed Shirley Banks, and more recent advances in DNA analysis have proved this beyond doubt. But, the question remains, did he murder Suzy Lamplugh?

ONE

Prince Charming

THE motto of the Duc de Guise, 16th-century head of the Catholic League, was '*á chacun son tour*' (my turn will come). The Duke's name was given to John David Guise Cannan born in Sutton Coldfield, Warwickshire, on 20 February 1954.

John was born to loving parents. His mother doted on him and, despite having an older sister and, in due course, a younger brother, it was 'little Johnnie' who occupied centre-stage in the Cannan home. His father, Cyril Cannan, was an exacting man with a quick temper. He had been a flight lieutenant in the Royal Air Force during the Second World War and served as an instructor on aircraft engines. Cyril Cannan was widely respected in Sutton Coldfield and was well known in the motor trade throughout the Midlands, although he was considered by some to be a tough individual.

John's mother was short and fair-haired, neat in her personal appearance and also in the well-ordered way she ran her household. She provided a comfortable, stable home for her husband and their three children. John probably acquired his habits of personal neatness and sense of good taste from his mother.

'Little Johnnie' was a boy with dark hair and piercing blue eyes beneath dark eyebrows that would converge over his nose as he grew older. He reacted quickly if he did not get his own way, and soon became something of a young tyrant, with the whole household revolving round his whims and wants. John grew up expecting to have his own way in everything.

Mrs Cannan was frequently the peacemaker between a strong husband and a wilful son. Her calming influence reflected an inner strength, which was to be amply tested by the tragedies that were to come. John may have interpreted his mother's acquiescence as weakness in the face of dominant forces. Certainly, he, like so many of his evil breed, would grow up with an ambivalent emotional attitude towards women. They were to be controlled and, when they reacted independently, he took violent steps to control them. He was capable of loving relationships but, when he was thwarted, he preyed on female vulnerability as a means of releasing his frustration.

John was a loner with a strong sense of his own power. As an adult he would say, 'I always wanted to be "Top Gun" and, because I was talented and worked hard, I always was "Top Gun".'

No shrinking violet, he regarded his abilities as second to none and despised weakness, and saw other's resentment of him as being the product of their own inferiority. In a letter to me, he characterised himself as 'big-head – big mouth', while his colleagues called him 'Billy Liar'.

He also regarded himself as a sensitive personality and developed a liking for reading philosophy. Perhaps he realised that the power to be derived from knowledge would lend strength to his already burgeoning self-confidence. When he played truant from school, he did not waste his time but, with admirable self-motivation, spent hours in public libraries learning about the things that interested him. Others have indulged in this kind of random education which can create specialised knowledge but often at the expense of structured learning.

John Cannan matured as a person with an unshakeable faith in his own abilities. He believed himself to be knowledgeable, he became aggressively competitive and had a taste for the finer things in life. He also became aware of the magnetism of his own personality. As a boy in his parents' home, he had always got his own way; as a youth, he enjoyed the power bestowed by driving fast, shiny cars and, as an adult, he discovered his sexual power. To his handsome looks and self-confidence, he added the civilities of good taste. He dressed well, favouring smart business suits and, once he had acquired his own flat, he furnished it tastefully. He also knew how to charm his way into the affections of his female companions with gifts of champagne and roses. In every sense of the word, John Cannan was a ladykiller.

After a period in which he indulged all his considerable attributes of charm, knowledge and self-assurance – a time which he later described as consisting of 'a hundred one-night stands' – John's confidence was sky-high. He could do everything he wished. He was also living in cloud cuckoo land. In reality, he had little ambition –for most of his time he was a shady second-hand-car dealer, who portrayed himself as a businessman. Self-deception began to emerge and, with it, a fatally flawed personality who believed that he was always right.

John's education began when he was four years old and his parents sent him to a private school for boys. They chose Keyse, situated high on a hill overlooking parkland, nor far from his home. It was a place, he said later, where 'the better-off sent their prodigal sons'. Among his first childhood memories were feelings of excitement about going to school.

In a nostalgic reference to these early school days, he spoke about his form teacher who had a weakness for eating biscuits during breaktime. In an early demonstration of his blue-eyed charm, John wheedled his way into her affections: 'She melted,' he said, 'and our morning breaks were nearly always spent sitting next to each other with yours truly chomping away at her "bikkies" and looking up at her adoringly. And adore each other we did.'

His mature recollections of the first year at Keyse were of happy times but of tough discipline. But then the headmaster at Keyse moved on, and his successor brought in a new regime and new staff to enforce it. Beatings became a regular part of the school regime and a threatening atmosphere pervaded the classrooms. But worse was to come.

John was seven or eight years old when, he later alleged, he suffered an experience which marked him badly. He claimed that a man took him into a vacant classroom and told him to drop his trousers. He then touched him between the legs and wanted John to feel him as well. John was very wary of the person concerned anyway and, in total fear, did as he was told. 'It went on for months,' said John, 'and it was something I couldn't share with anyone. It was dirty and horrid and I felt ashamed.'

After that, school became a place of horror and, not surprisingly, John employed every dodge he could think of to avoid going there. He became a nervous, highly strung child and developed a bad stammer. His mother took him to the family doctor and, at nine years of age, he was taken away from Keyse School and the misery it held for him. The experience affected him greatly, particularly because he felt unable to discuss his feelings with his parents.

Many years later, writing from prison, he recalled the original headmaster at Keyse whom he described as a 'super bloke', and spoke of how things later went sour. During a visit to the family home in 1987, he had gone for a walk on his own and could not resist the temptation to amble up to the old school. The Victorian building which had stood at the top of Wyndley Lane had been demolished by then but the memories came flooding back, 'the fear, the canings, the assaults … everything'.

He had an uneasy relationship with his father, who was quick to criticise. The parental philosophy, like that at Keyse, was to cope with life's trials. John remarked of his father, 'He was only ever proud of me when I came first. Any complaints about ill treatment at school obviously did not fall into a prize-winning category.'

John was 12 before he understood the unsavoury experience to which he had been subjected. He said that he began to feel 'somehow estranged from other people. It felt as if I had done something so terribly wrong.' There were times when he suddenly felt very low, unhappy and totally worthless. These feelings began to affect his behaviour and he found he could not apply himself consistently to any activity. Following another visit to the family doctor in his early teens, he was referred to a psychiatrist at Good Hope Hospital. Of the consultation which took place, he said he was 'too embarrassed to really open up'.

He believed his problems went far deeper than will-power or strength of character. 'I realised,' he wrote later, 'that emotionally I had a problem and one which meant I tended to hold people away at arm's length.'

He did not have any close friends, and developed no close bonds with his brother or sister. He blamed what happened at Keyse for making him different from other people. 'Different,' he explained, 'because I'd been involved in something dirty, despite being involuntary. From Keyse onwards, I've always harboured humiliation and shame and, arising from them, anger and a simmering resentment.'

Claims, true or otherwise, of childhood sexual abuse are one of the standard means that perpetrators of sexual violence use to justify their acts.

John's rationalisation of these events came after his life was shattered by his conviction for the murder of Shirley Banks. In Wakefield Prison, contemplating his chances of a successful appeal, he had plenty of time to examine those experiences which might have contributed to his failure. Blaming the system or the actions of others for his own misfortunes has been part of John's *raison d'être* since conviction. But there can be little doubt that he felt traumatised by those early events.

Denied a family environment in which his feelings of shame could be properly explored, he felt anxious and alone, a very unhealthy prospect for a young boy. 'It was after this period,' he said later, 'that I began to commit crime.'

A measure of his disorientation lay in the indecent assault which he committed when he was 14. He accosted a young woman in a telephone kiosk and put his hand up her skirt. His parents were utterly shocked and their son was given 12 months' probation.

John continued his education, although he frequently played truant. He was unhappy at home due, chiefly, to the strict attitude of his father. The time spent in public libraries perhaps helped him to gain five Certificates of Secondary Education (CSEs) and three Ordinary Level General Certificates of Education (GCEs). His athletic prowess won him an offer of a Sports Council grant to train with the Birchfield Harriers, a leading athletic club, but John's father was against the idea.

John left school at 17 and joined the Merchant Navy. This was perhaps a bid to escape from his unhappy family life, but lasted only three months. It is possible that joining the Merchant Navy was an attempt to break the family bonds but, having gone to sea, he may well have found life too restrictive and subject to discipline. He respected his father's engineering background and, through him, developed a life-long love of cars. Mr Cannan was general manager at Reeve & Stedeford, whose prestigious showrooms in Birmingham were filled with the latest models of the famous marques in British car manufacturing. Young John was taken on visits to car factories and later acknowledged his father's influence. 'Through him,' he said, 'I grew enchanted with such names as Austin of England, Morris of Oxford and MG at Abingdon.'

So John became a car salesman in his father's firm but at a difficult time for British manufacturers. Foreign imports, particularly from Japan, were affecting home sales. He regarded it as a matter of pride that he was selling British cars while many of his fellow salesmen had defected to sell imported models.

Those were happy times and he enjoyed the glamour and the people associated with the motor trade. Nevertheless, as he acknowledged later, his real ambition was to have qualified for university entry at 'a really great university like Oxford or Cambridge. Academia is where I really at heart wanted to be.'

As we have seen with Gacy and Bianchi, and it most certainly applies to America's most notorious serial killer Ted Bundy, this unrealistic ideal of one's own potential is frequently a characteristic of men committed to serial violence.

The life of a car salesman had its advantages, of course, and access to cars was one of them. He recalled enjoyable times with the Sutton fast crowd, 'dancing at The Belfry and screaming through the back lanes of Sutton in our Jag, TR7 and Company demonstrators'. John had not the slightest doubt about his abilities at this time. 'We were factory-trained sales executives and responsible for six-figure sales turnovers.'

However, the sad account of his traumatic school abuse and his description as a sales executive come only from the mind and pen of John Cannan. Maybe he was abused at school – we can only take John's word for that. John's bloated opinion of himself is evident in his description of his job; in reality, he was simply a car salesman in the used-car department. He was not 'factory-trained' in sales or motor engineering, nor was he responsible for 'six-figure sales turnovers'.

These 'happy and vibrant times', as John described them, came to an end when he married in May 1978. June Vale, a pretty, home-loving girl with light-brown hair, worked in a florist shop near the garage. She was his one and only steady girlfriend and their engagement lasted seven years.

He claimed later that he had suggested she had other boyfriends before committing herself to marriage, believing this might have alleviated later difficulties, the nature of which he does not explain. The unusually long engagement to June seems at odds with John's later promiscuous activities, but he was very much a loner with few, if any, really close friends.

When they married at Four Oaks Methodist Church, Birmingham, John's younger brother Anthony was the couple's Best Man. John had the customary stag night celebration, but those who attended were mainly Anthony's friends, not his. Yet, if style was anything to go by, the couple had a good start. 'My marriage was motor-trade blessed,' said John, 'with two beautiful dark-blue Rolls-Royce Shadows provided by the company.' Such a blessing it was that no one from the motor trade attended his stag night.

In his view they were 'rushed into marriage', chiefly by June's parents. After seven years, this might be thought rather an odd statement. With all the benefits of hindsight, John claimed, 'I never would have married her but everybody was trying to hassle me into it, her side especially.'

The newlyweds did not have a home of their own, so they went to live with John's parents. They also came under pressure to start a family. John alluded to differences in status between the two families and suggested that his mother-in-law wanted to consolidate her daughter's position with the Cannans.

According to John's account, his wife became pregnant against his wishes and, while he acknowledged that pregnancies could be accidental, he said, 'that one wasn't'. He claimed that June was meticulous in taking the pill, so he thought, 'it was strange that she forgot two weeks after her mum had asked me about when we planned to start a family'. The couple were trying to buy a flat in Minworth and John was seeking to establish a career for himself in the motor trade. 'I really could have done without all that extra trouble,' he said.

Later, writing to me from prison on November 1989, John recalled the pressures of marriage as a turning point in his life. 'That ruined all those previous years of happiness and success.' He said that, from a spiritual point of view, things got on top of him at this point 'and I began to slide downhill'.

Instead of going home after work to join his wife and daughter, Louise, he would lock up the showroom and drive into Birmingham. There he would buy dinner at The Albany or go to The Opposite Lock, a nightclub and rendezvous for the motor trade. He was smoking and drinking heavily. As he put it, 'Booze there most certainly was, and a string of girls and one-night stands.' By 1980, at the age of 26, John was practically an alcoholic.

So already we can see a fatal flaw within the personality of John Cannan, for he lives in a world of psychopathic self-denial. He blames his father for being too authoritarian; he claims to be the victim of his teacher at Keyse for sexually abusing him; he argues that he was pressured into getting married; and he blames his wife for becoming pregnant. And, in this respect, he is like so many other emerging and full-blown serial offenders with an overinflated ego, he is psychologically unable to apportion any of the blame to himself. So, apart from the bitter tragedy he was building for himself, he was also about to snare others in a web of violence.

Partially blaming his family life for ruining his life, John had effectively deserted his wife and daughter by the end of 1979. He worked six days a week and frequently put in two evenings a week at the showroom as well. Social drinking became something more serious and he had begun to slide into alcoholism. 'If you've ever wondered why the Scots are so aggressive,' he wrote, 'it's because whisky has a capacity to affect and radically change your personality and behaviour. Gin, it's true, can make you depressed; whisky, however, just makes you plain nasty, at least to some people it can.'

In February 1980, John thought his fortunes had changed for the better. He walked into an off-licence in Sutton Coldfield and bought a case of wine. It was Valentine's Day and he and the girl behind the counter, Sharon Major (her name has been changed to protect her identity), were immediately attracted to each other. She told me that she remembered John as 'the best-looking man I'd ever met and immediately I had a physical attraction towards him'. They laughed and joked and agreed to meet after work. He followed up by sending roses to the shop and she was won over by his charm. But this was the charm of a budding homicidal maniac and Sharon was lucky to escape with her life.

Sharon was, and still is, a vivacious woman with an open, trusting face, framed by longish fair hair. Aged 32, she was six years older than John. She was married with two children but was on the verge of separating from her husband, although they continued to share the same house. When John asked her out, she accepted and he explained that he was divorced, which was not true at that time, and that he worked as a sales manager at a local car showroom, which was not strictly accurate either. Had he told her the truth, then things might have worked out better.

When his father learned of his son's extra-marital liaison, he took an uncompromising moral line, which John described as 'supercilious'. There was a showdown. John left his job, and he left his wife and daughter.

'I packed my bags,' he said, 'and checked in at Sutton House [a guesthouse in Chester Road, Erdington].' He had stayed there before with one of his previous conquests, and explained his technique by saying, 'Buy 'em a drink, tell 'em I love them, tell 'em they were the best thing since sliced bread, them take them to the Sutton House guesthouse for a cheap night of easily forgettable passion.' However, for a man who could not enjoy his own company, on this occasion, there were no cheap pleasures – he was broke and craving alcohol.

Despite his low state, he and Sharon hit it off and became regular companions. In April 1980, he left the guesthouse and moved in with her and her children. By this time, her husband had left home. For the next six months or so, their relationship seemed to prosper. John had acquired a ready-made family with Sharon's two youngsters, a boy aged four and a daughter aged six. Quite forgetting that he had a wife and a daughter himself, John later wrote, 'I took very seriously my role as their surrogate dad.' He says he bought them toys occasionally and took the little boy to his first football game, Aston Villa v Birmingham City. 'We sat munching hamburgers,' John recollected, 'and he learned how to call the referee a "pillock".' He said the girl was backward for her age and he and Sharon took her to see a specialist at the children's hospital.

They went on trips as a family, including a visit to Blackpool and to Sharon's parents at Ilfracombe. John discovered, as all dads, surrogate or otherwise, know, that entertaining children was expensive. He bought them each a bicycle for Christmas 1980, second-hand machines which he painted up, because funds would not run to new ones.

Their financial problems became more acute when John lost his job through taking a vehicle without authority from the car firm which employed him at the time. Sharon began to realise that a great deal of what John had told her about his background was untrue. She encountered June Cannan in a local Safeway store, who told her that she was still married to John. She had baby Louise with her in a pushchair. Sharon did not challenge him about this immediately as he was busy looking for another job, but she had a new insight into his character. She later described him as 'extremely plausible and convincing'.

Sharon described their sexual relationship as being 'normal, healthy and active'. She regarded him as a demanding lover and he varied his technique. They did not use any sexual aids and bondage was never employed. 'John was what I would describe as a very physical lover,' she said after their relationship had finished. More recently in an interview, she was to alter her previous accounts by stating that he was no great shakes in bed. Harsh words and accusations would later be voiced about the use of 'prosthetics', as John likes to call sexual aids, and of attempts to indulge in anal intercourse. But, by then, their relationship had long been over.

If John was an attentive lover, he was also a jealous one. He claimed that he became fed up with men telephoning Sharon at home while he was there and also with men calling at the house when he was out. One evening, he became so incensed when a male acquaintance phoned Sharon from The Belfry that he leaped into his car and drove off to confront him. He walked into the golfers' lounge at the club and called out the man's name. He was told that he had left. According to John, the man turned up at the house on the following evening and a row ensued in the street. No blows were exchanged, but John, somewhat hypocritically, felt he had done enough to demonstrate that, as he put it, Sharon could not have her cake and eat it, too.

In one of his many letters from prison, John talked of his strong desire to keep the family together 'to forge a more constructive future for us all'. But the odds were not running in his favour. He took a job with a car firm in Bideford, Devon, which Sharon believed was in expectation of her moving to live with her parents in Ilfracombe. Indeed, John spent his weekday nights with her parents and commuted to Sutton Coldfield at weekends.

Sometimes he would stay with his parents in order to see his wife and daughter. The financial implications of sustaining this complicated existence were crippling him. He was, in effect, trying to support two families while living apart from both. He described it as 'pressure with a capital P'. Something had to give and the cracks began to widen in his relationship with Sharon.

John was besotted with Sharon Major and her maturity appealed to him. He was frank about his drinking but he lied to her over his finances. 'She was, or seemed to be, the answer to a prayer,' he said when he moved in to live with her in April 1980. But, as his financial situation crumbled, so his drinking accelerated. He claimed he was paying maintenance to June, supplementing Sharon's income when he could while paying rent on a cottage in Devon in the hope of moving there with Sharon and her children. In addition to this burden, he had to finance his drinking, which now amounted to a bottle of Scotch daily.

Circumstances added pressure to their relationship. They argued about the slightest thing and John was jealous and getting even more paranoid over Sharon's other relationships, which, in reality, amounted to nothing more than mere friendships. On one occasion, he punched her in the face and she got a black eye. 'I realised that there was an extremely evil streak in him,' she said later. She now wanted their relationship to finish but she did not know how, or was too scared, to end it. 'One part of me still wanted to be with him, but common sense told me it had to end.'

Matters came to a head with the approach of Christmas. There was an argument because Sharon's husband was coming to the house to visit the children on Christmas Day and Boxing Day.

'He wasn't going to stay at my house,' said Sharon, 'just visit.'

John took exception to the idea. 'That I strongly objected to,' he said, and he pleaded with Sharon to make a clean break with her husband. After much argument, he lost his case and, as he later described it, 'The upshot was that I spent Christmas alone in a small hotel in Erdington.'

Sharon did not see John again until he turned up at the house on 30 December in the early afternoon with a bottle of wine. She said he suggested 'that we have one more time in bed'. She yielded and he opened the bottle. The way John put it was that Sharon did not want the relationship to end. 'It was me who alluded to it,' he said. 'We went to bed and tried to patch up our differences but we'd both been drinking and started to argue. She said the wrong thing and suddenly I snapped.'

John's description of events seemed to take account of the brittle nature of his own temperament.

What followed was the subject of much bitterness and later recrimination. Sharon's account was that, during intercourse, John put his hands around her neck so that she had difficulty breathing. 'I told him to stop, saying, "Don't, you'll kill me doing that." He said, "I mean to kill you. I'm going to kill you. You've hurt me so badly, I'm going to hurt you, too."'

Sharon was terrified by the fierce expression on John's face. She tried to get off the bed but he held her down by placing his body across hers. She reacted by screaming and punching him about the head; she pleaded with him to stop and think about her children. 'I don't give a fuck about them,' was his menacing reply.

Sharon's recollection was that John then reached out for the plastic bag which he had brought with him into the bedroom and emptied the contents on to the bed. 'There was a vibrator,' she said, 'a gun and a pair of black rubber pants with a false male penis fitted to it.'

He picked up the gun, pointed it at her face and said, 'This is loaded.'

Sharon was now convinced that he intended to kill her. She struggled to seize the weapon and direct it away from her. 'Between us,' she said, 'we pulled the trigger.' As a result, the gun fired an air pellet which lodged in the wall. She recognised the gun as the air pistol they had used during the summer to shoot at targets in the garden. 'I knew that it fired one pellet at a time,' she said.

After Sharon managed to throw the gun on the floor, John tried a different tactic. 'I'm going to screw your backside,' he shouted. He failed in his attempts because she struggled furiously, but he did succeed in twice penetrating her vagina with the vibrator. She began to bleed heavily but, undeterred, he had sexual intercourse with her wearing the false penis.

'He made extremely violent love to me with this thing which hurt me a great deal,' she claimed.

Sharon's screams were heard by neighbours but they turned up their record player to drown out the noise.

The couple were engaged in a grim struggle, with Sharon several times trying to get off the bed. She was bleeding internally and also from the mouth and nose where he had struck her in the face. She grabbed his testicles to try to stop his continuous attack, 'but that just made him more violent than ever... John was so evil,' she said, 'looking almost possessed'.

At one point, she lost consciousness and remembered coming to with John slapping her face, saying, 'I haven't finished with you yet.'

He called her a whore and a bitch and renewed his attempts to penetrate her. Nearing exhaustion after two hours of trying to fend him off, Sharon consented to his demands, provided she could use a lubricant. 'Let me get some Vaseline,' she asked. This was a ploy to get out of the bedroom in the hope of making a dash down the stairs.

With one arm across her neck and the other holding her arm across the back, John 'frog-marched me towards the other bedroom', said Sharon. She found the Vaseline and he began to manoeuvre her back to the main bedroom.

Thinking that he was going to kill her or at least subject her to further sexual abuse and physical attack, Sharon made her move at the top of the stairs. She said afterwards, 'I'd be better off dead or paralysed than face going back into that bedroom.'

Sharon pushed John, causing him to lose balance, and they both fell down the stairs. They tumbled into the stairwell and Sharon hurt her back. 'I couldn't have fought with him any more. I was so physically drained.'

At this point, she recalled later, John reverted to his old self. He was caring and full of apologies. 'Oh my God,' he said, 'what have I done? I'm sorry.'

While he telephoned for an ambulance, Sharon tried to stand up, thinking he was still going to kill her, then she blacked out.

On the way to the hospital in the ambulance, she asked him, 'You really did mean to kill me, didn't you?'

'Yes, I did,' he replied.

Sharon was treated in Casualty and John remained with her until the police arrived. She gave him her house keys and told him to remove 'all his horrible things'. She called a woman friend who drove to the hospital and took her home. By then John had collected and removed the contents of his plastic bag, leaving the house keys behind.

Sharon said that she was battered and bruised with a swollen face and two black eyes. Her facial injuries necessitated treatment on her front teeth and she said that John had pulled out so much of her hair 'that you could have made a wig with what came out'. Her parents travelled up from Ilfracombe to look after her. 'I told both of them about the physical attacks,' she said, 'but I omitted to tell them about the sexual side of the assault.' Her father was shocked at her appearance and hardly recognised her.

Sharon did not report the assault to the police on the grounds that she had no faith in the legal system. She felt that she had only just escaped being killed and that if she lodged any complaint against John 'he might get only a few years' imprisonment' and might 'track me down and finish off what he had started'.

She added that she was afraid he would try to get to her through the children. 'I was absolutely terrified of John.' She regarded the day of the attack as the end of their relationship and resisted John's subsequent attempts at reconciliation.

Her account of the stormy and painful conclusion of her affair with John Cannan came seven years after the event and at a time when he was in police custody. In even the most timid of lovers' tiffs, the partners will disagree over the circumstances. This far more serious encounter was to prove no exception and John's account differed substantially.

In correspondence with me, Cannan referred on many occasions to the assault on Sharon, repeatedly denying that he had made a sexual attack on her. He admitted making what he called a 'serious assault' and acknowledged using a sex aid in the course of lovemaking, which he though probably accounted for the difficulties she subsequently encountered with her vaginal coil. 'The truth is,' he alleged, 'she was an instructive, older and enthusiastic partner.'

He called Sharon's version of events 'tripe', and maintained that she suffered 'terrible emotional insecurity and [sought] acceptance and comfort from as many people as possible, especially men, which tend[ed] largely to make her stray'. Sharon, he said, 'wasn't sugar and spice and all things nice ... but a devious and calculating woman, who frankly couldn't be trusted'. He maintained that her failure to report a sexual assault to the police in 1981 was because no offence had occurred.

His version of events was that he had been incensed over Sharon's decision to have her husband home at Christmas. He also claimed to have discovered that she had been a 'little more than a friend', as he put it, to a male acquaintance. 'Never have I been so angry,' he said, 'I really slagged her off.' He told her their affair was over; they shouted at each other and blows were struck. 'I hit her and I hit her hard ... I wanted to hurt her, I did hurt her.'

John claimed that she exaggerated her injuries and denied that any of her hair had been pulled out. 'So serious were her facial injuries,' he said sarcastically, 'that neither the ambulance man, the hospital doctor or her doctor ... had any recollection of her condition.' He alleged she had 'told a tissue of lies and made herself sound and look extremely silly'. He believed that 'anybody with a modicum of common sense and experience of people and life could not fail to deduce her malice and spitefulness'.

These recollections of events came in letters written to me by John from prison ten years afterwards, while he was facing the prospect of serving a life sentence. He blames Sharon for precipitating the end of their relationship which 'occurred against the background of considerable provocation'. Yet he claimed that he had tried to repair their relationship, using what little money he had to hire a car to drive down to Ilfracombe to find her. 'What I wanted to do,' he claimed, 'was to apologise and get us back as a family again'. This trip proved futile because Sharon was not at her parents' home. In February 1981, he returned to the house at Sutton Coldfield. 'We sat in the kitchen and I begged Sharon to forgive me for hitting her, I was truly sorry.'

Of John's character, Sharon's assessment was that he was really in love with himself. He was 'always looking into the mirror', was vain about his appearance and was clean and well groomed. In fact, women have described John Cannan as being too pretty. She described him as a complete loner, 'very deep, with no friends at all, male or female'. He was a person who lived in a world of his own, but the things he said 'were so plausible and with a degree of the truth in them ... I didn't know what to believe in the end,' she said despairingly. John's vanity was perhaps an outward sign of his inner emptiness and feelings of rage. His self-obsession was clearly indicated in subsequent interviews with the police.

Sharon denied having any other male friends during the time she spent with John. 'I was too scared and frightened of him to do that.' John was always eager to go out when he was with Sharon, whether he had money or not. She paid her share of the expenses and said that she never saw him with large amounts of money.

Of his moods, she claimed, 'As long as everything was going his way, he was nice and charming. He could sell sand to the Arabs, he had that much confidence. When things were against him, then he changed. The evil side of him showed through. He used to flick from one mood to another.'

Having been on the receiving end of his violent mood swings, Sharon was clearly aware of the danger of staying loyal to such an extreme personality.

John was first questioned officially about the sexual assault on Sharon three months afterwards on 14 March 1981 while in custody at Sutton Coldfield Police Station in connection with a later offence. He was interviewed by Detective Sergeant Barry Butler and Detective

Constable Brock Harrison. He acknowledged that he and Sharon had had 'a terrible argument, finishing up with us having an awful fight … I admit that I went too far and hurt her'.

Butler told him that a letter had been found in his flat after a police search. It was addressed to him from Sharon and was dated 26 February 1981. She referred to the incident on 30 December the previous year and described John's conduct as evil, wicked, brutal and depraved. 'From enquiries we have made,' said Butler, 'we believe that you forced Sharon to have sex with you in various positions. Is that right?'

'Well, it's not quite as simple as that,' John replied. He went on to say that they were having a great time in bed when Sharon brought up the subject of her other male friends 'as if to try and upset me'. The result was that he lost his temper and hit her about the head and body. 'I just lost control and went stupid,' he said, and added, 'Looking back on it now, I am ashamed of it and it seems that, although it was me, that it was someone else.'

This was a significant admission which, at face value, was simply a convenient way of making himself remote from the attack. But perpetrators of serial violence are known to experience such feelings. Indeed, Ted Bundy, the US serial killer, talked about his victims as if he were watching a film. DC Harrison asked John if he was saying that, after losing his temper, he assaulted her and forced her to have intercourse against her will and that she objected strongly. He said, 'Yes, she was shouting and hysterical. I just tried to hurt her as she's hurt me.'

DS Butler then asked, 'You are clearly admitting then that you raped her, aren't you?'

In a clear acknowledgement of his actions, he replied, 'Yes, I suppose I did.'

In an effort to be fair to both John Cannan and Sharon Major, I spent much time in researching their accounts and claims of the time they spent together. A great deal of what John has written and said is factually untrue, although he actually believes it to be correct. Sharon Major was undoubtedly swept off her feet by John, a man who could not live up to his overinflated ego. As their relationship developed, so the pressure increased on John to live up to the expectations he had so romantically portrayed to his lover. Slowly, the sands of time expired for him and this resulted in the release of pent-up frustration, culminating in a terrible sexual assault on the young woman.

Cannan has alleged that Sharon's behaviour was a 'contributory factor' and he believes she holds herself partly responsible for the circumstances that led up to another serious sexual offence. In a moment of vehement bitterness, he stated, 'And so in part she bloody well should!'

The incident, which he conveniently externalised by saying, 'We both had to share the blame,' was his rape of a pregnant woman in front of her mother and young son.

At the time of writing, Sharon Major still lives in fear of John Cannan.

True Lies

JEAN was 37 years old and married with a 17-month-old son. She ran a ladies' knitwear shop in Sutton Coldfield. On Friday, 6 March 1981, she opened the shop as usual at 9.30am and served a trickle of customers during the morning. At 12.30pm, she closed the shop and turned the 'Closed' sign round on the door. Her husband collected her and their son and they went off to lunch. They returned at about 2.00pm and Mr Bradford left his wife and toddler in the shop. Forty-five minutes later, Jean would be living the nightmare of her life.

The premises were compact, the shop itself being a room ten feet wide and some fifteen feet deep. At the rear of the premises was a tiny office with a separate door opening on to an alleyway leading to a cluttered backyard. The rear of the shop was dimly lit, the only natural light coming from the front window and through a small skylight. Mrs Bradford found it necessary to have the fluorescent ceiling light switched on all the time she was open for business.

At about 2.15pm, the woman from the shop next door called in for a few minutes' chat and, when she departed, Jean Bradford was left alone with her son. Thirty minutes later, at around 2.45pm, a man entered the shop. He was holding a handkerchief over his face as if to blow his nose. Just at that moment, the telephone in the back office rang and Mrs Bradford made her apologies before going to answer it.

She came out of the office to make sure the customer had not left the front door open, as she was afraid her young son might wander out into the street. Having satisfied herself on this point, she offered further apologies and returned to the telephone. The man mumbled something in reply and kept the handkerchief up to his nose and mouth.

With her son by her side, Jean Bradford had to hold the line while her caller was connected. She put her head round the door of the office and said, 'I'm sorry to be so long. Can I help you?'

The man gave a nervous sort of laugh and walked into the office. He was holding a knife which he pointed at her, saying he would cut her unless she kept quiet.

Then he threatened to cut the boy and, putting his finger on the telephone rest, disconnected the call. Mrs Bradford picked up her son and held him protectively. The man instructed her to go into the corner of the office and face the wall. Still holding her son and with the intruder's knife at her ribs, she did as she was told.

His commands were emphasised by the repeated use of the expletive 'fucking'. He asked her where the cash was kept. She turned round to show him but he made her face the wall again. She explained that the cash box was behind the curtain which screened the office from the shop. Mrs Bradford's son, sensing his mother's fear, began to scream.

'Stop your little girl,' the man told her.

She explained that it was a little boy and the child was frightened and asked if she could give him a drink which was on the table in the shop. The man stood close to her, touching the knife to her face and telling her not to 'fucking move'.

He went into the shop and returned with the child's bottle which he thrust into Jean Bradford's free hand. After having a drink, the child calmed down. The intruder located the cash box and spilled its contents on to the floor where he sorted through the change. He then asked where more money could be found, and she told him there was some in her purse in the shop. Mrs Bradford found difficulty in articulating her words, all the while being threatened with a knife.

Suddenly, the front door of the premises opened and in walked Jean Bradford's mother.

'Tell them that you're closed,' the man instructed.

Jean followed his instructions but her mother only laughed and made straight for the office.

'Who's this?' the man asked.

'It's my mother,' Jean replied.

The two women stood close together while the intruder asked again about money.

'Let my daughter go with the baby,' requested the older woman.

'No,' came the curt reply, accompanied by the threat that he would cut her if she did not keep quiet.

She persisted in her request and Jean could see the man was becoming increasingly nervous. She told her mother to shut up and do as she was told.

The intruder retrieved the purse from the table and brought it into the office. Jean thought it contained £20 in a brown envelope but he couldn't find it. She suggested that it might be in the writing case on the shop table but he couldn't find it there either. 'He was getting really panicky,' said Jean, 'and his voice went up a tone.'

At that moment, the telephone rang. The caller was Jean's husband, who was concerned when his wife did not answer the call. The intruder rendered any discussion meaningless by slashing the telephone wire. Then his mood changed. He told Jean's mother to move into another corner of the office. Then, having cut the cords used for hanging up clothes in the office, he tied her hands together behind her back. Jean could not see what was happening because she was facing the wall, but she gathered from his instructions what he was doing. Having secured her feet, he made the older woman shuffle back into the corner and stand facing the wall.

He then turned his attentions to Jean and began fiddling with her dress. She asked him what he was doing and he replied, 'The best way to tie your legs is to get your tights by your feet.' He then pulled her tights down to her ankles and, lifting her skirt, said, 'Beautiful.' He had already told her to put down the child and now instructed her to lower her knickers. She later told police that she refused but changed her mind when he said, 'Well, you don't want your baby cut.'

He then moved behind her and put his left arm around her neck while holding the knife to her face. He whispered that if she didn't want to 'fucking well get hurt' she was to undo his trousers and give him oral sex.

'Please don't,' she begged, but he became more threatening and ordered her to kneel down in front of him.

He undid his trousers and told her to take out his penis. When she resisted, he pointed the knife towards her child and repeated, 'You don't want the baby to get hurt.'

She complied with his instructions as minimally as possible. 'I did as little as I had to,' she later said in her statement.

The intruder then told her to take off her clothes. Fearing what was to come, she pleaded, 'Please don't, I'm pregnant.'

Jean's mother added, 'Yes, she's pregnant.'

'I don't care what you are, it doesn't matter to me,' he said.

Again, she complied with his instructions but still sought to deflect him. 'Please, no, why are you being so mean?

'You fucking do it or else,' he snapped.

When she was stripped naked, he told her to lie on the floor but, when her son cried, she instinctively leaned across to comfort him. The man shouted, 'All right, stand up,' and, putting an arm around her neck, raped her where she stood in the presence of her son and mother.

On finishing, he told her to pull up her tights and, at that very moment, the front door of the shop rattled as someone tried to attract attention from the street. Jean surmised that it might be a customer.

'Do you know a bearded man?' the attacker asked, having looked out towards the door.

Jean said it might be her husband. She was correct. The door shaking became even more frantic but then stopped. Pointing to the rear door of the office, the man asked, 'How do I get out of here. Is that the way out?'

He was told that it led into an alleyway. Jean found the key and opened the door. Undeterred by the noise which had returned at the front door, the man lingered to tell Jean, 'You might want to know about this … you'll realise later because I'll be dead within a fortnight.' He asked her if she was really pregnant; her mother replied for her, 'Yes.'

He said, 'Well, this won't hurt you then.'

When he asked for her name and address, Jean gave him the details. 'After all,' as she explained later, 'he'd looked into my purse.'

He still lingered, asking where the alleyway led and, on being told it gave access to a car park, asked the two women if they had a car. Jean's mother gave him the keys to her Rover. He then pushed Jean, still half-naked, into the alleyway and told her not to tell the police what had happened for at least two weeks or something would happen to her little boy because he knew where they lived. He then hurried into the yard, vaulted a fence and disappeared.

After this terrifying ordeal, Jean rejoined her mother and son, then let in her husband who was still frantically hammering on the front door. They telephoned 999 and Jean later completed a statement in which she described her rapist.

The description matched John Cannan.

John subsequently rationalised his actions leading up to the rape. Where previously he had blamed his father for provoking him to violence, he now blamed Sharon Major for triggering his aggressive outburst. 'It wasn't the real John Cannan in that shop,' he said, 'but a wretched and distressed one.'

As he had done previously, he sought to distance himself from the event. But he admitted choosing the knitwear shop as a target for robbery because, apart from money, he thought there might be fur coats that he could steal and sell. For a shop that sells only balls of wool, cotton and knitting needles, his explanation is less than convincing.

He further claims that he had no intention of raping anyone when he entered the shop but, when he could not find money or cash that the unfortunate Jean Bradford told him was in the shop, he felt as if nothing was going right and 'I just blew'. In 1987, John would enter another woman's shop in Leamington Spa with rope and a knife, with robbery and rape in mind.

> In some ways, I didn't want at heart to be there. I was scared and I was upset, but I needed money. Everything suddenly rose to the surface, all the bitterness and secret personal misery. I wanted her to feel and share my pain. I wanted to humiliate her like I had been humiliated, I wanted her to lose her innocence. I wanted to make her understand. And there was, of course, only one way to do it. I know how she must have felt.
>
> *John Cannan in a letter to the author*

John was remanded in custody by the Sutton Coldfield magistrates; his solicitor did not apply for bail. On 26 June 1981, he appeared at Birmingham Crown Court where he was jailed for a total of eight years by Mr Justice Stephen Brown. He was sentenced to five years for the rape with consecutive sentences totalling three years for taking a car and stealing money.

Two Appeal Court judges in London heard his appeal against the sentence in November. In rejecting the appeal, Mr Justice Skinner commented that the psychological scars of the rape must be very great. John himself acknowledged this, describing what he had committed as 'an appalling offence'.

Prison apparently gave John Cannan further time for reflection. At Horfield Prison, Bristol, where he was transferred in February 1982 following his conviction for the rape of Jean Bradford, he was housed in 'B' Wing which was reserved for prisoners serving five years or more. It is John's inflated claim that he took pride in being considered sufficiently trustworthy to be given what he called 'the top job in the nick', as the Governor's 'red-band' (trustee). Again, this provides a valuable insight into the workings of his mind. The trustee's job entails acting as an intermediary between the inmate population and the prison staff, similar to that of a foreman on a factory shop floor. The red-band has to be trusted by the cons and screws alike. The nature of John Cannan's offence, the rape of a pregnant woman in front of her child, would have been made known to the prison population on his admission to Bristol Prison.

In reality, John Cannan asked for protective custody (Rule 43) in an effort to save him from harm and assault freely administered by the inmates to known sex offenders. He was labelled a 'nonce' and a 'wrong 'un' by his fellow cons and prison staff. More than once, he was attacked on the landings and had salt tipped into his pudding, sugar thrown over his dinner and was spat at when collecting his meals. John Cannan was never a 'trustee'.

While locked up, Cannan met Annabel Rose. She was a solicitor working for a law firm in the city and she advised him about access rights to his daughter, Louise. Cannan was moved from Horfield and, two days after he arrived at The Verne Prison, Dorset, John received a visit from his father. It would prove to be the last time they saw each other, for Cyril Cannan was terminally ill with cancer. Father and son knew that this would be their last meeting. Much bitterness had passed between them and this was an opportunity to make peace with each other. Mr Cannan passed away peacefully at his home in February 1985 soon after his son embarked on his pre-release programme. 'Did I love him?' asked John in one of his letters. 'Yes, but we fought terribly.'

The good that prison did for John was acknowledged by him when he said, 'It did at least wean me off alcohol, albeit painfully.' For the rest, he found that all his previous ideas about the honesty and fairness of the system were overturned.

One may wonder how a man facing the prospect of eight years in prison will cope with the loss of liberty and how he will use his time. No doubt, John quickly came to terms with being confined; being a loner and very self-contained probably helped. With his keen brain, the world of books and debate appealed to him more than sport or craft pursuits. While these activities might occupy his intellect on a superficial level, the deeper recesses of his mind had to get to grips with his emotions, his ambitions and his sense of self-esteem.

The prison system encourages self-improvement and social rehabilitation in those who opt for it, but it also provides fertile soil for those who turn inwards to the realm of fantasy. There is little doubt that John dreamed of fame and fortune. He wanted to 'be someone' and to acquire the trappings of success – smart clothes, a stylish car and a well-appointed flat, with a lifestyle to match. There is nothing wrong with such aspirations, which are shared by millions, but John started from a poor base in seeking to acquire them.

For one thing, although he was a bright, articulate and plausible person, the only training he had was that of a car salesman, which was a route whereby he could achieve his ambitions quickly. For another, he tended to overrate his talents to the point where he alienated people, instead of drawing them along with him, because he always had to prove he was right; humility was not one of John's virtues.

As he emerged from his term of imprisonment, he probably

realised that the only way he could savour the good life quickly was by allying his natural wit and charm with criminal means. But there was a darker side to his fantasies, too. He bore deep-seated feelings of resentment towards the force which had alienated him from society. Whether he realised it or not, his emotions, while fuelling his ambitious drive, were also preparing to retaliate. He was a man primed for both action and violence, when the opportunity arose or when he was provoked.

Five years passed and, as the time approached for John's release from prison, he was eventually allocated a pre-release hostel in London which he would use as a base to 'start life anew, with the past, whilst not forgotten, put as far as possible behind me'. 'I wanted in short,' he said, 'to regain my dignity, to retain my self-respect.'

He thought his best prospects for work lay in the motor trade and he hoped to resume his career as a car salesman. He wrote to Jack Barclay, the prestige car showrooms in London, to the Bristol Rotary Club and also to car auctions at Poole in Dorset. 'Despite writing from prison,' he said, 'I received replies from them all.' Not surprisingly, they were all a 'no thank you'.

John also had ideas, as he phrased it, of putting 'some matters right'. This included a possible reconciliation with Sharon Major, whom he believed, in his warped mind, 'was only too aware of her own part in the events that led up to the rape offence'. She had written to him in prison and this gave him encouragement to think that future contact was possible.

On 25 January 1986, John Cannan was sent to Wormwood Scrubs Prison on a pre-release scheme. This lasted for six months and, while he was technically in custody, he lived in a hostel close by which gave him a degree of freedom and an opportunity to readjust to life outside prison walls. This prison hostel is seen as a means of relieving the overcrowded prison system and a way of helping low-risk offenders to rehabilitate themselves in the community. The offender's daily routine and movements are still subject to control, and the hope is that, by responding to this more sympathetic regime, the offender will qualify for full release on parole under the supervision of the Probation Service. It is also the case that the pre-release system can be abused. Supervision in the hostels can sometimes be fairly lax.

During this period, John worked for Superhire Limited, a firm which dealt with theatrical properties, whose premises, at that time, were in Telford Way, East Acton, a short distance from the prison. The firm has since ceased trading. John said, 'They thought the world of me, they didn't want me to go,' but, in truth, his employers had discovered that he gained employment with them by giving false references and that he was also a convicted rapist. As a measure of their deep-seated affection for John, they sacked him immediately.

Although he did not have a car of his own while he was lodged at the prison hostel, he borrowed one. John confirmed this in one of his letters, when he wrote, 'The hostel hired on a favour basis a red Ford Sierra belonging to the hostel inmate cook whose home was in London.' The owner of this vehicle is now dead; however, in the more recent investigation into the murder of Suzy Lamplugh, the police read John's letters, provided by the author, and were able to recover the car and subject it to a thorough forensic examination.

There is evidence to suggest that on May Day Bank Holiday weekend in 1986, John was either given a lift by the hostel cook, or he borrowed his car to drive to the Bournemouth area. He might have gone to Poole and the car auctions there, to follow up his application for employment, which would be refused.

John knew the New Forest and Southampton areas like the back of his hand. He would often walk through the woods for relaxation, and used to drink at Bucklers Hard, near Beaulieu. All this he subsequently confirmed in letters.

In his letters to this author, Cannan is adamant that he has only ever

JOHN DAVID GUISE CANNAN

visited Poole twice, once to a car auction in September or October 1986, and once on a trip with Gilly Paige, the ice-skater, whom he befriended a few months before abducting and murdering Shirley Banks. He consistently denies that he made three or more visits to Poole, and specifically the trip on this Bank Holiday weekend.

While rummaging through John Cannan's personal effects at Bristol Police Station, I came across a crumpled 'Pay & Display' ticket, which had been overlooked, or regarded as insignificant, by the Shirley Banks murder squad. This ticket is for Poole in Dorset over a Bank Holiday weekend, a time when Cannan denies being in the area.

On 3 May, the Saturday preceding Bank Holiday Monday, a 27-year-old woman, Sandra Court, was murdered. Sandra had been working for the Abbey Life Insurance Company in Bournemouth. At the beginning of May 1986, she left her job and planned to take up a post in Spain as a nanny. She attended a farewell party at the seedy Steppes Nightclub on Friday, 2 May, and got very drunk.

When the club closed, Sandra wanted to continue to celebrate, but her friends had had enough. Another woman, Carol Rylands, ordered a taxi for Sandra, who was so intoxicated she couldn't use a phone.

The cabbie, Stephen Williams, would tell the police that he dropped her off at the home of her sister Jennifer in Downton Close on the Muscliff Estate, at about 2.45am. The address was about a mile from her home where she lived with her parents. Jennifer's house was in darkness and no one would answer the door. 'I don't like leaving women alone like that at night,' the taxi driver later told the Coroner's Court, adding that he had offered to drive her to another address at no extra charge. Sandra had refused, so Williams drove away. He recalled that she was carrying a jacket, handbag and her shoes.

A number of other sightings were made of Sandra during those early hours, then, at about 4.15pm the same day, a group of schoolboys found the body of a dead woman in a stream not far from the Avon Causeway. The boys were standing by the side of a reasonably busy, narrow road which is bordered by meadows and light woodland. The lads were in an agitated state and, at first, tried to stop a man on a cycle, who strangely ignored them, so they flagged down a passing motorist, who called the police. The body was removed to the mortuary, although, in a somewhat remarkable blunder, scenes-of-crime officers did not attend the scene until the next day. Police who recovered the body of Sandra, who was partially naked, assumed that the woman might have simply fallen into the small stream of running water and drowned.

At the subsequent post-mortem examination, it was determined that the woman had died as a result of strangulation by ligature. The ligature was seemingly slight and there was no evidence of defensive marks around the neck caused by the victim's nails or hands, as would have been the case if she had fought to reduce the tightening of the noose as it encircled her neck.

There was no evidence of rape or sexual intercourse. But this did not mean that some form of sexual assault did not take place, for the cold running water may have rinsed away any intimate trace material. There was a slight injury to Sandra's head and the police now believed that this may have been caused during the disposal of the body, as it was heaved over the railings and into the ditch.

The examination could not approximate the time of death. The chill factor, due to immersion in fresh running water, ruled out a body temperature reading, and an examination of the stomach contents and digestive system proved inconclusive. However, the pathologist could say that she was dead before entering the water because no evidence of drowning was present.

Ten days after the murder, a letter posted in Southampton was sent to DCI Rose of Dorset CID who was leading the murder inquiry. Its contents suggested that the death was an accident and that the killer was truly sorry. Examination of the letter revealed that the writer, although right-handed, completed the note with his left hand in an effort to disguise the authorship.

In due course, Cannan was interviewed about his movements that weekend. He has said that the police are satisfied that he was not involved, and this is patently untrue. DI Stent did confirm that they knew that Cannan had been in Poole at the time of the murder, and that Dorset Police had interviewed the hostel cook.

John Cannan is adamant that he had never met Sandra Court. He has said that he has found it 'difficult to understand what basis people are using in trying to suggest my complicity'. But the coincidence of his knowing the area well, and of probably being there that very weekend, cannot be ignored.

John Cannan was released from prison and the hostel on 25 July 1986. Three days later, an event occurred in west London, a tragic mystery involving the disappearance of a young woman called Suzy Lamplugh, which commanded national headlines for several weeks.

Although not suspected at the time as being her abductor, suspicion against him grew to the point at which police said he was the only suspect. Once again, the nature of the incident, coupled with knowledge of his movements, drew John into the web of suspicion, as would his scores of letters to the author.

THREE

Desperately Seeking Suzy

JUST before lunchtime on Monday, 28 July 1986, a young estate agent left her office in Fulham Road, west London, to meet a client. Her name was Suzy Lamplugh and her disappearance has been in the news ever since.

Suzy, a vivacious 25-year-old blonde, was described as a 'smashing girl'. She had worked for Sturgis, the estate agency, for 16 months and was regarded as ambitious and responsible. Suzy was also a fun-loving, somewhat naïve young woman who lived on the edge of her financial means. She was sexually confident in male company, she enjoyed a number of lovers and had been known to sleep with two other men at one time.

Suzy Lamplugh enjoyed the company of men from all walks of life, and it can be said that she had a number of what might be called 'shady friends'. On the Saturday before she went missing, she was dancing with a stockbroker who had been fined for insider dealing. From this, we can establish that Suzy liked the rough with the smooth. From all accounts, John Cannan was certainly smooth.

Suzy's arrived at work that Monday morning at the usual time and busied herself with the office routine, then, shortly before 12.45pm, she received a telephone call from her bank. The previous Friday evening, Suzy had been dining at Mossop's Restaurant in Upper Richmond Road. When she left, she had inadvertently dropped her chequebook, pocket diary and a postcard on the steps. These items were found by Kenneth Heminsley, the acting landlord of The Prince of Wales public house in Upper Richmond Road, who duly reported the find to Suzy's bank on the Monday.

Upon receiving the bank's telephone call informing her that her property had been found, Suzy then called the pub and spoke to Heminsley. An arrangement was made for her to collect the pocket diary, postcard and chequebook at 6.00pm that evening. She never arrived.

When Suzy left her office for the last time on Monday, 28 July, she took with her the keys to a property at nearby 37 Shorrolds Road. Her office diary recorded the essential details of the appointment: '12.45, Mr Kipper – 37 Shorrolds Road o/s'. The annotation 'o/s' indicated that she planned to meet the prospective client outside the house. Mark Gurdon, the office manager, expected that Suzy would soon be back at her desk, probably bringing a lunchtime sandwich.

As the hours of Monday afternoon ticked by and Suzy still had not returned, her office manager's anxiety increased. Protracted absence without a contact telephone call was not Suzy's style. At about 5.00pm, Gurdon telephone Suzy's mother, Diana, and explained his concern. She asked if he had been to the house in Shorrolds Road. He had, of course, made this obvious check and established that Suzy was not there. The occupant of a neighbouring residence recalled seeing a young couple at number 37; he thought they were prospective buyers. He described the man as handsome, aged between 25 and 30 years, of medium height, clean-shaven with dark hair and wearing a dark suit. The man attracted his attention and he had taken little account of the woman.

Mark Gurdon did not know of a client named Mr Kipper. This was not unusual, for in a busy estate agent's office, prospective clients constantly called in or telephoned for appointments to view properties. Suzy had followed accepted practice by recording the appointment in her desk diary. Gurdon phoned the local hospitals to ask if an accident had been reported involving Suzy Lamplugh, but he drew a blank.

He telephoned Suzy's flat several times and returned to Shorrolds Road, all to no avail. His mounting concern was further heightened when he spoke again to the occupant of number 35, who now said that the couple he had seen were arguing and he thought that the man had bundled the woman into the car, although this later turned out to be an exaggeration.

Nevertheless, the police responded immediately. Details of Suzy's company car, a white Ford Fiesta, registration number B396 GAN, were circulated and two detective officers were dispatched to 37 Shorrolds Road. A search of the house produced nothing of significance and the detectives, accompanied by Mr Paul Lamplugh, Suzy's father, moved on to her two-bedroom flat in Putney. Again, nothing was found to help their search.

The first breakthrough, a disturbing one, was the discovery that night of Suzy's car, apparently abandoned, in Stevenage Road near Fulham football ground and running parallel to the Thames. It is a residential, no-through road. Fulham Football Club's ground and various warehouses and garages lie between Stevenage Road and the river. The spot was about a mile from Shorrolds Road and there was every indication that the vehicle had been left in great haste. It was badly parked, the handbrake was off and the driver's door was unlocked; the missing girl's straw hat was on the parcel shelf behind the rear seats and a purse nestled in the driver's door pocket.

Suzy's then boyfriend, a 27-year-old insurance broker, and her male flatmate were both questioned by police. They had each spent time in the company of business associates or friends and had well-corroborated accounts of their movements. Consequently, they were soon eliminated from further enquiries.

By this time, the police were treating the estate agent's disappearance as a major inquiry and DCS Nicholas Carter was appointed senior investigating officer. Police dogs and their handlers began to search the area around Shorrolds Road and Stevenage Road. Drains were opened in the hope of finding the missing keys to 37 Shorrolds Road and an artist's impression was created of the man seen with Suzy outside the empty house. It was possible that this might help to identify the mysterious Mr Kipper.

Forensic officers at the Metropolitan Police Forensic Science Laboratory at Lambeth subjected the white Ford Fiesta – which had been found directly opposite another house up for sale by Sturgis – to microscopic investigation. While fingerprint impressions and trace evidence were painstakingly examined, more immediate information was being gathered by officers conducting house-to house enquiries. Then an individual telephoned the police saying that she lived in a house in Stevenage Road, and almost opposite the spot where Suzy's car had been found. Mrs Wendy Jones told police that she had seen a white Ford Fiesta there on Monday at about 12.45pm. The vehicle was still there a couple of hours later and, when she returned from the cinema at about 10.30pm that evening, the car was surrounded by policemen.

These observations from a person judged to be a reliable witness put the cat among the pigeons. The timing was such that Suzy's car must have been driven straight to Stevenage Road immediately she left her office at 12.40pm; there was insufficient time to have driven first to Shorrolds Road and then to the spot opposite Wendy Jones's house.

The possible permutations of Suzy's movements on that afternoon were somewhat extended when Barbara Whitfield, a partner in a flat-finding company and a friend of Suzy's, claimed she had seen the missing girl on Monday afternoon. Barbara was cycling along Fulham Palace Road towards Putney when she saw Suzy driving in the opposite direction. 'I waved but she didn't see me,' she said. There was a man sitting next to Suzy and the time was about 2.45pm. 'I was absolutely certain it was her,' said Whitfield, who had known Suzy for five months. 'We would go and look at flats together and she was one of my best contacts.'

But there was something even more sinister that came to light. Some time during the afternoon that Suzy went missing from the streets of south-west London, a woman, who gave her name as Sarah, telephoned Heminsley at The Prince of Wales pub, and left a message for Suzy (apparently for when she turned up at the pub) to ring her at a number which he wrote down. A while later, a man also spoke to him on the phone, saying he was a policeman.

The genuine detectives to whom he told all of this were aghast, for they knew that no policemen could have phoned Heminsley on the afternoon she went missing – well before the disappearance had been reported to the police. Heminsley was adamant, too, that he had given the scrap of paper on which he had written the name and number to the police when he was interviewed a day or so later. But the squad certainly had no such piece of paper, which could possibly have been of immense importance. Nor could they trace the mysterious Sarah. Was the call made by Suzy herself, possibly under duress from 'Mr Kipper'? Was it a plea for help? Was the 'policeman' whom Heminsley said phoned him really the abductor himself?

It was all very baffling, especially as the two detective constables who had first interviewed Heminsley (soon after Suzy went missing) strongly insisted that they were not given any such piece of paper. The two officers were valued and trusted members of the investigative team.

From this, it is clear that only a very small number of people could have known that Suzy had made an appointment to meet Heminsley at 6.00pm that evening as her call to him was the last thing she did before rushing out of the office; it could only have been known to a member of the office staff, Heminsley, or a man and a woman whom Suzy encountered some time that Monday afternoon.

Today, the officers charged with investigating the Suzy Lamplugh case strongly believe that Kenneth Heminsley, a patently honest and straightforward person, was telling the truth. But the police also believe that the woman called 'Sarah' who made the first call was checking up on Suzy and a man she knew to be in her company. Indeed, Sarah was checking to find out if Suzy was with her killer. That man, they suspect, was John David Guise Cannan, the man who posed as the policeman.

Within hours, the Lamplugh family were besieged by phone calls from friends and the press started knocking on their door. Then, just 48 hours after Suzy disappeared, the Lamplughs received an unsolicited telephone call from John Bowron who was none other than the Secretary-General of the Law Society and Paul Lamplugh's boss. Bowron suggested the family consult a top lawyer – maybe someone like Sir David Napley. Lamplugh duly phoned Napley, the 71-year-old former President of the Law Society, who was one of the best-known solicitors in the country. A millionaire, Napley immediately agreed to cancel his appointments, urgently suggesting that Paul and Diana Lamplugh have lunch with him. That afternoon found the Lamplughs eating in a Chinese restaurant in Covent Garden with Napley, who was accompanied by two of his partners.

It seems that the Lamplughs were keen to employ the services of a private detective to search for Suzy, and Sir David dissuaded them. However, he assured them of his concern and said he was there if they needed more help. Suzy's disappearance had certainly aroused the interest of the world's media and the intervention of such distinguished solicitors as Bowron and Napley.

More evidence came to light when Suzy's office manager revealed that a bunch of roses had been delivered to Suzy at her office by a mystery man just days before she disappeared. Also, the owner of 35 Shorrolds Road now claimed that the man he had seen with Suzy was carrying what appeared to be a bottle of champagne. The plot was thickening and, as the hunt for Suzy dragged on with no results, the focus of attention inevitably shifted to her personal life.

She had trained as a beautician and worked at a Chelsea salon called Face Place. Her social aspirations probably classified her as a 'Sloane Ranger' but, after her 21st birthday, she decided to broaden her horizons by taking a job as a beautician on board the cruise liner *QE2*. The newspapers naturally speculated on her supposedly active love life.

Meanwhile, further confusing evidence came from eyewitnesses as the police reconstruction, which was broadcast on television, bore further fruit. Nicholas Boyle, an unemployed jeweller, claimed he saw Suzy on the day she disappeared standing outside number 37 Shorrolds Road with a smartly dressed man. He was vague about the time, saying it was between noon and 4.00pm, but precise about describing the man. Boyle's description was of a person wearing a charcoal-grey suit.

Another witness said he saw a young woman meeting a man outside the house in Shorrolds Road. His description fitted Suzy Lamplugh and the man was thought to be aged between 26 and 32. The man was described as good-looking and exceptionally well dressed. It is possible to see similarities between John Cannan and 'Mr Kipper', for apart from the photofit likeness between the two men, other similarities include an exceptional taste in clothing, a dark suit, dark hair, age, height, that they are handsome and their build.

New witnesses were coming forward at a bewildering rate but their well-intentioned information only accentuated the fragmented story the Metropolitan Police had already compiled. Some time before her disappearance, Suzy casually mentioned that she could be receiving approximately £3,000 on a property sale. In order for this commission to be received legitimately through Sturgis, the sale would have to well exceed the £1 million threshold. Sturgis had no such properties on its books at that time. This leaves the possibility of

Suzy being involved, without her employers' knowledge, in a private deal or something illegal. There was a massive Bristol–London mortgage fraud in progress at this time, and £3,000 would be commensurate with commission on a back-to-back property fraud.

There was also information received that Suzy was having a relationship with a man who claimed he lived in Bristol. It was alleged that Suzy said that this mystery man was a property speculator who had an expensive flat in London. However, when Suzy learned that this man, who liked to cook, might have been married, she dumped him. It is known that this man was still pestering Suzy with calls and flowers up to nine days before she disappeared.

The police theory at that time was that Suzy made the appointment to see Mr Kipper, when a man giving that name came into the estate agent's office on Saturday, 26 July because she was working at the weekend. On 28 July, she drove to Shorrolds Road to meet the prospective client as agreed and may have shown him around the property. Mr Kipper spoke to Suzy on the pavement outside and then used some ploy to persuade her to give him a lift to Stevenage Road, where there was another Sturgis property up for sale, and where his car was parked. At some point en route, his charm disappeared and, when they reached Stevenage Road, he threatened her sufficiently to force her into another vehicle which was parked in the street. At this point, she was spirited away and with her went the keys to 37 Shorrolds Road.

Like all such theories, it had inherent weaknesses and it did not – or perhaps could not – embrace all the evidence. The idea that an agile young woman could be abducted in a London street in broad daylight seemed preposterous. That such an incident could occur in a residential thoroughfare and within yards of two men working in the street seemed even more unbelievable. Moreover, there was the statement made by Barbara Whitfield that she had seen Suzy driving her car with a male passenger beside her at 2.45pm that same afternoon.

Nevertheless, the core of the theory, that Suzy had been lured away by a man demonstrating all the normal behaviour of a potential house purchaser, whose charm had turned to menace, had the sound of reality about it. Such a scenario could also explain the events leading up to the abduction and murder of Shirley Banks.

After Shirley Banks's disappearance from a busy shopper's car park in central Bristol on 8 October 1987, the telephones and telex machines began to hum between the Avon and Somerset Constabulary and the Metropolitan Police. Detectives from London visited the so-called 'Bride Squad' at the police headquarters in Bristol. Similarities were noted between the cases of the two missing women and the thought grew in the minds of the detectives that they might be looking for the same man. There the thought might have remained, but John Cannan's correspondence creates further suspicions.

John was sent to a pre-release hostel at Wormwood Scrubs in Du Cane Road, London W12, following his sentence for the rape committed in Sutton Coldfield. The hostel is situated about three miles from the office in which Suzy Lamplugh worked in Fulham Road, SW6. He started to work and, at this time, he was nicknamed 'Mr Kipper' by his fellow hostel inmates because of his preference for wearing kipper-style ties, which were fashionable at the time. The *Observer*, in its fifth-anniversary report of Suzy's disappearance, noted that John Cannan had borne the nickname 'Kipper' long before she made the headlines.

John was finally released from the hostel on Friday, 25 July 1986, three days before Suzy was abducted. He admits he used to frequent two local wine bars also visited by Suzy, one being the Crocodile Tears just across the road from where she worked. While the world of the Wormwood Scrubs hostel and that of Suzy Lamplugh may seem socially miles apart, geographically only three miles separated them.

In John, we are, of course, on face value, dealing with an opportunist.

But there is also the distinct possibility that Suzy's abduction was part of something much larger. And Suzy's mother, Diane, has gone on record as saying that she thinks that her daughter's abduction and murder was 'a professional job'.

If this was an opportunist abduction, while John was at the hostel he knew that the place to find wine bars and the kind of girls he found attractive was Fulham. John's favoured lifestyle encompassed the wine bar rather than the public house. Colonel Jasper's or the Crocodile Tears, with their 'yuppie' connotations, were much more his milieu than the Rose and Crown or Pig and Whistle.

When first asked to account for his movements during the period from 25 to 28 July 1986, he maintained he could not remember. After he was released from the hostel on Friday, we know that he didn't return to his mother's home in Sutton Coldfield until late Monday night or early Tuesday, so where did he stay and, more importantly, whom did he stay with?

The artist's drawing of a man seen in the company of Suzy Lamplugh could be taken for John. Moreover, the description of the man's height, age, build, colour of hair, good looks and style of clothing, though general in nature, are true of John.

We know from John's record that he was both an opportunist and a schemer. He often approached young women with spurious chat about property and talk of being a businessman. He was also perfectly capable of trawling for victims and effecting abduction as his later actions demonstrated. His easy charm was one of his most disarming characteristics. It worked with Sharon Major and every other girlfriend he met – this easy manner had been well polished.

At the time of her disappearance, John was moving around the general neighbourhood in which she worked. He was, to some degree, mobile to the extent that he had access to a borrowed car. It is hard not to wonder about the false number plate which he had made up and fixed to Shirley Banks's Mini. John claims in his letters to the author that he chose the number SLP 386S, at random. Is it pure fantasy to note that you can read the number plate as Suzy Lamplugh (SLP), who would have been his third victim (3) and the year of her abduction 19(86). By the same logic, Dan Kipper 'becomes' (kidnapper), all of which John strongly denies.

John has consistently claimed that the Metropolitan Police have ruled him out as a suspect. This claim somewhat flies in the face of more recent events as Cannan was recently arrested in Wakefield Prison, where he is serving a natural life sentence for the murder of Shirley Banks, and taken to Belgravia Road Police Station in London, where he was interviewed at length by DI Stuart Auld of the Metropolitan Police Serious Crimes Group.

Suzy's mother, Diana, was reported as saying she suspects Cannan killed her daughter. As more recent events now prove, Cannan has been named by the police as their only suspect.

In a letter referring to an article in a Sunday newspaper highlighting the circumstance around Suzy's murder, John stated, 'Everybody is now firmly convinced I killed Suzy Lamplugh. I haven't.'

Making straightforward statements that can be readily corroborated is not John Cannan's style. After all, even the skills of a senior detective over 20 hours of questioning in the face of incontrovertible evidence of guilt regarding the murder of Shirley Banks could not elicit an admission from him. His continuing denial of her murder is unbelievable and unacceptable, even when new developments in DNA analysis have proved beyond any doubt that Cannan murdered Shirley Banks. So should we accept his denial over Suzy?

John has admitted to the author that he is withholding certain information about a number of unresolved issues. His reason for doing so is to enable him to remain in control. 'Information is power' is how he puts it.

John fears that, if he releases his 'information', he might be murdered in prison, and this has a ring of truth about it. In the light of his remark – 'information is power' – his letters clearly point the finger of guilt at others who were known to him, and that is why he cannot, or will not, account, for his movements during the three days before and encompassing Suzy's abduction. But the police suspect Cannan was in the area of Suzy Lamplugh's office around the time she disappeared.

FOUR

Sex Drive

ON Monday, 6 October 1986, at about 1.00pm, an attempt was made to abduct a young woman in Whiteladies Road, Bristol. This offence took place a few minutes' walk from Leigh Woods where John Cannan eventually took up residence. This attempted abduction occurred a year to the day before a similar attempt to abduct Julia Holman in Bristol.

The victim, who was not named by the police, reported the attempted abduction and made a statement including a photofit description. The photofit was not unlike John Cannan. A suspect was rapidly arrested, interviewed and then released. This man was not John Cannan. Nevertheless, John's bank statements reveal that, at 1.31pm that day, he withdrew £25 from a cashpoint dispenser at Lloyds bank in Clifton. This transaction placed him close to the scene of the offence and within 30 minutes of its occurrence. Later in the day, he withdrew cash from an ATM in London. Then he returned, via Reading, to Bristol.

During the late evening of Monday, 6 October, a rape occurred in the Berkshire town of Reading. Donna Tucker had been watching a video recording of the disgraced Sir Jeffery Archer's *First Among Equals* with a neighbour at her home on the outskirts of Reading. At about 10.30pm, she retired to bed, but an argument ensued with her husband, Gerry. They had recently returned from a holiday in Egypt where they had picked up a gastric infection. As a result, they were both tired and the argument concerned Gerry's decision to go to bed earlier than usual.

Donna climbed into bed but could not settle down. Eventually, the 30-year-old decided to get up. She dressed in a yellow jumper and blue skirt, then went out of the house to calm down. It was a cool night and Donna reflected that she and Gerry had been married for four years and, although their relationship was a good one, they occasionally had tiffs for which their antidote was that one of them went out to 'cool off'.

On this particular occasion, Donna took a book with her and went for a drive in the family's Vauxhall Cavalier. She drove down Langley Hill, along the A4 and turned into Chantry Green off the Sava Centre roundabout. After parking under a street lamp, she turned off the engine and listened to the radio while reading her book. She recalled hearing the midnight news on BBC Radio 2 and, afterwards, heard footsteps approaching the car.

Looking into her rear-view mirror, Donna noticed a man walking along the footpath on the opposite side of the road. He walked past the car. About three or four minutes later, she saw the man again walking towards the Sava Centre roundabout. She went back to her book and looked up again when she was aware of someone approaching the car.

Her driver's side window was open. The man spoke to her. 'Excuse me,' he said, 'can you tell me where Balfour Drive is?'

Donna replied, 'I'm sorry, I'm afraid I don't…'

'It's supposed to be around here somewhere. I've been walking around here for quite a while.' They conversed briefly about Balfour Drive with the man looking up and down the road.

'Have you got an *A to Z* in the car?' he asked.

Donna glanced over her shoulder into the back of the Cavalier and, as she did so, was aware that he was reaching for the door handle. He opened the door and said, 'Don't make a fucking move, or noise... See this knife? If you don't do as you're told, you'll get this in your gut.' He was holding a knife with a blade four inches long.

Donna was terrified, but she had worked in a building society where staff were advised always to give in to any demand rather than risk violence. She had also worked for the Red Cross in Uganda where threats of violence were commonplace. She said, 'What do you want?' thinking the man was after money or her jewellery.

'I just want sex,' he replied. 'Get in the back of the car. Get down on the fucking floor.'

She did as she was ordered as slowly as possible in the hope that a passer-by might appear whose attention she could possibly attract. She clambered into the back seat with some difficulty due to her heavy build and the position of the passenger seat which was set back as far as it could go. The man climbed into the driver's seat and started the car. She noted that he was carrying a carrier bag, and had pulled a blue-knitted balaclava over his head. He asked where the headlamp switch was located, then, after making a U-turn in Chantry Green, drove towards the A4. He repeated that she would not get hurt if she did as she was told.

As they drove away, the attacker asked Donna what her name was. She replied 'Jane', but then thought better of it, for she realised he would discover the truth if he rifled her handbag. 'No, I'm sorry,' she said, 'I lied to you... it's Donna.'

When they reached the A4, he asked, 'Where's the fucking countryside?'

She asked what kind of countryside, and he replied, 'Somewhere dark and quiet. Just carry on along this road.'

She asked him what his name was, and he replied, 'Don't be silly,' and then said, 'No, OK… you can call me Horse.'

When they reached junction 12 on the M4 motorway, Donna directed him towards Theale. They turned off into the Theale Industrial Park and stopped next to a rubbish skip. There were a few security lights around the factory premises adjacent to the car park where they stopped, leaving the car in partial darkness.

The attacker instructed Donna to remove her knickers and he climbed over the front seats to join her in the back. Lifting his balaclava, he kissed her several times on the mouth and then ordered her to perform oral sex. She attempted to masturbate him first in the hope of relieving his sexual tension. He told her to stop fooling around and then attempted sexual intercourse with her lying awkwardly in the back seat. This failed, so he forced Donna to move into the front passenger seat which was now racked down into a reclining position. Straddling her, he said, 'You've not been raped yet.' Then he entered her, groaning and calling her by name. 'Now you've been raped,' he panted.

When he had finished, he sat back in the driver's seat. He told her not to look at him; she was so distressed she could not close her eyes and, to comply with his wishes, put her hands over her eyes. While she rearranged her clothing, she asked him what he was going to do. He said he would take her back to the place where he had found her, adding, 'But we're not finished here yet.'

From the carrier bag he produced a pair of white gloves. Donna recalled that they were too large for his hands. He wiped the steering wheel, the window winders and handles on the driver's and passenger side of the car.

He then asked, 'Has your husband ever fucked you up the arse?'

Donna said, 'No,' to which he replied, 'I haven't got AIDS.' He produced a tube and explained that it was KY jelly. He applied it to her anus and told her she would have to guide him in. Having enquired if he was 'on target', he entered her, groaning in excitement before he ejaculated.

When he finished, he gave her some tissue to wipe herself and fumbled around on the floor looking for the cap of the KY jelly tube. Donna lit up a cigarette and offered him one. Then he started the car and began to drive back towards Reading. At some point in their conversation, he mentioned that his wife had died two-and-a-half years previously.

'I'm sorry about that,' Donna replied. 'Have you any other children?'

'I had,' he replied. He seemed anxious to talk and kept asking Donna if she was all right. For her part, she was keen to keep the conversation going in the hope of finding out more about her rapist. But he wouldn't say whether he lived in the area.

As they approached Reading town centre, Donna asked him where he wanted to go, suggesting the railway station or perhaps the bus station. He said he knew where he was, explaining that he had come to Reading to see someone and had parked his car in the town. He drove on to the inner distribution road and turned left into Abattoir Road just before the railway bridge. Abattoir Road is a dead-end running parallel to the railway line. He stopped the car a little way down the road and instructed Donna to 'get out and brush down the seats'. She did as she was told while he once again wiped the steering wheel with his gloves. Kissing his rape victim on the lips, he said, 'Goodbye, Donna, take care and be good… and if you can't be good, be careful.' With that, he strolled off into the night clutching his carrier bag.

Gerry Tucker had dozed off after Donna left the house but woke up at about 1.25am when the family dog started to bark. Donna had returned. He stood on the landing as she mounted the stairs calling out to him, 'I've been raped.' She was terribly distressed, although coherent, and told him in detail what had happened.

Before contacting the police, Gerry looked inside the car. He noticed that the towel normally kept on the rear seat for the dog to sit on had been screwed up in a corner. Realising there might be important evidence in the vehicle, he decided not to use it to drive

Donna to the police station; instead, he went to the phone and reported the incident.

In her statement to the Thames Valley Police, Donna described the rapist as a white male in his late twenties or early thirties. He was of average height and slim build; he had collar-length dark hair and dark 'five o'clock shadow' around his face. His eyes were dark and his eyebrows 'met in the middle'. He was wearing a dark, two-piece business suit with a light-coloured shirt which was open at the neck as he had loosened the knot on his striped tie. The plastic carrier bag in which he kept the KY jelly and the gloves were plain white. Donna said that he was well spoken and, although she could not place his accent, the way he said 'somethink' or 'nothink' suggested a northerner.

Within five hours of the rape, Donna and her husband accompanied WPC Angela Balcombe to the KUKA factory car park at Theale Industrial Park and pointed out the location where she had been raped. Later that day, detectives visited the scene and conducted a search of the area in which Donna's car had been parked. Scenes-of-crime officers collected a number of cigarette ends and two used tissues.

At Reading Police Station in Castle Street, Donna Tucker was asked to hand over the clothing which she had worn when she was assaulted. The yellow jumper, blue skirt, slip, shoes, bra and pants were sealed into clear plastic crime bags. Her pants, labelled AJB/6 – a pair of white M&S white knickers – were later destined to become a crucial item of evidence. Donna also handed detectives another tissue which she had used to wipe her vagina. This, too, was sealed in a bag and labelled AJB/7.

Next, Donna was examined by the police surgeon, Dr Manhar Lal Swami at his surgery in Russell Street. WPC Balcombe was present during the examination. The doctor found no injuries or bruises either on her body or around the genital area. Specimens taken for forensic purposes included saliva, vagina and anal swabs, blood, head and pubic hair and fingernail scrapings.

The Tuckers' Vauxhall Cavalier was taken to the Home Office

Forensic Science Laboratory at Aldermaston where it was minutely searched for trace evidence. No semen was found but tapings of loose debris on the car seats were taken and retained for future reference. All the samples collected at the scene of the crime, together with Donna's clothes and the specimens she had provided, were examined by John Bark, one of the laboratory's forensic scientists. He discovered traces of semen on the anal swabs and semen staining on the slip, skirt and knickers. Tests showed the presence of type-A blood group substance in the semen traces.

DNA would later link directly to John Cannan. In the meantime, he remained at large.

John moved into a bedsit in Richmond Hill in Bristol and on 30 November 1986 he returned to Sutton Coldfield where he stayed with his mother. In August 1987, he had a telephone call from his solicitor, Jim Moriarty, asking him to drop in at the office. He was told that the Reading CID wished to see him again. After speaking to DC Higgins, he agreed to travel down to Reading with Moriarty on 30 April. The next day, he attended an ID parade and Donna Tucker failed to pick him out.

Further trips to Bristol were financed by a gift of £5,000 from a distant relative, John Perks, who had been the chairman of a successful engineering company in Sutton Coldfield. In addition, when his father died, John inherited £2,000 which had been set aside to help him get back on his feet.

Despite these windfalls, John had no compunctions about his resolve to make money illegally. He claimed that his return to Bristol was largely due to solicitor Annabel Rose, who offered him the prospect of some work which involved setting up financial investment channels. This, according to John, was due to begin in December 1987.

One of John's favourite haunts in Bristol before he took the flat at Foye House in Bridge Road was the Avon Gorge Hotel. It was there, on 14 June, that he met Gilly Paige, an attractive, 24-year-old showgirl. She was a former Olympic ice-skater and was taking time off from the *Holiday on Ice* show. John had met Annabel Rose earlier that day and, after she had returned home, he left his room and went down to the restaurant for dinner where he spotted Gilly.

As she put it later, he 'kept making eye contact with me'. According to John, the restaurant staff were aware of the signals and the waiters were taking bets on whether or not he would seduce her. 'It's a well-remembered incident,' he later said with his ego getting the better of him.

He sent her a bottle of champagne with a note giving his room number and saying, 'I'd love to see you. Don't disappoint me.'

Gilly thought, 'What the heck!' and decided to accept the invitation. She said later, 'I have never met anybody so charming. He had this way of making a woman feel very special.' She remarked on his good looks and 'amazing eyes'. John liked the Avon Gorge Hotel because it was the only hotel in the area that offered a suite with a jacuzzi. 'It was in the jacuzzi that I first made love to the ice-skater,' he claimed.

The following day, John gave Gilly a lift to Birmingham in his hired Ford Escort. They chatted during the journey and touched on some rather odd subjects. He talked about the police searching for bodies in woods and rivers, but suggested that the best way to get rid of a body was to put it in concrete on a construction site. John added to this bizarre conversation by venturing to say that that was probably what had happened to Suzy Lamplugh. John also asked her if she knew the name to describe people who had sex with dead bodies and talked about bondage and anal intercourse. He volunteered the information that he enjoyed sex with other people watching.

When they pulled off the motorway and drove into a service station, they sat talking in the car and, at one point, John put his hands round Gilly's neck and said, 'You know I'll never hurt you... you're much too nice to hurt,' then rather ominously he added, 'Maybe this is the way Suzy died.'

At some point in the trip, they drove off the motorway into country lanes and Gilly was questioned as to whether anyone knew where she was. Despite being scared, she was sufficiently entranced by John to meet him again, which she did twice in Bristol and also in Poole.

Their relationship was brought to an abrupt end by Gilly's skating commitments which required her to return to the *Holiday on Ice* show. They parted on good terms and John spoke of the interlude as 'another brief flirtation'.

Gilly wrote to John from France six weeks later, inviting him to fly out to see her in Grenoble. He declined because he was again short of money and was planning trips to India and the West Indies. John said that she kept telephoning him from abroad but, by the end of July, he was busy moving into his new flat at Foye House.

The day after John was convicted at his trial at Exeter Crown Court in April 1989, the *Sun* newspaper carried an interview with Gilly Paige, whom the paper described as an 'ice show beauty'. She talked about her encounter with John and of her nightmares in which she was haunted by his hypnotic eyes. She told a reporter that, during her car ride to Birmingham with John, he'd spoken about his interest in buying property and his insistence on being shown around by a woman. He mentioned Suzy Lamplugh who had disappeared and said the police were searching for someone called Mr Kipper. His opinion was that Mr Kipper had got rid of the body by putting it in concrete. Gilly was reported as saying, 'It gave me the creeps.'

John completely denied the remarks attributed to him and called Gilly 'a liar and an opportunist'. Never short of a theory, he later told the police that 'she was a bit of a moody girl', and put this down to her unhappy upbringing.

Julia Holman finished work at 5.30pm on Wednesday, 7 October 1987, and went with three colleagues to the Colonial Bar at the Watershed in central Bristol. She stayed drinking and chatting to her friends until 6.50pm when she decided to leave.

Julia had left her car that morning at Canon's Marsh car park, a short distance from the Watershed. She walked alongside the harbour for a short distance and then used an alleyway to reach Canon's Road. Using a gap in the fence, she entered the open-air car park and strolled towards her light-blue Ford Fiesta. She took the keys out of her handbag as she approached it, unlocked the door and slid into the driver's seat and pulled the door shut.

As she put the key into the ignition, her driver's door was wrenched open and she found herself looking at a total stranger. He produced what she took to be a handgun with a barrel about six inches long. Bending his head into the car and thrusting the gun against her side, he said, 'If you do what I say, you won't get hurt.' He pushed her as if he wanted her to move across into the front passenger seat while continuing to point the gun at her.

With great presence of mind, Julia swung her legs round to the right and kicked out at him, at the same time pushing him off-balance with her hands. She also shouted at him and let out a loud scream. As the man straightened up, she slammed the car door shut, started the car and rapidly drove out of the car park. She noticed that he casually walked off in the direction of the city centre.

Julia told detectives that she did not notice anyone following her while she made her way to the car. She described the man as aged about 30 to 35 years of age and about five foot eight to five foot ten inches tall. He had a dark complexion which she described as Latin or Italian, clean-shaven but with side-burns level with the bottom of his ears. His hair was black, collar-length but tidy. He was wearing an unbuttoned grey or beige mackintosh with epaulettes, underneath which she saw a dark-coloured business suit, a light-coloured shirt and a dark tie.

When he was arrested months later, Julia identified Cannan during an identification parade.

During the early evening of Thursday, 8 October 1987, John Cannan spotted a vivacious blonde called Shirley Anne Banks who was shopping for a dress in Debenhams, Bristol. He stalked her around the store and, when she left to get into her car, he abducted her.

Cannan imprisoned the terrified woman in his flat that night, then, the next day, he took her into nearby woods and beat her to death.

On Thursday, 29 October 1987, John Cannan went into Ginger, a boutique in Leamington Spa. It was about 3.55pm and the owner, Carmel Cleary, was arranging clothes on the rails, while her manageress, Jane Child, sat at a desk in the front of the shop. They were the only people in the premises which was situated at 20a Regent Street.

Cannan, who was wearing black trousers and a grey zip-up bomber jacket, had a silver-grey crash helmet on his head with the visor raised. His jacket was bulging as if there was something bulky in it and a pair of blue-grey gloves poked out of the top left-hand pocket.

Cannan stood beside one of the clothes rails and said, 'I'm looking for some gift ideas.'

Carmel Cleary walked over to where he was standing and produced some jumpers.

He said, 'She's a size 38.'

Carmel drew his attention to one of the garments and explained, 'This is a medium, this will fit her.'

'I could tell,' she said later, 'that he was not interested in the jumpers.'

The man said he wanted something brighter and walked over to the display rails near the desk. 'She's only 24,' he said, before pausing to look at more of the items for sale.

Sensing that the man did not appear genuine in his browsing, Carmel Cleary moved over to the desk and casually spoke to Jane Child. She asked her to phone Room Service, a nearby shop, on the pretext of settling an account. This was a ploy to bring someone else into the shop. Suddenly, the man was standing next to the two women. He held an orange-handled knife with a serrated blade in his left hand with which he threatened Carmel. Holding the weapon close to her stomach and speaking to Jane Child, he said, 'Turn out the lights, lock the door and, if you scream, I'll knife her.'

Mrs Cleary picked up the shop keys from the desk and Jane Child walked to the corner of the boutique where the light switches were located.

The intruder said, 'What are you doing?' and, still brandishing his knife, walked over to her.

At this point, using great presence of mind, Carmel Clary dashed across to the front door of her shop and ran out into the street screaming, 'Help! Help! There's a man in the shop with a knife.'

Her desperate screams attracted the immediate attention of Andrew Riley, a builder, who had just entered Regent Street from Portland Street. He ran towards her, asking, 'What's up?'

The shop owner gasped out, 'He's got a knife.'

As they spoke, the man rushed out of Ginger, turned left and ran down into Portland Street.

'I decided to chase him,' said Riley later, and 'almost immediately I was joined by another man [Robert Filer]... the two of us ran down Portland Street towards Portland Place.'

Soon the police were hunting for the would-be robber, and shortly thereafter they arrested John Cannan and took him into custody.

Cannan's black BMW car was found parked near to the incident. In the vehicle were found handcuffs, a replica revolver, several lengths of washing line and a tax disc for an Austin Mini car. It was a vehicle that belonged to newlywed Shirley Anne Banks, who had been missing since Thursday, 8 October 1987.

Later in the day, police searched Cannan's home, Flat 2, Foye House, Clifton, Bristol. In the garage was a crudely repainted blue Mini car with false number plates – SLP 386S. Inside, officers found a riding crop. The car and the crop belonged to Shirley Banks. He was charged with the attempted robbery at Leamington Spa and, later, the abduction and murder of Mrs Banks. However, her body was not found until Easter Sunday, 3 April 1988, when it was discovered by a family walking in the woods. It was badly decomposed and lying in a woodland stream deep in the Quantock Hills, Somerset.

The charges before John Cannan included raping and inflicting grievous bodily harm on Sharon Major; kidnapping, raping and indecently assaulting Donna Tucker; attempting to kidnap and rape Julia Pauline Holman; stealing Shirley Anne Banks's car; abducting and murdering Shirley Anne Banks; and assaulting, imprisoning and attempting to rape Carmel Cleary.

The jury deliberated for ten hours before bringing in their verdicts. John Cannan stood impassively in the dock, dressed, as he had been throughout his trial, in a blue blazer and grey flannels. His face betrayed no sign of emotion as the jury foreman told the court that unanimous verdicts had been reached on all charges. Guilty to the charges of abducting and murdering Shirley Banks and guilty to the other charges of rape, buggery, abduction and attempted kidnapping – six verdicts in all.

Sentencing John Cannan, the judge told him, 'I have to bear in mind mercy, but I also have to deter others who might be minded to have the inclination to attack and violate women. Above all, my duty is to protect others from you and the possibility that you may ever have the opportunity to commit such offences again.

'The sentence for the murder of Shirley Banks is that fixed by law – imprisonment for life. But I add the recommendation that the period you serve in prison shall be the period of your life. You should never again be allowed liberty outside prison walls. Take him down.'

John Cannan the killer paled and staggered to the top of the steps leading down to the holding cells beneath the court. It was one of the few signs of emotion this homicidal sexual psychopath had portrayed throughout the entire proceedings.

'I put my faith in you to preserve me some measure of dignity,' John Cannan told the author. He also said that it was important he should not lay down any preconditions for his co-operation. 'You should write it as you see it.'

John David Guise Cannan, the 'ladykiller', went into prison a lean, good-looking young man. Today, his weight has ballooned, and he is almost unrecognisable as the handsome criminal of 18 years ago. Podgy and unkempt, he has been stripped of his style. The only things he retains are his dreadful secrets and, perhaps, the key to the whereabouts of Suzy Lamplugh's remains.

This chapter is based upon a thousand case papers supplied by John Cannan and the Avon and Somerset Police; two years' correspondence with John and extensive interviews with the principal characters.

PATRICIA WRIGHT

17 July 1951–

Black, petite and not unattractive, Patricia Wright is no serial killer. However, this devious woman, along with the aptly named Larry Slaughter, stabbed her former husband to death for a double-indemnity insurance fraud. This case is of great interest to the criminology-orientated mind in that it took 15 years to come to trial.

This homicidal canvas is the work of no routine amateur, for the mind-twisting case of Patricia Wright may be likened to a masterly woodcut completed by MC Escher, a Dutch graphic artist most recognised for mind-bending visual illusions and impossible buildings. Like Escher, Patricia Wright was a wizard at deceiving the eye. Hers is also one of the most interesting cases I have come across.

I am no stranger to the California correctional system, having been a frequent visitor to San Quentin State Prison. I had never been, though, to the Central California Women's Facility (CCWF), Chowchilla, which was opened in October 1990.

Housing over 3,200 female inmates – many of whom are serving life – CCWF is the largest women's prison in the USA and covers a massive 640 acres. I was to pay just one visit and that was to speak to Patricia Wright, who is currently serving natural life for the brutal stabbing death of her former husband, Willie Jerome Scott.

Patricia Scott (*née* Wright) has always firmly denied this; moreover, in letters to me, she claimed that a *single* 'double-indemnity' insurance policy covered her husband's life, and that, after his death, she collected just over $30,000.

Arletta, Patricia's sister, is adamant, too, that her sister is innocent. Indeed, in a letter from prison, dated March 2003, Patricia Wright wrote these words:

Now, I not only know that I did not kill my ex-husband, the actual killer has now confessed to doing the killing. He is my brother [Larry Wright]. This saddens me greatly. He has now told the family. While I do not wish to harm him, he did this, not me. I want my life back.

… I have been incarcerated about six years for a murder I did not commit. I am innocent. My brother has now told why he had to kill him … because he is a straight man and this gay man came on to him and he couldn't allow that. So, I am at another loss here. Now, that of my brother as I cannot forgive him for what he has done to our family, my children and me. I am a good person. I don't deserve this. Please help me.

… My brother [Larry Wright] says he'll never go to prison for this murder, that he's sorry but he can't do it – confess. Rather let me rot. I don't know what to do about him and his confession. How can I get him to tell the authorities? He'll get life in prison and it may not even exonerate me and set me free. All this is really upsetting.

Patricia Wright to the author from prison

Patricia Wright forcibly maintains that she was 'fitted up' for the murder by relatives and crooked detectives. She says she is mentally ill and legally blind.

I soon discovered that some of Patricia Wright's claims are true, notably that, on Monday, 17 September 1990, Wright was examined by Raymond E Gaylord, OD, who confirmed that she was 'blind due to pigmentary degeneration, with a best-corrected visual acuity in both eyes at 20/400'.

Because of her poor eyesight, since 1974, Wright had 'qualified for Supplementary Security Payments until her monthly payments of $705.40 were terminated as from Sunday, 1 March 1998'.

It is also true that, by the time of her trial, which took place 18 years after the murder had been committed, the police had destroyed the weapon – a knife.

It would be correct to say that the 911 caller who had alerted law enforcement to the body was never located and the tape of the call has been misplaced or lost.

True, too, that no fingerprints or blood were found linking Wright to the murder. Since the conviction, two material witnesses have died, along with the coroner and an arresting officer – all of which add some weight to the desperate pleas of Patricia Wright.

Nevertheless, this is where the truth ends. In a nutshell, Patricia Wright is quite sane and arguably earns the distinction of being one of the most duplicitous female killers in prison today.

There was not *one* insurance policy covering her ex-husband's life, as she claimed, but two. Unfortunately, thousands of California citizens believe her, and with the support of several newspapers, they are raising considerable funds in their campaign to set Patricia Wright free.

With no evidence, physical or otherwise, to link anyone to this brutal murder, the trail leading to Scott's killer ran cold. Although the police had their own suspicions, nothing else happened, although Chinese whispers indicated that Patricia Wright and Larry Slaughter had murdered Willie Scott for an insurance payout.

Then, after 17 years, someone 'coughed' to the police. On the evidence provided, Patricia Wright and Larry Slaughter – whose single fingerprint was found on the van where the victim was found – were arrested and found guilty of conspiracy to murder. Currently, they are both serving natural life in the California penal system.

Slaughter has said nothing and he has refused to discuss the case with me or anyone else. Conversely, the garrulous Patricia Wright claims she is innocent. She says that, although she collected on one double-indemnity life insurance policy, it was never a motive. She insisted to me that only *one* policy ever existed.

Today, thousands of well-meaning citizens believe her. They are raising money for her attorneys and, as an investigative criminologist, I was asked to support their cause.

ONE

Insufficient Evidence

FIRST-degree homicide frequently visits 'The City of Angels'; at the end of autumn, in 1981, another murder was added to the statistics.

At about 2.15pm on Tuesday, 22 September, following an anonymous 911 call, LAPD Sergeant Thompson was tasked to investigate a 1977 Dodge 'Harvest' three-door motor home parked facing east at the south kerb in front of 436 E Temple.

The veteran cop knew that this seedy downtown location was a well-known hangout for gays and male prostitutes, yet on this stiflingly hot afternoon the area was uncharacteristically deserted.

Pulling his sleek cruiser to the side of the street, Thompson stopped. He had just been involved in a high-speed pursuit that had resulted in a drunk driver, high on smack, being forced from the road. Hot engine oil from the police car dripped on to the road, and one of the hubcaps was now missing.

Leaving the V8 ticking over and the air-con running, the officer switched on his strobe bar, made a note of the camper's plate – 407 TSZ – and called it in.

Sergeant Thompson tried both front doors of the camper; they were locked with the windows up. Fingering the grip of his sidearm, he cautiously walked around the vehicle and found that all of the other windows were open. The rear door was unlocked but closed. He had been around dead bodies all his career and he could not fail to smell the unmistakable sweet, gullet-clenching stench of decomposing flesh emanating from inside.

Placing a handkerchief over his nose, the officer peered through one of the windows and saw the badly decomposing body of a white male. The deceased was grotesquely slumped on a bench seat next to a fold-down table.

The cause of death was immediately obvious – a black-handled 9-inch knife was sticking into the unfortunate man's chest, and a plastic trash bag had been thrown over his head. The sergeant immediately realised that he was dealing with yet another homicide and that the victim had suffered an appalling number of stab wounds.

After calling for support, Sergeant Thompson was soon joined by other blue uniforms to secure the scene and, at 3.30pm, detectives Timothy Dotson and William Adrian from Central LAPD Homicide turned up. Inseparable in their work, the two men were now destined to become the lead investigators in a case that would take 18 years to come to trial.

A driving licence, number JO809154, revealed that the deceased was 37-year-old Willie Jerome Scott. A check through vehicle licensing records showed he had owned the beaten-up camper for 20 years. The VLR clerk pointed the officers to an address at 4331 Alonzo, Encino. So, while the police contacted the house, the vehicle was taken away for impounding at Viertels Tow Yard where it would be forensically examined.

Detective Dotson would later say to colleagues, 'The guy looked and smelled like he had been cooked in a fuckin' oven. It [the inside of the camper] stank to hell.'

Miss Doreen Hudson had been a supervising criminalist

employed by the LAPD Criminalist Laboratory for approximately 21 years. It fell upon her shoulders to gather evidence from the camper that might assist the investigators. Once inside the vehicle, and directed by the other detectives, she collected up 'numerous items including several towels, cloths with stains on them, various items of clothing, and two shoes ... 49 cents, a brown purse, pills, a key, toothbrush, various papers and cheques'.

Moving slowly through the cramped interior of the camper, Miss Hudson searched a small bathroom and the kitchen area where she reported finding 'a stove'. But many years later at trial, she said that she 'could not remember if I looked in any of the drawers containing the utensils and knives'. That meant a crucial question could not be answered. Had the knife come from the camper's kitchen drawer, or was it the property of the killer?

People who plan to kill someone usually bring a weapon with them. If the knife had not belonged to the deceased, it would have indicated that the murder might have been planned in advance, maybe by a stranger. Had the knife belonged to the dead man, it could have indicated that killer and victim were acquainted, thus narrowing down the search for a suspect. This issue would remain unresolved for 17 years.

An officer searching the sweltering van pointed to an ashtray in the console of the engine housing. Mrs Hudson took out a butt and placed it in a plastic evidence bag. The theory behind this recovery was that someone other than the deceased might have smoked the cigarette, and perhaps saliva typing might reveal the identity of the smoker of this particular cigarette, though saliva testing was not completed.

While all this was going on, the camper was being dusted for fingerprints. Thirteen different sets of prints were found and it goes without saying that the owner's dabs were all over his property. The knife was clean. However, on the LHS rear-view mirror, a Crime Scene Investigation officer found a single print, which later proved to have been left by a man with the entirely appropriate name of Larry Slaughter.

Later that afternoon, detectives Dotson and Adrian arrived at 4331 Alonzo, Encino. It was a predominantly black neighbourhood squatting over Ventura Boulevard located off Highway 101 in the San Fernando Valley.

The detectives knocked on the door and it was opened by a slightly built, not unattractive woman, who introduced herself as Patricia Wright.

'We are making enquiries about Mr Jerome Scott,' said Dotson, flashing his shield. 'He lives here?'

'No,' came the blunt and suspicious answer. 'Willie and I were married once... he comes here a lot, but he ain't here at the moment.'

'You know where he is right now?' asked the beefy Adrian, who resembled the actor Brian Dennehy.

'Nope. Last saw him Saturday... somethin' wrong, uh huh?'

'Yes, ma'am. May we come in?'

Patricia Wright's statement was as follows:

The last time I saw Jerome [Willie Jerome Scott] was last Saturday morning at about 10.00am at my house in Encino. Jerome was with another black man in his early 20s. They were both in the motor home, and they were drinking. The other man was a sissy that Jerome met.

Jerome is a homosexual and has been hanging out with a lot of sissies. He has not been living with me for some time now because of the men he has been seen with. He met this man he was with Saturday about three weeks ago. I think his name was Ralph or Roger. Just before they left, Jerome came into the house and got a bucket, because he wanted to wash the motor home. They left about 11.30 or 12.00 and he said he would be back later, but I never saw him again.

I don't know too many of his friends because Jerome would never tell me much. His cousin, Lillian Black, knows them, and his play mother, Billie Neil, knows some of them, too. There are others who know some of his sissy friends, but you will have to check with them. I can't think of anyone who would want to kill him. He did live with a homosexual named Herman Cross for a long time, and another man by the name of John Bell from Atlanta, Georgia.

Jerome's mother, Mable Goffe, may know some of his homosexual friends. I think Lorenzo introduced Jerome to Ralph, but you will have to talk to Billie to get Lorenzo's address.

Patricia Wright in a statement to the police

The remark 'I can't think of anyone who would want to kill him' aroused the officers' suspicions because they had made no mention of Jerome being dead.

Over the following days, the officers interviewed a number of witnesses who knew the deceased. Betty Joyce Hill, a family friend, said,

On 15 September 1981, Jerome and Lillian came over to my house for a visit. They got here about 7.30 pm and stayed for approximately one-and-a-half hours. When they left, they were in Lillian's car, and that was the last I saw of them.

Jerome lived her for about a month-and-a-half in June and July. The next time I heard anything about Jerome was when Pat called on Tuesday night about 9.00pm, and told me that Jerome was dead. On Saturday morning, 19 September 1981, at approximately 10.30pm or 11.00pm, Pat called me and asked if Jerome was here. I told her no, and she said that he left her house to wash the camper and he never came back. She also said that he was with a male Negro with an earring, and that he was with Jerome when they left the house.

When Pat called me Tuesday night, she was at her sister's

house on 64th Street. She said that the Coroner called her at her sister's house.

Betty Joyce Hill

Lillian McConico, a friend of Jerome's, stated,

Willie Scott spent the night at my house last Wednesday, 16 September 1981. He left his camper on Thursday at about 12 noon. That's the last I saw of him. He said he was going to Pat's house. She lives in Encino. On Saturday, 19 September 1981, at about one in the afternoon, he called me. He was in Encino because he said he was home. That's the last I heard from Willie.

About one hour later, Pat called … she said she would be over as soon as Willie got done washing the camper. At about 4.00pm, Pat called me again. She asked if Jerome was there. I told her no. She told me that he wasn't down there washing the camper. The first time she called me she had said that she went and offered to help Willie wash the camper. Willie told her no, that the kids would just be in the way. She told me there was another 'little black dude' with him that had an earring in his ear. She said that she thought it was strange that this guy was with Willie, but she didn't get a good look at him.

At about five minutes after 8.00pm, Pat called again. She asked if Jerome had got there yet. I told her no. She then said she was at her sister's house on 64th Street … She told me that she had left a note at the house for Jerome. She told me to tell Jerome if I saw him. On Sunday at about 8.00am and 3.00pm, Pat called again and asked if I had seen Jerome. I told her no.

Lillian McConico

After taking their statements, detectives Dotson and Adrian considered if one of Scott's male prostitutes could have robbed and killed him – his jewellery, wedding ring, 18-carat gold necklace, diamond watch and diamond ring on his right finger were missing. They also learned that he had just cashed his IDS American Express Disability Insurance. It amounted to just over $4,350, and that money had gone, too.

They reasoned that it was highly possible that someone close to the deceased had known about the money, and murder for financial gain was now very much a possible motive.

However, perhaps the blitz-style overkill of the murder ominously added another dimension. If robbery was the motive, just a few stabs – the first being lethal anyway – would have been sufficient to terminate life. However, the person who had murdered this man had done so in a homicidal rage. In other words, the killer did not like Willie Scott at all.

At the post-mortem examination, it was established that Willie Scott was terminally ill from cancer and he had just a few months to live. The ME also determined that the man would have lost consciousness within a minute of the first stab to his throat; the carotid artery had been severed, blood loss would have been immense and anoxia (lack of oxygen to the brain, resulting in blacking out) would have quickly ensued. This first stab, however, was followed by a 'blitz of 15 other stabs to his body'. The ME noted, 'There was no evidence of a struggle and no defensive wounds were found on the dead man's hands or arms.'

The Crime Scene Investigation report stated that 'there was little blood "splashing" around the camper, which is usually associated with such a ferocious attack. There was no evidence of a struggle. Mr Scott had been helpless when the knife was driven into his body time and again. In scenarios such as this, it is highly probable that the attacker would have been splashed with blood and his clothes either had to be washed or thrown away.'

With all of this evidence, it was now clear that someone hated Willie with a passion. The killing was 'personal', and only a person who despised him could have committed such a heinous crime.

As the picture started to unfold, it became obvious to investigators that the deceased had been drinking heavily, as witnesses testified to, and he might have fallen into a drunken stupor, dying without putting up a struggle for his life. Willie could have been murdered at the location where the vehicle was discovered, or murdered elsewhere and the vehicle driven by the killer/s to 436 E Temple, where the police found it.

Semen recovered from the dead man's enlarged rectum, which suggested that he had had gay sex with someone before he died, was not tested for a DNA profile. Two tests on blood found in the camper proved that one of them matched Scott, and the other was from an unknown person. The latter was never traced.

But what of the 911 call alerting the police to the camper and the decomposing body? Of course, anyone could have peered in through the window and seen the carnage after noticing the smell of rotting flesh. However, the police could not rule out the possibility that, as the corpse had been there for some days, someone wanted the body to be discovered; if so, why?

Born on 29 December 1943 in Texas, five-foot-nine-inch Willie Jerome Scott enjoyed a bisexual lifestyle, getting drunk, picking up male prostitutes and having sex with them in his van. In fact, he even made sexual advances to male members of his own family, including Gerald Singleton, the husband of his sister-in-law, Sherry Wright Singleton, and he had made other sexual advances to young Larry Wright, Patricia's brother. Eventually, Willie's behaviour prompted a divorce.

In a letter to me, Patricia Wright's sister, Arletta, wrote:

Jerome Scott was a flamer; at times he wore lipstick, nail polish, ladies' earrings, and he tried to pick up on any man who he could talk to in private. My first husband was a Minister so Jerome Scott would never have had success in picking up on my husband but Jerome Scott tried to pick up on Gerald Singleton

and every man that crossed his path. He even tried to pick up
on my sister Carvette's husband, named Agee. He went through
our family trying to pick up on different sisters' husbands and
boyfriends. He drank a lot.

Arletta Wright in a letter to the author

Patricia was born on 17 July 1951. Marriage documents show she
married Willie Scott in June 1978, and they initially lived at South
Highland Avenue, Los Angeles.

As early as 5 June 1980, and two years after his marriage to Patricia,
papers prove that Willie Scott took out a 'double-indemnity' life
insurance policy – No. 40163159 – with the firm New York Life. The
$15,000 cover included 'Accidental Bodily Harm' to be paid, even in the
event of murder, to the beneficiary, his wife Patricia Scott, who would
receive the tidy sum of $30,000. The premiums were $29.65 a month.

Throughout the period of the policy, New York Life documents
show that Patricia paid the premiums through her own bank
account. And it is here the first red warning flag pops up. In letters
to me from the Wrights, they were adamant that this insurance
policy was taken out by Willie Scott 'years before he met Patricia',
while the insurance company's records conclusively prove otherwise
– that the policy was taken out two years *after* they were married.

This is puzzling, though, for the Wrights and their legal advisers
have had this insurance policy document in their possession for
years. Surely, someone, at least one professional employed by the
pro-Wright campaign since her incarceration, would have noted
this contradiction? It is almost inconceivable that no one had
spotted it before I did.

Examining the trial transcripts, one of my colleagues noted that
an insurance company employee had produced the insurance policy
file in court. Why, I asked again, would the Wrights tell me, and the
American public, that this policy was taken out long before Patricia
and Willie had married when it patently had not?

Looking at the Wrights' correspondence more closely, I noticed something else. They had inferred that Willie had taken out this policy 'years *before he met Patricia*' (my italics). If Willie had taken out the policy before he had even met Patricia – and in the absence of a change of beneficiary recorded in the insurance file – this proved that the Wrights were being less than economical with the truth. You do not make a person a beneficiary if you have not even met them.

I knew that I was being spoon-fed a red herring. This was a wake-up call. Now I was under no illusion that the thousands of pro-Wright supporters were being led up the garden path, too.

On Tuesday, 30 September 1980, the address for all insurance company correspondence was changed to PO Box 78431, Los Angeles, and, on the very same day, Patricia's bank dishonoured a cheque payment for $29.65. There were insufficient funds in her account to pay the premium.

On Monday, 5 January 1981, a second cheque for $29.65 was dishonoured. Again, in March 1981, there were insufficient funds to meet the same amount.

So, it was quite clear that, during this period, Patricia and her husband were suffering financial hardship and, around this time, they learned that Willie had terminal cancer.

On Thursday, 26 March 1981, the couple moved to 3617 West 64th Street, LA, and Patricia brought the premium arrears up to date.

In 1995, 14 years after the murder of Willie Jerome Scott, Patricia's brother Larry Dion Wright started a 12-year sentence at the Corrigan Men's Facility Maximum Security Prison in Connecticut, for threatening the life of a social worker called Judith Castonuary at the Department of Children and Family Services. He had also been charged with physically abusing his son Larry Jr.

Larry Wright wanted out, so he schemed and, because he couldn't write, he dictated a letter to a cellmate who then posted it to the Los Angeles Police Department. In the letter, Larry explained that he had information about the Scott murder. If the law would cut him some slack and get his sentence reduced, he would tell them all he knew.

Larry Wright told detectives that, when he was a 13-year-old boy, he was watching television one evening and thought he heard a loud noise outside. He assumed that it was Jerome's motor home 'rocking and rolling' in the driveway at 4331 Alonzo, although he didn't bother to investigate until the following morning.

Larry Wright gave the following statement to investigators at 11.30am on Thursday, 30 March 1995:

I began living with Patricia Wright shortly after my mother's death. Since that time, Patricia was my legal guardian. Over the years, I have heard from different family members that Patricia had been involved in the death of my father, Charles Wright. My father died of an overdose of drugs.

In 1981, I was living with Patricia Wright at 4331 Alonzo Ave, Encino, California. On the day that I last saw Jerome Scott, I was in the house with Patricia Wright, Larry Slaughter, 'Billy' Torr, Lorenzo King and Jerome Scott as he talked with Patricia and Larry in the dining-room area. Some time during the evening, I saw Jerome walk out of the front door toward the mobile home parked outside. Patricia and Larry stood behind talking for a short while until Larry got up and walked out of the front door toward the mobile home. I don't recall when Patricia left the house, but I believe she walked outside shortly after Larry Slaughter walked outside. I remember hearing the mobil [sic] home rocking back and forward like if there was a great deal of movement inside. The noise from the mobile home was much more noise then I would hear of a person was just walking inside it [sic]. Not long after I heard the noise from the mobil home [sic], Patricia came inside the house and directly told me "Larry was not hear tonight" [sic]. I later realize that she was telling me not to tell anyone that Larry Slaughter was at the house that night. Patricia looked like something had occurred that made her cautious and suspicious. I felt that something had occurred, but I didn't know what. I went into my room and I again heard the noise of the mobil home rocking [sic]. I think Patricia went back outside and I went to sleep.

I recall that Larry Slaughter would carry a large knife stuffed in a cardboard case in his right rear hop waistband. Larry Slaughter had carried the knife in his waistband for several years. The knife had a wooden handle dark in colour and the blade was very long. In all the time that I have known Larry Slaughter, I have never seen him without the knife, until Jerome turned up missing. Since the day that I found out that Jerome was dead, I noticed that Larry wasn't carrying the knife that I had seen him with in the past.

The next morning I saw Larry Slaughter walking down the hill toward Patricia, who was waiting for him. I had not see the mobil home [sic] or Jerome since the night before.

Larry Wright in a statement to police

The police eagerly seized on this information, but failed to ask the obvious question: 'Why did it take you 14 years to tell us?'

Of course, the detectives and scenes-of-crime investigators who had initially entered the camper shortly after the murder found no evidence of any struggle at all. It had appeared that the victim had been stabbed to death as he slept or was incapacitated with drink, all of which started to discredit Larry's story... unless, of course, the man, unable to defend himself under any circumstances, surrendered after the first knife blow – which the post mortem confirmed – and this was followed by the stabbing and accompanying commotion that Larry Wright was referring to.

And there was another problem with Larry's statement. I have since learned that, at the time of the murder, the Wrights rented their home. It was an old property and Patricia and Arletta Wright strenuously claim in a document dated Thursday, 20 February 2003, 'not even a small car would fit into the narrow walkway to the front door, that it was common knowledge Willie's motor home was always parked across from the residence in Alonzo Street'.

This being the case, then Larry Wright certainly had remarkable hearing!

Patricia and Arletta Wright went quiet when I brought Larry Wright's claim to them, that he had heard the commotion in the van from inside the house. Their recollection of the parking situation was also completely at odds with the statement of Ephesian Waters, who remembered, 'When I got to the house on Saturday, there was a gold Cadillac in the garage and a two-door grey or silver Toyota in the driveway. On Monday, the Cadillac and Toyota were still there. Also I saw a black Lincoln parked in the driveway.'

Neighbour Lois Levy also said, 'Later that night, I heard a lot of cars driving up their driveway.'

Some time after the murder, Patricia Wright vacated the premises and new people moved in. Patricia Wright told me that the new residents hired a contractor to enlarge the walkway, converting it into a drive 'where they could park their small car', which is again totally at odds with the statements made by Ephesian Waters, Lois Levy and the garrulous Larry Wright.

For most of his school years, he was placed in a special education class for the emotionally disturbed and mentally retarded. He dropped out of school in the seventh grade. Patricia had raised Larry from the age of nine after their mother, Jeanette Wright, died. The lad obviously resented Patricia and he was almost beyond discipline. In later years, whenever he got annoyed, he would claim to anyone with a sympathetic ear that Patricia had killed her former husband.

Nevertheless, after speaking to the LAPD, and having served just two years of the twelve-year sentence, Larry Wright walked out of prison a free man. He was soon confessing again, this time saying that LAPD detectives had beaten him up and harassed him into signing his statements.

The LA District Attorney and the police have denied cutting a deal with Larry Wright, who, as might be expected, says otherwise. It is a fact, though, that, for some reason, Larry Wright served only two years of his twelve-year jail term. You can draw your own conclusions.

With one dubious informant now prepared to offer 'new' evidence, the LAPD wisely started fishing around for someone else to corroborate Larry Wright. So detectives decided to arrest Patricia's brother-in-law, Gerald Singleton, on suspicion of murder. They held him in custody for 72 hours and the Wrights claim that his photograph was flashed on every major news channel, and on the front page of the *Los Angeles Times*, until his release. Try as I could, I was unable to verify this claim, probably because murder is commonplace in LA, and Singleton's arrest would have hardly been front-page news.

Mr Singleton – like Larry Wright – now claims that the police offered him a deal, too. He would say to investigators that Patricia Wright had asked him to take a brown paper bag to one Lawrence Slaughter as payment for the killing of Jerome Scott. Oddly, after Singleton had signed his statement, he was immediately released. So I think we can all agree that the evidence suggesting that he might have committed murder was flimsy at best!

Singleton's statement was taken at 5.00pm on 18 May 1995. In it, he states,

Back in 1981, I was just released from Orange County Jail for conspiracy to commit robbery. I was out of jail for about (1) week when Pat (my wife's sister) asked me to do her a favor. She said that this man (I know him as Larry Slaughter) is bothering her for his clothes. Pat said that she would pay me $25 to take a brown paper bag, with clothing in it, to Larry Slaughter. I was to deliver it downtown, somewhere on Broadway, where Larry would meet me. I did the job. She gave me the bag but I never looked in it because I really respected Pat. I got off the bus and he was right there waiting for me. I handed him the bag and he just took off running. This really surprised me because Larry and me were friends. I hadn't seen him for a while and I wanted to talk to him but he just took off running so I just got back on the bus. I seen Larry off and on for years after that happened.

Then, in 1990 or 1991, I end up in the same jail dorm with him out at Wayside. I confronted him and told him I was pissed off about the way he has been treating me, and the time I took the bag. He tells me, 'Man, there was about $25,000 – it was $20,000 – in that bag. I was in a hurry.'

At this point, we got on the conversation about Willie Scott's murder. Slaughter said, 'Man, I'm tired of Larry Wright, Billie, Sandy, and them discussing this murder. They don't know how serious it is. The only ones who were there was me and Pat. Pat took the first swing. Pat's a crazy bitch. She acted like she enjoyed it.' Slaughter said that we [Willie, Pat and I] were all together in the camper 'somewhere downtown'. Pat takes some kind of knife and starts stabbing Willie in the chest, calling him a motherfucker every time she stabs him. Slaughter said that he just stood by and watched. After the stabbing, they just left him there and took off.

Gerard Singleton in a statement to police

This statement partially demolished the information given by Larry Wright, whom we know led police to think that the murder might have taken place in the driveway of his home, for Singleton claims that Slaughter confessed to the murder taking place 'somewhere downtown'. If Slaughter was telling the truth, why would he lie about the murder location?

If Singleton is correct, he cites Slaughter's version of events as a wild stabbing by a 'crazy bitch', which certainly seems to point to a frenzied killing. And are we being asked to believe, in respect to the statements made by Larry Wright, Gerald Singleton and this hearsay admission from Slaughter, that the police concocted the lot, although the forensic evidence found in the van, and at post mortem, does suggest that there could be some truth surrounding it? Singleton later retracted this confession.

Undeterred by Larry Wright and Singleton's retractions, the police turned their attention back to the camper van and the earlier fingerprint evidence. On the left-side rear-view mirror Slaughter's single print had been found. In itself this was of little evidential value, because Patricia Wright and her sister claim in a document dated 20 February 2003:

> Lawrence Slaughter was a close friend to Jerome Scott ... Mr Slaughter had been in the 1977 Dodge motor home hundreds of times also before Jerome Scott got murdered, no one can tell what date or time a fingerprint got on a object that's a well-known fact.
>
> *Patricia and Arletta Wright*

However, this claim is of interest insomuch as one obvious fact appears to have been overlooked. If Slaughter had been in the camper 'hundreds of times', why was only one of his prints found on the *outside* of the vehicle? Presumably, Patricia Wright had been in the camper many times, too. However, in the document mentioned above, Arletta Wright states, 'Thirteen fingerprints (sets of) were recovered from inside and outside the 1997 Dodge motor home, none of the fingerprints matched Patricia Wright.'

So, yet again, more red flags appear as a result of claims made by Patricia Wright. Research has proved that Larry Slaughter had not, in fact, been in the camper 'hundreds of times'. Slaughter was straight and he had no time for Patricia's ex-husband.

Having come up against several inconsistencies, perhaps it was now time to think laterally.

Paying a Premium

TAKING a step back, it seems worthwhile focusing on the obvious inconsistencies, mainly those of Patricia and Arletta Wright.

If Slaughter was a regular visitor to the camper, then surely at least one of Slaughter's dabs, a fingerprint, or a palm print, would have been discovered in the interior? They had not been found.

Despite the statements given by Larry Wright and Gerald Singleton – both statements being retracted as soon as these two men were released from jail – not a shred of physical evidence was found to say that Slaughter had ever been in the camper. Indeed, there was just the print on the outside door mirror to say that he had even touched the vehicle.

The police now started digging deeper. One not insignificant issue that caught their attention was Patricia Wright's unusual behaviour shortly after Willie Jerome Scott disappeared.

The first hint of Patricia Wright's unusual behaviour came from Larry Wright who told police that, within a day of Jerome's disappearance, Patricia started calling various hospitals trying to locate him. Larry claimed that this all seemed strange because Jerome had a habit of vanishing for several days, indeed weeks at a time, and that Patricia Wright had never seemed concerned about his whereabouts until the day he went off to wash his van.

A family friend called Betty Joyce Hill had told detectives that, on the day Jerome disappeared, Patricia had phoned her to say that Willie had gone off to wash his camper and hadn't returned. Patricia said she was worried about him.

Betty Hill's recollection corroborated Larry Wright's observation.

Detectives interviewed Lillian McConico who claimed that Patricia had phoned her, too – not once, but on two occasions, asking if her former husband was with her. He was not, but this was highly unusual behaviour for a woman who knew that her former husband would disappear for days, even weeks at a time, and had never concerned herself before.

If the police were going to tie this somewhat creaky case up, it would be finding proof of a motive for the killing.

Larry Slaughter and Patricia Wright say they certainly were not lovers, while other members of the family say they were. Nevertheless, this matters little because Willie and Patricia had already parted company before the murder, and there was apparently no animosity between them.

Sniffing around, although somewhat belatedly, the police finally got wind of the insurance payout to Patricia. This alleged motive supposition was slightly rocky at the outset, for why murder a man who was suffering from terminal cancer with a few months left to live? Nevertheless, when detectives made more thorough enquiries at New York Life, the company who had issued the policy, they were surprised to discover the existence of a *second* double-indemnity policy – No. 37645648 – a policy that, to this very day, the Wrights argue never existed.

The police officers' suspicions were further aroused when they learned from New York Life that Patricia Scott had made the claim on the first policy with somewhat indecent haste on Tuesday, 23 September 1981 – the second working day after the murder – and before Willie Scott was cremated on Monday, 28 September at the Forest Lawn Cemetery in Glendale.

She picked up a cheque for $30,352.81 less than a month later, so the first insurance policy had been paid. When I asked Patricia Wright how she had spent the money, she wrote to say that she had reinvested it into an annuity and, with the balance of $10,000, she had bought a car. This was a complete lie.

We know of Patricia's unusual concern about Willie's whereabouts the day after he vanished – she had never worried before. We also know of the anonymous 911 call alerting police to the body. I asked myself, could this call have been made by Patricia Wright or Larry Slaughter, who wanted the money as soon as possible?

In investigations where circumstantial evidence plays a large part in justice being meted out, a jury takes into consideration acts indicative of guilty consciousness or intent; the anonymous 911 call and Patricia's unusual concern for Willie most certainly fit into this category.

Scanning the second policy application, the detectives took down the details and followed up a few leads. It transpired that James Alley, the insurance agent who sold the policy, hadn't actually seen Willie Jerome Scott complete or even sign the application form.

Alley, who knew Patricia and Willie, took Pat's word that Willie would sign the form when he returned later in the day. However, Patricia Wright forged the signature and passed it off as genuine.

And, as a further example of the integrity of public-spirited Patricia Wright – probably due to an innocent oversight – she conveniently failed to tick the appropriate box indicating that Willie was less than 100 per cent fit. In fact, as we know, he was dying of cancer with just a few months left to live!

The homicide investigators also noted that the second double-indemnity life policy – this time to the tune of a $55,189.77 payout in the case of accidental death or murder – had been taken out on Wednesday, 26 August 1981, a year after the couple's divorce and just 24 days before the man's murder.

The investigators learned that it was Patricia Scott, not Willie, who had paid the first and only premium payment. Coincidentally, too, she was the sole beneficiary. She had received the full payout of $55,189.77 on Friday, 21 January 1983, and not told a soul.

Further detective work proved that she had reinvested $30,189.77 of this money back into an annuity with New York Life, and had spent the balance on, among other things, a mini-van.

Technically, and this is a vital red flag, Patricia and Arletta Wright are correct when they say that 'the second policy never existed'. I have since confirmed that the second insurance policy document was not issued before Willie Scott's murder. Indeed, the document was never issued at all because, by then, the man was dead and cremated.

However, despite their knowledge to the contrary, what the Wrights conveniently failed to point out to the police, or me – and they most certainly have not informed their thousands of supporters – is the fact that Willie's life was covered under New York Life's 'Temporary Conditional Coverage Agreement' from the date of signature and the first payment. In her own letter, she states, 'The DA said I had two insurance policies, yet they could not find a second insurance policy anywhere because there was always only one.'

Obviously, and crucial to her claims of being an innocent woman, Patricia is trying to hide from everyone the existence of the second policy taken out shortly before the man's murder, because the payout sum of $30,352.81 is closer to the figure of $30,000 – that of the first policy. But in arguing this she has made a fatal mistake, an irrevocable error in which she foolishly admits the lie. Patricia Wright claims specifically that, using the $30,000 payout from the first policy, she purchased the mini-van for $10,000 and used the remainder for the annuity.

However, the insurance company's records are accurate. They prove beyond any doubt that Patricia Wright only purchased one annuity with them and this was done on payment of the second policy. If so, she could have given the money to Larry Slaughter as suggested by Singleton.

In a document supplied to me by the Wrights, dated Wednesday, 19 March 2003, item # 34, Arletta Wright poses this interesting question: 'Why would Patricia Wright want to murder her husband – in fact, they were divorced – knowing that he was the sole financial source of income for their two children and herself at the time?'

This observation was somewhat disingenuous because Willie Scott did not support his family at all. Patricia was receiving $705.40 a month in social security benefits.

Of course, we recall that the claim on the first policy was made just three days after Willie Scott's murder and, maybe because of financial hardship, Patricia did need the money urgently. And we know that Willie Scott had terminal cancer, so why did she and Slaughter kill him? The answer can only rest with the 'double-indemnity' clause. $30,000 would only be paid out if cause of death were accidental bodily harm or homicide. If Willie Scott had died through natural causes, and he had terminal cancer with just months to live, then the payout would have been a mere $15,000. The very existence of a second double-indemnity policy being taken out under extremely dubious circumstances merely sets Patricia Wright's motive for murder in stone.

It has since been confirmed by several witness statements, and supported by police documents, that Larry Slaughter paid a number of unannounced visits to Patricia Wright's residence directly after the murder, demanding that some of his clothes be returned. When he turned up, she hid behind locked doors.

Patricia Wright had never washed Slaughter's clothes in the past, although immediately after the murder she had washed a pair of his trousers, a sweatshirt and a lightweight jacket. Arletta and Patricia further confirmed this in letters, as did Slaughter and Singleton in their police statements.

The suggestion is that these items could have only been the bloodstained clothes worn by Slaughter at the time of the murder. However, this being the case, one has to ask why Patricia did not give them to him, rather than hide behind closed curtains. Indeed, Slaughter was extremely keen to have his clothes returned to him because they had been contaminated with physical evidence that tied him to the murder and he was fearful that the cunning Patricia Wright – as another form of insurance – might use this against him.

But it was not just his clothes Slaughter wanted. He needed his cut of the first insurance payout and this dovetails somewhat neatly into the statement given, then retracted by Gerald Singleton, who told detectives that, after his release from prison in 1981, and after the payout of the first policy, that he ran an errand for Patricia Wright, to deliver 'clothes' in a brown bag to Slaughter.

Singleton also claimed that Slaughter later confessed to the murder, adding that the bag had also contained his split of the insurance money.

Whether the $20,000 figure is correct, we may never know. However, with Slaughter having got his slice of the action, Patricia Wright would have been left with just $10,000 from the first policy payout and, as she herself admits, she used the $10,000 to buy a car, which was a lie. She bought the car after the second policy was paid.

While Patricia Wright had possibly been plotting the murder of Willie Scott with her accomplice for some time, she would have been wise not to inform Slaughter of the second policy she had discreetly taken out just 24 days before Jerome was murdered.

Indeed, until this very day, Patricia has apparently convinced her family, as well as her supporters, that a second policy never existed. Technically, she is correct, but as we now know she had reinsured Willie's life anyway.

Patricia Wright claims she is a good woman, and wouldn't you say you were an angel if you were trying to extract yourself from a life sentence? She says that she loved Willie and that she would never have harmed him. But the fact remains that whoever conspired to murder Willie Jerome Scott for the purposes of collecting his life insurance, and other monies, as well as the expensive jewellery, were very devious, manipulative and evil people indeed.

Having completed my investigation into the case of Patricia Wright, out of courtesy I emailed a copy to Arletta Wright for her comments, and the results were truly amazing.

She stated that I was 'absolutely 200 per cent right', and that she [Arletta] had written all of her letters to me, and compiled her meticulously presented files 'believing 200 per cent' that the information she had received from Patricia Wright was honest. She added:

> Please forgive me if you feel I have deceived you. I didn't mean to be taken that way. I have asked my sister how much insurance she got and she guaranteed me it was only $30,000. She said someone else must have cashed it [the second policy].
>
> *Arletta Wright in a letter to the author*

All of which proved that, even at such a late stage, the duplicitous Patricia Wright was still denying the existence of a second policy.

When I pointed out in reply that for someone else to cash in the policy was impossible – the insurance company's records were accepted by both prosecution and defence as totally accurate, and that Patricia had cashed both policies because the money had been deposited in her bank account – Arletta had to concede:

> I agree. I believe you 100 per cent ... my sister should have been straightforward right up front ... It makes me look like a fool, to go to bat with my sister if I don't have the truth. It definitely hurts a lot ... Patricia should have been straight from the beginning and said 'Yes, I got the insurance but I didn't kill him.'
>
> *Arletta Wright in a letter to the author*

I reminded Arletta, a deeply religious person who quotes scripture in her letters, that she had obviously carefully studied the court transcripts because she always had any other information I required at her fingertips. Surely, I suggested, she *must* have noticed the discrepancy over the insurance policies; she had been a fraud investigator for a telephone company in the past. Did she not attend the trial and hear all of this before? Obviously, I suggested, motive for financial gain lies at the root of the matter.

Arletta's reply was interesting:

> I didn't get a chance to read the transcripts all the way through, though I do my best. I had my hands full for the past two years … my daughter had a baby girl. I didn't read all the transcripts. But I believe in my sister's innocence. I strongly believe the truth will come out.
>
> The truth will set Patricia free. This is the first time I have heard about my brother Larry Wright confessing to a murder. I have never ever heard of such. Where did you get that statement from? My brother was a little boy when Jerome died.
>
> *Arletta Wright in a letter to the author*

I told Arletta that this statement had come from none other than Patricia Wright, who had told me in a letter that Larry had confessed to the murder.

Arletta's reply was immediate. 'My sister never tells me what she writes in her letters.'

Like an insect struggling to extricate itself from a Venus Fly Trap, Patricia Wright is also fighting for her freedom. However, in doing so she attempted to conceal the truth, not only from me, but is still concealing the truth from the people who believe she is innocent – including the person she claims to love above all others, her sister, Arletta.

First, Patricia lied about the insurance policies and, it seems, deceived Arletta into the bargain. Then she lied about Larry Wright admitting to the murder, and that all the family knew that Larry had confessed, when he had not and they did not.

At the time of writing, Arletta says she is deeply shocked, especially as for years she has convinced herself of Patricia's innocence, and has gone to considerable lengths and financial expense through well-meaning efforts to prove it. Indeed, such is the deep-seated belief in Patricia's innocence that, even now, Arletta says she holds out hope that her sister is telling the truth and prays to God that this is so.

In one of Patricia Wright's letters to me from prison, she states, clutching at straws, 'There was no physical evidence, real or imagined, to say that I had committed this murder.'

On the face of it, Patricia Wright seems convincing enough; however, a closer look under the covers reveals that she was convicted on overwhelming circumstantial evidence.

It is the cumulative effect, the 'arithmetic of circumstantial evidence', which causes so many juries to say that, even though the evidence before them is entirely indirect, they are 'satisfied beyond any reasonable doubt' of the safety of convicting, as was the case with Larry Slaughter and, at a separate trial, that of Patricia Wright.

Patricia Wright's final plea to me was:

I am fighting for my life. I simply received insurance money, now long gone, because of his death. I never wanted him gone or dead. We had loved each other. We have a son who needs both his parents. We stayed friends till the end. I did not commit murder. I am innocent. I am a good person. I don't deserve this. Please help me.

Arletta Wright in a letter to the author

In desperation, Arletta phoned her sister in prison. During the short conversation, Patricia finally admitted to the second policy, and Arletta confirmed this in an email dated Friday, 30 May 2003:

> Chris, thank you, I appreciate your help. I spoke to my sister Patricia Wright on Wednesday by telephone. I advised that I needed the truth. My sister did say that, yes, she got all the insurance money. And I knew all along.
>
> *Arletta Wright in an email to the author*

Having seen the meticulously presented files and documents sent to me by Arletta Wright, and having received much correspondence from her and speaking with her over the telephone, I am sure she is, or was, convinced of her sister's innocence. 'And I knew all along' might also refer to her strong suspicions.

Like a visitor viewing one of Monet's grand works, and as the closest relative to Patricia Wright, Arletta, a God-fearing woman, stood too close to the larger picture and, through no fault of her own, she couldn't see the wood for the trees.

Arletta Wright comes from home-grown and simple stock, and it is not uncommon for relatives – even when faced with the obvious fact that one of their family is guilty – to revert to denial. They simply cannot allow themselves to imagine that someone they love and hold dear to their hearts could commit such terrible crimes for such cold-blooded reasons. I am of the belief that Arletta is no exception. For years, her thoughts and feelings would have cemented into one of almost total belief in Patricia's claim of innocence. She has been surrounded by citizens, various journalists and lawyers who have supported Patricia Wright, and all of this has combined to strengthen Arletta's resolve. But herein lies the problem.

Arletta, and all of Patricia's supporters, have been predisposed – for their own personal reasons – towards this woman in prison. They have, in effect, their own well-meaning agendas. The newspaper articles reporting on the case are most certainly biased towards injustices perceived – rightly or wrongly – to have been carried out by a largely white California law and criminal-justice system upon the black community.

Larry Wright insisted that he wanted to help his sister get out of jail. Then, in his second letter to me, he said he would only do so for $10,000 – cash up front! I believe that, in desperation, Arletta Wright turned to me in an honest attempt finally to uncover the truth. She offered payment at the outset. I declined, saying that, if I took the case, I would remain unbiased and I did not want to be influenced in any way. I explained that the chips would fall as they may, and that my findings would be published for the public record, either to support Patricia's claim of innocence or to confirm her guilt.

I have no feelings either way for Patricia Wright, who now sits in a cell at Chowchilla Women's Facility in California. I do, however, wish Arletta Wright all the best for the future.

This chapter is based upon 1800 case documents and personal correspondence.